AF837549

Collaborative Translation

Innovative Practices and Interactions Towards the Future

Valentina Baselli and Francesco Laurenti (eds.)

Collaborative Translation

Innovative Practices and Interactions Towards the Future

PETER LANG
Bruxelles · Berlin · Chennai · Lausanne · New York · Oxford

Bibliographic Information published by the Deutsche Nationalbibliothek
The Deutsche Nationalbibliothek lists this publication in the Deutsche Nationalbibliografie; detailed bibliographic data is available online at http://dnb.d-nb.de.

Library of Congress Control Number: 2025913031

This book was funded by the International Center for Research on Collaborative Translation (IULM).

ISSN 1663-9367
ISBN 978-3-0343-5424-0 (Print)
ISBN 978-3-0343-5742-5 (E-PDF)
ISBN 978-3-0343-5379-3 (E-PUB)

DOI 10.3726/b23053
Dépôt légal D/2025/5678/42

© 2025 Peter Lang Group AG, Lausanne (Switzerland)
Published by Peter Lang Editions Scientifiques Internationales – P.I.E.
SA, Bruxelles (Belgium)

info@peterlang.com

All rights reserved.
All parts of this publication are protected by copyright.
Any utilization outside the strict limits of the copyright law, without the permission of the publisher, is forbidden and liable to prosecution.
This applies in particular to reproductions, translations, microfilming, and storage and processing in electronic retrieval systems.
This publication has been peer reviewed.

www.peterlang.com

Contents

List of Figures

List of Tables

Acknowledgements

The editors would like to express their gratitude to the reviewers who participated in the review process, Allegra Mancini, Julia Mary Scilabra, Clara Pignataro and Silvia Velardi. They would also like to acknowledge the ongoing financial, logistical and organisational support provided by the International Center for Research on Collaborative Translation (IULM), as well as the Department of Humanities of IULM University.

Beyond Tradition. New Horizons in Collaborative Translation: A Preface

Francesco Laurenti

Although collaborative translation has existed for centuries, only recently has it become a specific research focus. Given the prevalence of collaboration in translation practices since at least the third millennium BC, it is surprising how little attention historians have paid to its study. Considering the crucial role collaborative translation has played in disseminating texts, information, and cultural products, as well as in facilitating interactions between cultures, it is remarkable that twentieth-century Translation Studies portrayed translation mostly as an individual activity.

Today, after the so-called information age, in a time where concepts like network society, semantic web, digital media, Virtual Reality, Augmented Reality and Metaverse are part of everyday life, communication constantly evolves alongside the growing production of information. In this context, translation remains essential for understanding the world and communicating in real and virtual worlds, with the demand for translation in the market greatly exceeding the supply of qualified professionals. Overall, the resort to collaborative translation has been a constant feature in human cultural history. The recent and significant rise in scholarly interest in collaborative practices is largely attributed to the widespread adoption of new media and tools that enable collaboration between participants (both in person and online), resulting in transformative changes in the translation process.

Therefore, a systematic re-examination of these processes has become more urgent today, and such scrutiny may have a lasting impact on conventional ideas regarding both the nature of translation and the status of the translator[1].

[1] Cf. Michael Cronin, 'The Translation Crowd', *Tradumática* 8 (2010), 1–7.

The discussion of emerging collaborative practices in the global language market must begin by examining the different forms of collaboration in translation. It is of fundamental importance to map out these practices and attempt a definition that spans the many interpretations of 'collaborative translation' within Translation Studies. What exactly makes a translation 'collaborative'?

While 'collaborative translation' is not a new topic, its definition still sparks varying opinions[2]. The broadest description seems to be that of Sharon O'Brien, who suggests that translation is collaborative when two or more agents somehow cooperate to produce it. This can refer to situations where multiple translators work together on a single translation, as well as when human agents collaborate with both human and non-human tools[3]. The term 'collaborative' thus encompasses both human teamwork and the use of technology.

Other scholars have also proposed diverse definitions, reflecting a range of views. Alain Désilets and Jaap van der Meer[4] use the term in a broader sense to describe the tools that support collaboration, such as software for shared terminology resources[5], platforms for sharing translation memories[6], online marketplaces connecting translators and clients[7], and crowdsourcing[8] or agile translation systems. Differing from traditional top-down models, these systems enable multidisciplinary teams to collaborate through simultaneous workflows. They also refer to 'crowd post-editing'[9] where a community of

---

[2] Marcel Thelen, 'Collaborative Translation in Translator Training', *Konin Language Studies* 3 (2016), 255–257. I am indebted to Thelen's list of definitions for these two paragraphs.

[3] Sharon O'Brien, 'Collaborative Translation', in Yves Gambier, Luc van Doorslaer, *Handbook of Translation Studies*, Vol. 2, (Amsterdam/Philadelphia: John Benjamins Publishing Company, 2013), 17.

[4] Alain Désilets, Jaap van der Meer, 'Co-creating a Repository of Best Practices for Collaborative Translation', in *Linguistica Antverpensia*, 10/(2011), 29–30.

[5] Cf. Platforms such as Wikitionary, ProZ's Kudoz forum, Urban Dictionary, TikiWiki and Reverso Dictionary.

[6] Tools for the sharing of multi-lingual *corpora* are TAUS Data Association, MyMemory and Google Translator Tolkit.

[7] As in the case of ProZ.com, TranslatorsCafe and Translated.net.

[8] Through systems that allow for the translation of content on the part of volunteer translators, as is the case of LinkedIn, Facebook, Firefox, TED Talks, Adobe TV, Translators without Borders and Kiva.org, to mention a few.

[9] As those collaborating with Google Translate, Microsoft Bing Translator and Asia Online.

amateur translators revises machine-generated translations. Désilets and van der Meer's definition focuses more on the tools that enable such collaboration, rather than the practices themselves.

Jeremy Munday refers to 'collaborative translation' as a synonym for 'crowdsourcing', explaining that collaborative translation often involves 'large groups of non-professional translators'[10] and Anthony Pym argues that 'collaborative translation' and 'crowdsourcing' refer to the same practice[11].

Despite the various attempts, the definitions mentioned above[12] do not provide a clear, unified answer to the question 'What makes a translation collaborative?' Therefore, how can we reach consensus on the definition of collaborative translation that reconciles these differing perspectives? A shared definition is potentially essential to promote theoretical exploration and foster further research on collaborative translation practices.

Collaborative translation today, as a process, involves multiple actors that work together to translate a text or speech or environment, although not always simultaneously or in the same location. Such collaboration often implies modern technologies, advanced digital tools and online platforms that support real-time collaboration and collective intelligence while fostering a shared work environment. It relies on knowledge sharing, teamwork, and clear, effective communication among contributors, all of whom may not be professional translators and may resort to synergy between humans and machines. There are different forms of collaboration within the field of translation, and this diversity may be one reason why scholars have not always agreed on what should be included under the umbrella term 'collaborative translation'.

To categorise the different types of collaborative translation practices, scholars have generally focused on the question 'Who is collaborating with whom?'.

10 Jeremy Munday, *Introducing Translation Studies. Theories and Applications*, (London/New York: Routledge, 2012), 282.

11 Antony Pym, 'Translation Research Projects 3', *Intercultural Studies Group*, Tarragona (2011), 78.

12 The author agrees with Thelen (Cf. Thelen, 258).

In literary translation, for instance, some of the most common collaborative practices involve two or more translators with complementary language skills working together on a text. Additionally, translators may work directly with the author of the original text whenever possible or work in different languages on the same text, collaborating to create a shared resource. Moreover, practices such as the translation of a drama piece, from script to stage, typically involve a collective effort from various people, including translators, actors, directors, set designers, musicians, and the audience[13].

Translation Studies have traditionally mainly focused on such human relationships, but there is a growing need for a more inclusive approach. This would allow for a reconsideration of both human and non-human agents, especially in the translation practices influenced by technology and innovative translation tools. For translators, the current environment marks a crucial turning point driven by the need to meet market demands, adapt to rapidly evolving technologies and address the challenges of increased global communication. Translators must first acknowledge —and ideally embrace— that it will soon be limiting to view the 'translation' work in a narrow sense. Instead, they should begin to appreciate the collaborative, cooperative, and multifaceted nature of translation, which is embodied in a team setting that includes managers, coordinators, terminologists, consultants, supervisors, and subject matter experts who can provide real-time support to the translator.

It is not uncommon for some agencies to promote their use of the traditional TEP model (an acronym for the three conventional stages of translation work: translation, editing, and proofreading) as a guarantee of the quality of their services. However, this model has clear limitations, particularly within the context of today's globalized translation market. One key issue is that

---

[13] Cf. Susan Bassnett, 'Translating for the Theatre: The Case Against Performability', in *TTR: Traduction, terminologie, redaction*, 1 (1991), 99–111; Eva Espasa, 'Performability in Translation: Speakability? Playability? Or just Saleability?' in C.A. Upton, ed., *Moving Target: Theatre Translation and Cultural Relocation*, (Manchester: St. Jerome Publishing, 2000), 49–62; Margherita Laera, 'Theatre Translation as Collaboration: Aleks Sierz, Martin Crimp, Nathalie Abrahami, Colin Teevan, Zoe Svendsen and Michael Walton discuss Translation for the Stage', *Contemporary Theatre Review*, 21 (2001), 213–225; Francesco Laurenti, 'Shakespeare on Stage for the Screen and Collaborative Translation: Cesare Deve Morire', *Lingue e Linguaggi*, 52 (2022), 117–191.

editors operate at the final stage of the process and do not always possess greater expertise or a deeper understanding than the translators themselves. This may lead to the risk of introducing new errors into the translation text instead of simply correcting the existing ones. Another limitation lies in the sequential and asynchronous structure of the workflow, as well as the rigid division of translation stages, which risks prolonging the process by adding extra steps without necessarily enhancing the final product—and potentially increasing the likelihood of errors. Additionally, in the TEP model, error-checking is often reserved for the final stages, a point at which corrections typically demand the greatest—and frequently avoidable—investment of time and resources.

An alternative model that has been at least partially adopted by major translation agencies is the model designated by the acronym PCTP ('plan', 'coordinate', 'translate' and 'publish')[14]. In this case, translations are produced by 'communities' of translators working together on a specific project through digital tools that manage translations via web-based gateways, allowing for collaboration through a series of modules to optimize productivity.

Recent developments in the translation practice further reveal even more significant changes due to the integration of artificial intelligence (AI) into the field, increasingly positioning it as a vital collaborator. The interaction between human translators and AI is changing both the methods and the results of translation, combining human creativity and contextual knowledge with the speed and efficiency of algorithmic processing.

AI-powered tools are revolutionizing the translation industry by offering rapid automated translations of large volumes of text. However, if on the one hand technologies driven by neural networks and large language databases can generate translations that are mostly accurate in basic grammar and semantic content, AI masters standard and formulaic translations, while tending to struggle with subtleties, idiomatic expressions and context-dependent meanings, all of which are crucial to high-quality translation. Consequently, human expertise remains essential for enhancing AI-generated translations,

---

14 Renato Beninatto and Donald De Palma, 'Collaborative Translation', in *Multilingual* 2008, <http://www.scribd.com/doc/4069269/Structuring-Collaborative-Translation-20-Less-Delivery-TimeBetter-Quality≥, accessed 31 December 2024.

ensuring that these translations are culturally and contextually suitable. Consequently, a collaborative methodology termed 'post-editing of machine translation' (PEMT) is emerging. Here, human translators assess, modify, and enhance AI outputs, thereby effectively reconciling automated efficiency with the need for human discernment and creativity.

This combination of human translators and AI in the collaborative translation process marks a significant shift in Translation Studies and brings about the inclusion of human translators and AI together in the translation process. Although AI tends to fasten the translation and increase efficiency, it does not, most of the time, compete with the quality and contextual understanding offered by a human translator. Collaboration between AI and human translators will therefore probably become more complex as AI technology develops, offering the translation industry both new opportunities and challenges.

With the continuous evolution of virtual environments and immersive digital experiences, the Metaverse has emerged to be the realm in which physical and digital worlds converge in a collective virtual space that integrates augmented reality, virtual reality and other digital experiences, with great potential for global interactions. In such an immersive digital realm, effective communication across cultures and languages will soon become even more crucial and, in this multilingual environment, collaborative translation will meet new opportunities to ensure seamless communication and promote inclusive interactions in real-time. In the context of immersive experiences, translation involves the interpretation of non-verbal signals, gestures and symbols that are culturally relevant in virtual environments. Given the complexity of the Metaverse, with all its dynamic and immersive nature, translation must evolve beyond traditional methods to adopt innovative approaches that can cater to these multiple dimensions of interaction.

This poses a significant challenge for current translation technologies and practices, which are built for traditional two-dimensional means of communication. A significant challenge in translating into and out of the Metaverse, for example, is that it requires continuous translation among different communication channels and the use of a mixture of text, spoken words, gestures, or even visual elements such as signs or virtual objects. In this new setting, traditional translation methods, which typically depend on text or audio inputs, may not be able to keep up with the diverse and multimodal nature of communication.

Moreover, the immersive and cross-cultural dimensions of the Metaverse require translations to be context-sensitive and culturally appropriate. Virtual environments often offer unique, culture-specific experiences driven by the social and cultural contexts of their user: a virtual game, a digital art exhibition, or social interactions in the Metaverse can include cultural references, jokes, or idiomatic expressions that are hard to translate accurately. The greatest challenge is to ensure that the translations in the Metaverse maintain the cultural context and nuances through which the interaction is enhanced. Furthermore, the Metaverse is decentralized and changes rapidly, meaning that languages might change swiftly or evolve within these virtual worlds: new slang, specialized jargon, or technical terms may become common as users develop their own virtual cultures and communities. Thus, translators (be they human or AI-driven) will need to stay abreast of such swift linguistic changes to ensure communication remains accurate and relevant in this fast-evolving environment.

Translation tools powered by AI, including machine translation and NLP systems, have already made notable progress in facilitating real-time translation in conventional online settings. In the Metaverse, AI is expected to play a fundamental role in facilitating seamless, multilingual interactions in different languages and modes of communication through real-time speech-to-text and speech-to-speech translation, enabling users with diverse language backgrounds to communicate easily during live virtual events or interactions. Advanced NLP systems could automatically identify and translate spoken languages while also accounting for subtleties (tone, emotion, and context) and more sophisticated linguistic and cultural nuances (humour, metaphor, or idiomatic expressions), and AI-powered tools could translate even non-verbal communication, like gestures or visual symbols, by understanding their cultural significance and providing suitable translations within the virtual environment.

However, in the Metaverse, where there is a diversity of cultures and contextually meaningful communication, artificial intelligence may find it difficult to give precise and culturally appropriate translations without human intervention or subsequent editing, and a human-driven multilingual localization is becoming increasingly essential for the fruition of the Metaverse experience.

For this reason, the Metaverse will benefit from an integrated approach where AI performs basic translations in real-time, while human translators or moderators review the accuracy and cultural appropriateness of the interactions. As the digital realm of the Metaverse continues to grow in breadth and complexity, it also provides promising opportunities for collaborative translation methodologies.

The Metaverse is likely to change our understanding of translation: traditional frameworks in translation will need to change in response to the diverse and multimodal forms of communication that characterize virtual worlds. Translators will need new skills and will have to use innovative tools to faithfully represent non-verbal, visual, and cultural features in the Metaverse, ensuring that communication retains its meaning and cultural appropriateness. As this virtual landscape continues to evolve and diversify, effective communication across languages and cultures will be crucial to the experience of the Metaverse (opening new frontiers to Translation Studies, redefining what translation itself means and forcing translators to acquire new skills) and the future growth of the Metaverse remains closely dependent on a multilingual localization performed through a synergy between human translator and AI.

References

Bassnett, Susan, 'Translating for the Theatre: The Case Against Performability', *TTR: Traduction, terminologie, redaction*, 1(1991), 99–111.

Beninatto, Renato S., and De Palma Donald. A., 'Collaborative Translation', in *Multilingual* 2008, <http://www.scribd.com/doc/4069269/Structuring-Collaborative-Translation-20-Less-Delivery-TimeBetter-Quality>, accessed 31 December 2024.

Désilets, Alain, van der Meer, Jaap, 'Co-creating a Repository of Best Practices for Collaborative Translation', *Linguistica Antverpensia*, 10(2011), 27–45.

Espasa, Eva, 'Performability in Translation: Speakability? Playability? Or just Saleability?', in C.A. Upton ed., *Moving Target: Theatre Translation and Cultural Relocation*, (Manchester: St. Jerome Publishing, 2000), 49–62.

Laera, Margherita, 'Theatre Translation as Collaboration: Aleks Sierz, Martin Crimp, Nathalie Abrahami, Colin Teevan, Zoe Svendsen and Michael Walton discuss Translation for the Stage', *Contemporary Theatre Review*, 21(2001), 213–225.

Laurenti, Francesco, 'Shakespeare on Stage for the Screen and Collaborative Translation: Cesare Deve Morire', *Lingue e Linguaggi*, 52(2022), 177-191.

Munday, Jeremy, *Introducing Translation Studies. Theories and Applications*, (London/New York: Routledge, 2012).

O'Brien, Sharon, 'Collaborative Translation', in Gambier Yves and van Doorslaer Luc, eds., *Handbook of Translation Studies*, Vol. 2, (Amsterdam/Philadelphia: John Benjamins Publishing Company, 2013), 17–20.

Pym, Anthony, 'Translation Research Projects 3', *Intercultural Studies Group*, Tarragona, (2011).

Thelen, Marcel, 'Collaborative Translation in Translator Training', *Konin Language Studies*, 3(2016), 253–269.

Collaborative Translation Innovative Practices and Interactions towards the Future: An Introduction

Valentina Baselli

This book provides an overview of innovative collaborative translation practices and the growing impact of new human-technology interactions in translation and interpreting. While collaborative translation can be traced back to ancient times, it is in recent eras - characterized by the technological turn[1] in translation and interpreting - that this practice has undergone significant evolution. Various aspects of collaborative translation have been explored over time, including multilingual texts, historical collaborative translations, the relationship between authors and translators, collaborative editorial translation, and teamwork in translation and proofreading. However, the rise of new technologies and artificial intelligence (AI) has led to a new type of collaboration between human translators/interpreters and technology, i.e. human-computer or human-machine interaction.

> Human-computer interaction (HCI) lies at the intersection between the social and behavioural sciences on the one hand and computer and information technology on the other. It is concerned with understanding how people make use of devices and systems that incorporate or embed computation, and how such devices and systems can be more useful and more usable[2].

HCI has developed methods that boost work practices, help organizations and assess the utility of devices, interfaces and programmes. Therefore,

---

1 Claudio Fantinuoli, 'The technological turn in interpreting: the challenges that lie ahead'. *Proceedings of the conference Übersetzen und Dolmetschen 4.0. – Neue Wege im digitalen Zeitalter* (2019), 334-354.

2 John M. Carroll, *HCI Models, Theories, and Frameworks: Toward a Multidisciplinary Science* (Burlington: Morgan Kaufmann Publishers, 2003), 1.

HCI research has broadened its scope to examine how humans interact with technologies and computer, e.g. in the case of new user interfaces and technologies designed to support human activities.

From this perspective, human translators or interpreters and machines are two forms of intelligence, collaborating and enriching each other. HCI covers scenarios where a variety of technologies and human actions coexist and can be conceived as a unified system[3]. This results in what could be described as a form of collaboration, in a broader sense, between an individual and technology. Among all forms of human-machine interactions, the relationship between humans and AI cannot go unmentioned. AI represents a matter of discussion in every field of scientific research and has begun to permeate the fabric of our daily lives. Its impact is felt everywhere, sparking conversations and driving innovation like never before. As a matter of fact, at the time of writing, it stands as the most significant technological revolution of our time. Narrowing it down to the scope of this volume, the rise of AI has introduced new approaches to translation, interpreting and content creation resulting from human-machine interaction.

In Translation Studies, the relationship between translation and AI has been widely researched[4]. However, although the use of AI in translation can enhance the translator's efficiency and access to information, it also raises ethical issues as regards the role of human translators, the presence of biases

---

3 Du Ziqiang, *Bridging the gap exploring the cognitive impact of Interpretbank on Chinese interpreting trainees* (Bologna University: Ph. D Dissertation), 14.

4 Just to mention a few example, see Sanjun Sun, Kanglong Liu, and Riccardo Moratto, *Translation Studies in the Age of Artificial Intelligence* (London: Routledge, 2025); Chan Sin-wai, *Routledge Encyclopedia of Translation Technology* (London: Routledge, 2023); Felix Do Carmo, and Joss Moorkens, 'Differentiating editing, post-editing and revision', in Maarit Koponen, Brian Mossop, Isabelle S. Robert, and Giovanna Scocchera (eds.), *Translation Revision and Post-editing: Industry Practices and Cognitive Processes*, (London: Routledge, 2020); Kaifang Fan, and Chunlei Wang, 'Translation Studies in the Era of AI: Characteristics, Fields and Significance', *International Journal of Translation and Interpretation Studies*, 3/4 (2023), 58-67; María del Mar Sánchez Ramos, 'Public Service Interpreting and Translation Training: A Path towards Digital Adaptation to Machine Translation and Post-Editing', *Interpreter and Translator Trainer 16 (3)*, (2022), 294–308.

in translations, and the impact of AI on the workforce[5]. Despite the above-mentioned challenges, new opportunities for innovation and collaboration between Translation Studies and AI have been explored. These include the development of hybrid models that combine human and machine translation[6].

In the field of collaborative translation, 'fully automatic machine translation struggles to meet the expectations of its users since there are more or less translation faults brought on by data bottlenecks. Therefore, we require collaborative assisted translation technology for human-computer interaction'[7] and human oversight in the content creation process. According to experimental findings, the translation accuracy of the collaborative translation system for AI-based human-computer interaction ranges between 95.6% and 98.2%. Hence, the quality of translations is enhanced after human-computer contact and cooperation[8].

Furthermore, as Muñoz[9] highlights, computer-assisted translation contributes to easing and distributing the cognitive processes involved in translation among individuals as they work together with computers towards a new type of translaboration[10], thereby demonstrating how beneficial HCI can be in translation processes and practices.

---

5 Firat Soysal, 'Enhancing Translation Studies with Artificial Intelligence (AI): Challenges, Opportunities, and Proposals', *International Journal of Philology and Translation Studies*, 5/2 (2023), 177.

6 Jichen Zhu, Antonios Liapis, Sebastian Risi, Rafael Bidarra, and G. Michael Youngblood, 'Explainable AI for Designers: A Human-Centered Perspective on Mixed-Initiative Co-Creation', *2018 IEEE Conference on Computational Intelligence and Games (CIG 2018): Maastricht, Netherlands, 14-17 August 2018 (ss. 1-8)*. (Piscataway: IEEE, 2018).

7 Yunzhi Shao, 'Human-Computer Interaction Environment Monitoring and Collaborative Translation Mode Exploration Using Artificial Intelligence Technology', *Journal of Environmental and Public Health*, (New York: Wiley onlinelibrary, 2022) <https://onlinelibrary.wiley.com/doi/10.1155/2022/4702003>, accessed 20 September 2024.

8 Yunzhi Shao, 'Human-Computer Interaction Environment Monitoring and Collaborative Translation Mode Exploration Using Artificial Intelligence Technology'.

9 Ricardo Muñoz Martín, *Traductología cognitiva. Tratado general*. (Las Palmas De Gran Canaria: ULPGC Ediciones, 2023) < https://spdc.ulpgc.es/libro/traductologia-cognitiva_150298>.

10 Translaboration derives from blending 'translation' and 'collaboration,'. For more details, see Cornelia Zwischenberger, Alexa Alfer, *Translaboration - Translation and labour, Translation in Society*, 1/2, (2022), 200 – 223.

The recent technological turn and the new pervasive AI paradigm have also strongly affected Interpreting Studies and the interpreting practice. Indeed, interpreters daily interact with at least two types of interpreting technologies, i.e. technologies used to deliver interpreting services, such as Simultaneous Interpreting Delivering Platforms (SIDPs) for remote interpreting assignments, and those that can be applied to support the interpreters' workflow and enhance their performance. From this perspective, HCI mainly focuses on the user experience, exploring how technology can support cognitive processes. In relation to the latter type of technology, HCI can serve to understand how computer-assisted interpreting (CAI) tools can enhance interpreters' performance, which significantly improves with the use of CAI tools, while potentially reducing their cognitive load. Therefore, artificial intelligence has been integrated into third-generation AI-based CAI tools[11] to support human interpreters during both in-person and remote interpreting assignments.

Furthermore, in Interpreting Studies and interpreter training, Virtual Reality (VR) gives rise to a new type of interpreter-technology interaction. Especially in the wake of the pandemic - which accelerated the global adoption of distance learning and remote events - the demand for more immersive experiences from both academia and event organisers has led to a rise in projects and events hosted in VR. To immerse in these virtual realities, users wear VR headsets and join virtual worlds with their avatars, thus creating a new type of human-machine interaction as well as a new player, the 'avaterpreter'[12]. Although it may seem futuristic, interpreter training in VR is increasingly gaining popularity and interpreters are starting to practise interpreting in virtual reality and in the metaverse using VR headsets. In

---

11 Claudio Fantinuoli, 'Towards AI-enhanced computer-assisted interpreting', in Bart Defrancq and Gloria Corpas Pastor (eds.), *Interpreting technologies. Technologies – Current and Future Trends*, (Amsterdam/Philadelphia: John Benjamins Publishing Company, 2023), 46-71.

12 Valentina Baselli, 'The Avatar-Interpreter: Simultaneous Interpreting using VR Headsets', in Sara García Fernández, Fátima Gómez-Cáneba, Beatriz Guerrero García, Francesca Placidi, Margarita Savchenkova, and Susana Schoer-Granado (eds.), *Traducción y sostenibilidad cultural II: retos y nuevos escenarios* (Salamanca: Ediciones Universidad de Salamanca, 2025), pp. 309 – 316.

this context, the intersection of VR, AI and interpreting paves the way for the integration of virtual reality/augmented reality and CAI tools, thereby advancing the field of augmented interpreting. On the other side of the coin, even in Interpreting Studies the adoption of new technologies, especially AI, inevitably raises ethical concerns, including privacy issues and the rise of machine interpreting aimed at replacing human interpreters.

Therefore, while the use of AI leads to ethical questions around human workforce, privacy and creative content creation, it is only through ongoing dialogue between human translators/interpreters and new technologies that accuracy and confidentiality can be ensured.

Hence, the wide-ranging variety of collaborative practices and human-machine interactions previously mentioned also reflect the multifaceted content of this volume, which originates from a collection of contributions presented during the *Collaborative Translation Award* and the conference *Training Translators and Interpreters Today: Perspectives and Evolutions* held at IULM University in 2024. While the essays are varied in scope, they are all united by the overarching theme of collaborative translation and human-machine interaction, our focus of research at the International Center for Research on Collaborative Translation (IULM).

The first part of the volume explores new collaborative practices in retranslation, quality assurance of collaborative translations, extreme translations and audio description. The volume opens with Francesco Laurenti's essay, which investigates the impact of translators' subjectivity on retranslation. This essay presents the dynamics of collaborative retranslation by analysing a corpus of literary retranslations into Italian of George Orwell's *Homage to Catalonia*, comprising different translation strategies and issues, e.g. the translation of orality, errors and multilingualism. Laurenti concludes his essay by highlighting the importance of considering subjectivity's implications in collaborative retranslations to ensure effective, accurate and new translations.

This essay is then followed by a discussion around collaborative translation evaluation and quality assurance by Federica Villareale. Her examination includes a model for organising work in collaborative translation, categorizing collaborative translation (communication, coordination, or collaboration) tools and a self-evaluation questionnaire for translators working on collaborative projects. The core of her contribution lies in a questionnaire purposely designed to assess the effectiveness of collaborative translation practices, specifically in terms of promotion, time-saving, and quality improvement.

Lara Delle Foglie follows Villareale's contribution with an examination on transcreation and extreme translation of texts that do not conform to conventional rules, including poems, experimental prose, proverbs, tongue-twisters, songs, audiovisual content and marketing copy. Extreme translations and transcreation share several common elements, which confirm their status as translation practices, bringing the translator to visibility. Through the analysis of selected case studies, including Joyce's *Finnegans Wake* and Queneau's *Exercices de style*, Delle Foglie underscores the significance of acknowledging these practices as a form of translation, emphasising their inherently collaborative nature.

The subsequent contribution, an essay by Laura Giordani, addresses the importance of teamwork in audio description, highlighting the benefits of collaboration between professionals with different skills, including writing and cinematic language experts, narrators, sound technicians and, ideally, blind and visually impaired people who can provide direct feedback. In an era where authorship is regarded as a solitary endeavour, a series of guidelines and indications of good practice for a new collaborative approach can generate a faster and more effective method that will support the end user.

The second part of the volume addresses the new above-mentioned type of interaction between technology and human translators or interpreters.

The first contribution by Fabio Morotti draws upon the fields of computational creativity, adaptation studies, generative culture, and AI cinema. In this work the author explores the intersection of generative AI and intersemiotic and collaborative translation, applied to the creation of an audiovisual version of Virgil's *Aeneid* through human-AI interaction. In addition to presenting the challenges and opportunities associated with integrating AI into creative practices, the author discusses the potential benefits and limitations of this approach. Indeed, his work highlights the role of AI in creating innovative adaptations, where faithfulness to the original source requires deep understanding of both the literary text and generative AI capabilities. This underscores the need for human oversight and creative input in the generative process.

In the following contribution, Gatto and Villareale narrow the focus of the audiovisual version of the above-mentioned Virgil's *Aeneid,* to a linguistic analysis of the intersemiotic translation carried out. After describing the project and the plot of the video, they report on the creative process of generating this video from a written text, underlining the importance of the creator's input. For this project, the Latin source text was first translated into English, with the aim of generating AI images to eventually create a video. The video was manually edited and subtitles in several languages were added to make the project accessible to a broader audience. The process was carried out through continuous human-AI interaction.

This volume would not have been complete without mentioning a new form of collaborative oral translation. Therefore, the last contribution of the volume delves into a relatively new area of collaborative interpreting and interpreter training. In their paper, Baselli, Comoglio and Russello describe the interaction dynamics between conference interpreters and virtual reality (VR), presenting the results of a case study conducted during a training session organised by the International Center for Research on Collaborative Translation at IULM University. Activities such as sight translation, shadowing and simultaneous interpreting were performed using VR headsets in immersive virtual environments, allowing for experimentation with human simultaneous interpreting in VR conference settings. The authors emphasize the potential of integrating VR and AI as a promising avenue for further investigation.

As new collaborative practices and technological changes are driving human interaction in entirely new directions, translators and interpreters must keep up with these rapidly evolving settings, reinventing their roles and reshaping old perspectives. 'After all, next-generation technologies will need next-generation interpreters'[13] and translators.

References

Baselli, Valentina, 'The Avatar-Interpreter: Simultaneous Interpreting using VR Headsets', in Sara García Fernández, Fátima Gómez-Cáneba,

---

13 Bart Defrancq, and Gloria Corpas Pastor, *Interpreting Technologies – Current and Future Trends*, (Amsterdam/Philadelphia: John Benjamins Publishing Company, 2023), 4.

Beatriz Guerrero García, Francesca Placidi, Margarita Savchenkova, and Susana Schoer-Granado (eds.), *Traducción y sostenibilidad cultural II: retos y nuevos escenarios* (Salamanca: Ediciones Universidad de Salamanca, 2025), pp. 309 – 316.
Carroll, John M., *HCI Models, Theories, and Frameworks: Toward a Multidisciplinary Science* (Burlington: Morgan Kaufmann Publishers, 2003).
Defrancq, Bart, and Corpas Pastor, Gloria, *Interpreting Technologies – Current and Future Trends*, (Amsterdam/Philadelphia: John Benjamins Publishing Company, 2023).
Del Mar Sánchez Ramos, Maria, 'Public Service Interpreting and Translation Training: A Path towards Digital Adaptation to Machine Translation and Post-Editing', *Interpreter and Translator Trainer 16 (3)*, (2022), 294–308.
Do Carmo, Felix, and Moorkens, Joss, 'Differentiating editing, post-editing and revision' in Maarit Koponen, Brian Mossop, Isabelle S. Robert, and Giovanna Scocchera, eds., *Translation Revision and Post-editing: Industry Practices and Cognitive Processes*, (London: Routledge, 2020).
Fan, Kaifang, and Wang, Chunlei, 'Translation Studies in the Era of AI: Characteristics, Fields and Significance', *International Journal of Translation and Interpretation Studies*, 3/4 (2023), 58-67.
Fantinuoli, Claudio, 'Towards AI-enhanced computer-assisted interpreting', in Bart Defrancq and Gloria Corpas Pastor, eds., *Interpreting technologies. Technologies – Current and Future Trends*, (Amsterdam/Philadelphia: John Benjamins Publishing Company, 2023), 46-71.
Fantinuoli, Claudio, 'The technological turn in interpreting: the challenges that lie ahead'. *Proceedings of the conference Übersetzen und Dolmetschen 4.0. – Neue Wege im digitalen Zeitalter* (2019), 334-354.
Muñoz, Martín Ricardo, *Traductología cognitiva. Tratado general* (Las Palmas De Gran Canaria: ULPGC Ediciones, 2023) <https://spdc.ulpgc.es/libro/traductologia-cognitiva_150298>.
Sin-wai, Chan, *Routledge Encyclopedia of Translation Technology* (London: Routledge, 2023).

Soysal, Firat, 'Enhancing Translation Studies with Artificial Intelligence (AI): Challenges, Opportunities, and Proposals', *International Journal of Philology and Translation Studies*, 5/2 (2023), 177-191.

Sun, Sanjun, Liu, Kanglong, and Moratto, Riccardo, *Translation Studies in the Age of Artificial Intelligence* (London: Routledge, 2025).

Yunzhi, Shao, 'Human-Computer Interaction Environment Monitoring and Collaborative Translation Mode Exploration Using Artificial Intelligence Technology', *Journal of Environmental and Public Health*, (New York: Wiley onlinelibrary, 2022),

<https://onlinelibrary.wiley.com/doi/10.1155/2022/4702003>, accessed 20 September 2025

Zhu, Jichen, Liapis Antonios, Risi Sebastian, Bidarra Rafael, and Youngblood G. Michael, 'Explainable AI for Designers: A Human-Centered Perspective on Mixed-Initiative Co-Creation', *2018 IEEE Conference on Computational Intelligence and Games (CIG 2018): Maastricht, Netherlands, 14-17 August 2018 (ss. 1-8)*. (Piscataway: IEEE, 2018).

Ziqiang, Du, *Bridging the gap exploring the cognitive impact of Interpretbank on Chinese interpreting trainees* (Bologna University: Ph. D Dissertation, 2024).

Zwischenberger, Cornelia, and Alfer Alexa, *Translaboration - Translation and labour, Translation in Society*, 1/2, (2022), 200 – 223.

PART I

The Evolving Nature of Collaborative Translation

1

Issues of Multiple Subjectivities in Collaborative Retranslation: George Orwell's *Homage to Catalonia* as a Case Study

Francesco Laurenti

Abstract

This essay investigates the impact of translators' subjectivity on retranslations, specifically on the sub-genre of collaborative retranslations. To do so, this essay examines the dynamics activated when retranslation is collaborative. As a case study, this essay considers a corpus of recently published literary retranslations of George Orwell's *Homage to Catalonia* into Italian. Namely, the issues that are described include the translation of orality, errors, and multilingualism; such issues are explored in a collaborative setting, highlighting some of the phenomena that come into play when different subjectivities work side by side in the process of collaborative retranslation.

Introduction

The implications of subjectivity on collaborative translation and more specifically on retranslations represent a challenging and stimulating topic for investigation. The questions that arise from this almost unexplored issue imply a shared definition of the concept of subjectivity regarding translation, and the notion of subjectivity as it applies to collaborative retranslations vs collaborative translations in more general terms.

What kind of and how many subjectivities are involved in the collaborative translation process? Are there different implications in the case of a work that has been collaboratively retranslated rather than translated for the first time? How do we mitigate subjectivity in collaborative retranslation? What are the implications on our notion of the subjectivity of those translations that are carried out collaboratively?

To investigate the dynamics that are activated when retranslation is collaborative, and to focus on subjectivity in such a process, this essay will consider a small corpus of recently published literary retranslations of George Orwell's *Homage to Catalonia*, focusing on the following matters: chapter order, orality, errors, and multilingualism.

1. Preliminary Definitions

To better investigate this specific field, an introductory distinction must first be made about what we mean by 'collaboration' when we speak of translation (and retranslation), distinguishing it from 'cooperation'. This is a distinction worth repeating, as it is not always easy to differentiate between collaboration and cooperation, and one word is often used to mean the other.

It is nothing new for individuals to come together to perform complex tasks, the purpose of which either cannot be achieved by a single actor or can be better achieved with the involvement of several actors. This is what happens in today's organizations, where collective work is based on sharing common interests and tasks in a *continuum* that ranges from cooperation to collaboration.

To distinguish between the two, it is essential to understand the nuances related to subjective responsibility and the means used to perform the task and to differentiate the level of interdependence between actors.

'Co-operative work' can be defined as collective work in which the task to be performed is divided into sub-tasks; each sub-task is then assigned to a different person (actor) based on their specific abilities. In other words, it is a rationalized distribution of tasks among several different actors who will act autonomously. Each participating actor knows what he or she must do from the outset and communicates, exchanges or shares elements to achieve his or her individual goal, which, in the end, will be juxtaposed against the achievements of the other actors to create a single product.

Co-operation focuses, in a nutshell, on working together by performing different tasks separately[14].

Collaborative translation, on the other hand, does not necessarily imply an *a priori* division of roles, but rather a situation in which tasks and goals are shared, so that each actor in the group works on the same points, whether synchronously or not. It is a matter of combining the contributions of the individual subjectivities during the work: responsibility is more inter-subjective and lies with the whole group. This way of working requires regular communication between group members and precise knowledge of the progress of the (collective) work.

Moreover, in collaborative translation, inter-subjective interactions must be constant to ensure the overall coherence of the work, which is a necessary condition for the efficiency of the action. Thus, it can be deduced that collaboration is a form of action that goes beyond that of the individual subject.

Collaboration happens when an organised group of different subjects directs their collective interactions towards a goal that everyone knows could not be achieved by a single actor. Therefore, individual contributions only make sense when they are integrated, when they merge with all others, and are not simply juxtaposed. In other words, it is a matter of combining the individual contributions of each subject with those of others.

Collaborative work implies a mutual commitment in a joint effort to perform the same task and solve the same problem together and thus requires more interaction by team members and more interpersonal motivation and trust.

Our analysis will primarily investigate collaborative retranslations; however, the works under investigation include retranslations that are more

---

[14] France Henri, and Karin Lundgren-Cayrol, eds, *Apprentissage Collaboratif À Distance – Pour Comprendre Et Concevoir Les Environnements D'apprentissage Virtuels* (Québec: Presses de l'Université du Québec, 2001), 34.

peculiarly co-operative (to highlight the different implications of subjectivity in divergent forms of collective translation).

When considering retranslation, it must be noted that some authors tend to differentiate between retranslations which are influenced (and thus shaped) by previous translations of the same work, and 'new translations' which may not take them into account and are simply published later chronologically. I have decided not to delve into this topic, as this differentiation still lacks universal acknowledgment. However, the specific examples I will focus on - collaborative retranslations of George Orwell's *Homage to Catalonia* - are analyzed precisely in their relationship with previous translations.

Subjectivity has been defined as 'everything that has to do with the subject as a creator and user of discourse'[15], and as 'the marks by which a subject interprets and judges the world and expresses his or her affinity to it'[16]. On a similar note, it has been argued that 'the translator's subjectivity, which is the status influenced by subjective and initiative ideas and personal views, is critical for the translator and translating'[17] as it determines the translator's understanding and rendering of the source text, as well as their translation strategy and methodology[18]. As explained by Zha Mingjian and Tian Yu, 'the essential characteristics of the translator's subjectivity refer to the translator's "active cultural consciousness", "human character" and "aesthetic creativeness"'[19].

What is particularly interesting about the translator's subjectivity is that it does not operate in an originally objective language. In the words of

---

15 Émile Benveniste, *Problèmes de linguistique générale I* (Paris: Gallimard, 1966). Also see Émile Benveniste, *Problèmes de linguistique générale II* (Paris: Gallimard, 1974).

16 See Catherine Kerbrat-Orecchioni, *L'énonciation : de la subjectivité dans le langage* (Paris: Armand Colin, 2002 [1980]); Anne Reboul, and Jacques Moeschler, *Dictionnaire encyclopédique de pragmatique* (Paris: Éditions du Seuil, 1994); Patrick Charaudeau, and Dominique Maingueneau, *Dictionnaire d'Analyse du Discours* (Paris: Seuil, 2002).

17 Shufen Huang, 'A Study of the Translator's Subjectivity in Literary Translation – Exemplified by the English Version of The Border Town', *Open Journal of Social Sciences* 7/5 (2019), 99.

18 Huang, 'A Study of the Translator's Subjectivity in Literary Translation – Exemplified by the English Version of The Border Town', 99.

19 Zha Mingjian, and Tian Yu, 'On the Subjectivity of the Translator', *Chinese Translators Journal* 24 (2003), 19–24.

Jean-René Ladmiral : « la subjectivité radicalement individuelle du traducteur, en tant qu'il est un scripteur, un ré-écrivain et co-auteur, [...] s'inscrit dans le cadre de l'intersubjectivité commune qui se trouve dans le langage, tant dans le texte-source ainsi que dans le texte-cible »[20] [as a writer, re-writer, and co-author, the translator's profoundly unique subjectivity is a component of the inter-subjectivity that permeates language in both the source text and the target text][21].

It is subjectivity that contributes to giving the field of translation its fascinating mark, as it is a fact that individual interpretation necessarily permeates translation at every level and stage[22].

2. A Hint of a Proposal for Operational Guidelines

Even though the inescapability of subjectivity in the act of translating has been widely recognised, Translation Studies still give the impression of wavering between accepting the realm of subjectivity and investing translations with a certain ideal of objectivity (with the risk that objectivist aspirations may not only be futile but also harmful)[23].

What happens then, if the translator's agency is intertwined with that of other parties, as in the case of collaboratively or co-operatively retranslated works? Hanne Jansen and Anna Wegener coined the term 'multiple translatorship'[24] to refer to the translation process and product and to describe the complex network of relationships among agents involved in the translation event.

---

20 Muguraş Constantinescu, 'La traductologie que j'ai développée est une réflexion qui s'appuie essentiellement sur mon propre travail de traducteur – Entretien avec Jean-René Ladmiral', *Atelier de traduction* 14 (2010), 18.

21 All translations are my own unless otherwise noted.

22 Inger Hesjevoll Schmidt-Melbye, 'Ambiguïtés et hybridité – de la subjectivité dans le domaine de la traduction', *Synergies Pays Scandinaves* 7 (2012), 32 and 40.

23 Schmidt-Melbye, 'Ambiguïtés et hybridité – de la subjectivité dans le domaine de la traduction', 32.

24 Hanne Jansen, and Anna Wegener, 'Introduction', in Hanne Jansen, and Anna Wegener, eds, *Authorial and Editorial Voices in Translation 1 – Collaborative Relationships between Authors, Translators, and Performers* (Montréal: Éditions québécoises de l'oeuvre, 2013), 1–38.

If we perceive the translator as a subject who leaves his or her mark on the text and relate this to the phenomenon of retranslations (the existence of several translations of the same work), we can more easily see how a series of translations is also a manifestation of the translators' subjectivity and how tracing the marks that a translator leaves in his or her text[25] represents an open field of investigation.

We refer here to the term 'subjectivity' both as the intentional, conscious or non-conscious, state of a subject and as a derivation of the term 'subject' (where the individual is considered as the medium of an action in which it leaves its mark). Every translation is thus the manifestation and result of the meeting of multiple subjectivities.

When it comes to collaborative retranslations, the subjectivity of the translators interacts both with that of their collaborators in the act of retranslating a text, and with the subjectivities that are conveyed by previous translations of the same work. This is potentially true, even if translators undertaking a retranslation need not necessarily be familiar with, or even aware of, the work of their predecessors.

Bearing all of this in mind, how do we intercept subjectivity when it comes to collaborative retranslations? How can we 'measure' it and clearly define the interactions between different subjectivities?

Quoting from Lawrence Venuti, 'retranslations typically highlight the translator's intentionality [and subjectivity] both because they are designed to make an appreciable difference'[26] and because the retranslator selects and interprets the foreign text according to a different set of values, to bring about a new and different reception of that text in the translating culture[27]. As claimed by several scholars[28], the more subjective the translations (and retranslations), the more they are considered authored. The idea behind this

25 See Elzbieta Skibinska, 'La Retraduction, Manifestation De La Subjectivité Du Traducteur', *Doletiana* 1 (2010), <https://raco.cat/index.php/Doletiana/article/view/148423≥, accessed 10 November 2023.

26 Lawrence Venuti, 'Retranslations: The Creation of Value', *Bucknell Review* 47/1 (2004), 3.

27 Venuti, 'Retranslations: The Creation of Value', 3.

28 See Willis Barnstone, *The Poetics of Translation: History, Theory, Practice* (New Haven: Yale University Press, 1993); Anthony Pym, 'The Translator as Author: Two Quixotes', *Translation and Literature* 14/1 (2005).

seems to be that the translator's relative independence from the source text is indicative of his or her subjective involvement in the translated text, with the assumption that: 'if the translator stays close to the original, there is little subjective involvement (little authoring), whereas if he or she departs from the original, there is a great degree of subjective involvement'[29]. However, even this idea cannot always be confirmed, given that the decision *not* to depart from the original 'is as much a matter of subjective choice as [is] the decision to depart from the original'[30].

Translation involves making decisions about how to convey the meaning, style, tone and cultural nuances of the source text in the target language. These decisions can be subjective and are often influenced by a translator's background, experiences and personal preferences. Indeed, as individuals with unique perspectives, translators imprint their subjectivity on their translations in several aspects:

1) Interpretation: Translators may interpret the same source text differently based on their understanding of the context, culture and language, and these differences in interpretation may lead to variations in the translated content;
2) Cultural Bias: Translators may unintentionally introduce cultural biases into the translation, and their cultural background may affect how they understand and convey certain concepts or references;
3) Tone and Style: Translators may have different preferences for the tone and style of the translation;
4) Language Proficiency: Differences in language proficiency among collaborators can result in variations in the quality and accuracy of the translation, and translators with a stronger command of the target language may have a greater influence;
5) Personal Preferences: Translators may have personal preferences regarding terminology or phrasing, which may lead to disagreements and discussions during the collaborative translation process;

---

[29] Annjo Klungervik Greenall, 'Translators' voices in Norwegian retranslations of Bob Dylan's songs', *Target* 27/1 (2015), 40–57.

[30] Greenall, 'Translators' voices in Norwegian retranslations of Bob Dylan's songs', 40–57.

6) Editing and Revisions: Collaborative translation often involves multiple rounds of editing and revisions; each revision may introduce new elements of subjectivity as different collaborators suggest changes based on their perspectives.

Thus, the translator's subjectivity,encompasses various aspects, 'including cultural awareness, reader awareness, personal attributes, social and ideological views, language competency, aesthetic propensity, and inventiveness'[31]. These elements can be observed through textual appropriation, adaptation and intervention throughout the translation process; when it comes to collaborative translations, they occasionally need to be monitored and addressed. To address issues of subjectivity in collaborative translation, the team should establish clear guidelines, maintain open communication, and prioritize consistency. But how do we mitigate subjectivity in collaborative (re)translations?

Several strategies can be adopted:

1) Create Style Guides: Develop style guides and glossaries providing specific instructions on preferred terminology, tone and style to ensure consistency across translations;
2) Technology Integration: Translation memory tools and terminology databases can help maintain consistency by storing previous translations and preferred terminology;
3) Peer Review: Encourage peer review within the translation team to cross-check and discuss translation choices, aiming for consensus, as regular feedback loops can refine translations and reduce biases;
4) Cultural Sensitivity Training: Ensure that translators are culturally sensitive and aware of potential biases when translating content from different cultural contexts; each translator's awareness and understanding of cultural differences is crucial;
5) Collaborative Decision-Making: Foster a collaborative environment, where translators can openly discuss and resolve differences in

---

31 Guo Xiaohan, and Mohamed Abdou Moindjie, 'A Perspective on the Translator's Subjectivity and its Constraints in Literary Translation: A Critical Analysis', *Journal of Positive School Psychology* 6/4 (2022), 3118.

interpretation, establishing open channels for discussing translation choices.

To understand some of the dynamics that characterise the encounter between several subjectivities (several subjects, each with their individual self-conscious perspectives) in collaborative retranslations, let us explore subjectivity as the manifestation of personal impressions, prejudices, interpretations, perspectives and ideology, by focusing on a corpus of recently published retranslations of George Orwell's *Homage to Catalonia*. This will serve as a paradigmatic example of how, through several concurrent translations of the same work, the specific subjectivity of an author can be better intercepted and reintroduced into the receiving culture.

3. Retranslating a volume undergoing several concurrent retranslations

If it is true that translations rarely happen by pure chance, this may be even more true when referring to retranslations, which often respond to the dynamics of the publishing market (as in the case of copyrights) and to different constraining factors (e.g. the pressure to target readers' interests and their 'horizon of expectations'[32]).

Upon the arrival of the 'long-awaited' seventieth year since the death of a specific author, an anniversary that becomes an automatic incentive to reproduce his or her texts, publishing houses contact translators and groups of translators – usually well in advance – so that they may have a retranslation ready for publication on the exact date of the forfeiture of rights.

In 2021, George Orwell was for this reason prominent in Italian bookstores, with several new editions and new translations of his works[33]. In such a publishing context, thanks to the comparison between several new translations, the subjectivity of the original author and the subjective approaches of the

32 Ya-Mei Chen, 'The Translator's Subjectivity and Its Constraints in News Transediting: A Perspective of Reception Aesthetics', *Meta* 56/1 (2011), 14.

33 The list of Italian publications is very long: one needs only to think that in 2021, some thirty translations of Orwell's works were published in Italy, including a dozen translations of *Homage to Catalonia*.

different translators and agents involved in the retranslations, can more easily emerge and be effectively examined. We can elaborate on how different subjectivities were involved in this massive retranslation activity, which in some cases was also collaborative.

In such a situation, some professional translators, who may already know each other well, may end up translating the same work for different publishing houses at the same time, and this was the case in the latest round of Italian retranslations of Orwell's works.

In such cases, it is not uncommon to see another form of collaboration, rarely surveyed, between translators who are translating the same work at the same time, but for different publishing houses, and who discuss their translation issues and solutions with each other. Such a collaborative dialogue between translators is usually founded on mutual trust, given that it can be compromising (when not contractually prohibited) to reveal one's translation choices before the actual publication of the work. This general tendency to avoid 'stealing' solutions from others is also driven by the desire not to produce a style and a 'voice' that are too similar to those of another retranslation, and thus produce 'replicas' rather than 'new translations'.

Through several concurrent translations of the same work, the specific subjectivity of an author can be better reintroduced into the receiving culture by manifesting its different nuances. Thus, when retranslations take place at about the same time (and are directed to broadly the same readership), it is easier to find out through comparative analysis whether or not the subjectivity of the original author "survives" in retranslations. It is also easier to observe how the influence of different subjectivities (translators/revisers/other actors) affects the translated work.

As a matter of fact, retranslation lends itself well to comparative analysis. If one or more of the observed retranslations are collaborative, this adds a further layer of analysis, since keeping track of those collaborations proves useful to investigate the subjectivity of each translator, as well as different interpretations of the author's subjectivity in the final work.

4. Collaboratively Retranslating George Orwell

Our translation of *Homage to Catalonia* was published within a collection of Orwell's selected works[34] translated into Italian by different translators, who already knew each other, discussed with each other, and translated each according to their subjectivity (after a collective debate among the translators of the entire collection, that left a trace in their individual choices).

For a more faithful rendering of the political dimension of Orwell's writing, we opted to form a team consisting of translators with different 'political subjectivities' to interpret Orwell's political ideals and principles. This required, of course, prior dialogue between the translators of different works, to harmonize the translations without making them excessively dull.

The heterogeneity of the translators provided different ways of interpreting Orwell's subjectivity through the translators' approaches that we wanted to coexist in the collection: in our opinion, the plurality of different translating subjectivities would have ensured a greater adherence to the heterogeneity of Orwellian writings.

How did the selection of the works to be translated within the volume come about? Was it an imposed or collaborative choice? The collaborative dimension of the work and the fact that the translators knew each other allowed for a discussion among the translators even before the selection of the works to be translated was made. This enabled Enrico Terrinoni, the project leader, and a member of the translation team, to select a corpus of works and suggest it to the publisher.

In this sense, the publisher proved to be very prompt in accepting the proposal by our team leader. Perhaps the fact that our choice was presented as being collective and was sponsored by one of the most authoritative translators from the English language in Italy, convinced the publisher to proceed in the direction we suggested. Thus, there was a subjective yet collaboratively reasoned choice underlying the retranslation, of who would translate what

[34] Original titles: *Down and Out in Paris and London*, trans. by Andrea Binelli; *Burmese Days*, trans. by Andrea Binelli; *Homage to Catalonia*, trans. by Francesco Laurenti and Fabio Morotti; *Animal Farm*, trans. by Enrico Terrinoni; *1984*, trans. by Enrico Terrinoni.

and why. Through this selection, we intended to convey the evolution of Orwellian writing and trace the development of Orwell's subjective creativity.

How did Morotti and I, translators of *Homage to Catalonia*, relate to the translators of the other works in the collection of Orwellian retranslations published by Newton Compton?

In my case, I considered being joined by Fabio Morotti, a scholarly anthropologist and a writer of travel and reportage books, translator, and a keen connoisseur of the English language, particularly of George Orwell, with the firm belief that our collaboration would result in an Italian rendering of *Homage to Catalonia* that was closer to the original than a single translator could have achieved. While such a collaboration was yet to come to fruition, it was clear to me that the translated text would benefit enormously from it.

Morotti would ideally provide his historical awareness concerning the events taking place in 1930s Spain. Most importantly, however, as a reportage author whose own work had been influenced by Orwell's writings, he could also offer an important stylistic contribution to the rendering of the dry Orwellian language, characterized by short periods, repetitions, and by a lack of metaphorical language. To represent Orwell's voice to Italian readers today, we felt we had to distance ourselves from certain choices made by the translators who had preceded us. Mainly, this concerned some specific aspects, such as the rendering of the plurilingualism, the approach to Orwell's errors in the original text and the peculiar marks of orality in Orwellian writing, as well as the very architecture of the work, which underwent a major restructuring between the first and subsequent English editions.

Let us now deal with the rendering of Orwellian orality, the translation of errors and our choices concerning the organisation into chapters of the original work.

The aim is to understand how collaboration allows us to reason together, providing us with greater confidence in our choices. Our choices, as we will see, exemplify some of the dynamics that can be established between the subjectivities of translators collaboratively retranslating a work vs the subjective creativity of both the author and previous translators.

5. Translating Subjective Implications in Chapters Organisation

In *Homage to Catalonia*, reality for Orwell represents the battleground between objectivity and ideological interest, which is also enacted through falsehoods, misrepresentations, and the instrumental use of sources by propaganda writers.

Such a discovery and new awareness is substantiated in Chapter V and Chapter XI, which in the first edition (1938) were published in the body of the work. These are important chapters, the most markedly political in the novel, representing an in-depth study of the Spanish situation accompanied by various sources and multiple excerpts from contemporary newspapers. These chapters will end up in the Appendix: first in the French translation, on which Yvonne Davet worked together with Orwell, and in later English editions of the work. What is important is that when the French translation was published in 1955 (Orwell, 1955, trans. by Yvonne Davet), after a dense and fruitful exchange of correspondence and sharing of reflections on crucial aspects of the text between the translator and Orwell himself, the translation was restructured in its architecture and division of chapters, and thus featured Chapters V and XI as appendices. As for the English editions of the original work, while they initially remained faithful to the first edition, from 1986 onward they would almost inexplicably move these two chapters outside the text in the form of appendices.

In our case, we had to choose whether to translate these chapters and place them into the body of the work (as was the case with the first edition of the *Homage*) or to place them 'outside' the *Homage* in the form of appendices (as will happen from a certain point onwards in the publication history of the *Homage*). How did we approach these chapters and the solutions of previous translators before making our choice? A deeper investigation was necessary. First, it was necessary to understand the reason why Orwell had wanted to place those chapters at the centre of the work at that specific moment in the evolution of his writing. We could 'interrogate' Orwell directly by looking at the paratext, but Orwell had never officially commented on this. We could alternatively investigate Orwell's private writings, with the hope of finding clues that might point us to a solution. Or we could seek comparison with the translators who had preceded us, to understand what solutions had already been taken.

To understand the thinking behind moving what were originally Chapters V and XI to the end of the book, an important collaboration provides us with relevant information: the one between the French translator Yvonne Davet and Orwell himself.

It was to the French translator, with whom Orwell exchanged letters for more than a decade, that the author would first reveal his intention, not yet final at the time, to reorganize the contents of the work. In a letter dated July 29, 1946, Orwell mentions that he is thinking of extracting 'one or perhaps two chapters' for the reprinting of *Homage to Catalonia* in England (1946, n.p.) by bringing them back at the end of the book in the form of appendices.

For Chapter XI, which refers to newspaper propaganda, Orwell notes that it is a chapter with historical significance that would risk being 'boring' to readers who were not particularly interested in the Spanish Civil War and could for this reason be moved to the end without damaging the text. In this sense, however, convinced Orwell was of the crucial importance of the chapter in the middle of the work, he was perhaps influenced by the publishing failure of the first edition and by his readers' expectations.

The collaboration between Orwell and Davet still stands as a valuable testimony to understand some of the collaborative dynamics established between authors and their translators, and in our case, it must be more carefully considered as the French translator's choices influenced subsequent retranslations worldwide.

However, we, as translators, had to understand whether it was the publisher who proposed to the translator (or to Orwell) some specific choices to make the work easier to read; the answer to this question came from the paratext. In a note that accompanied the French translation, the translator wrote that she had opted for moving these chapters to the appendix 'According to George Orwell's wish' because '[they deal with] the domestic politics of the Spanish revolution, Orwell wrote, and it seems to me that the reader would find them boring. But at the same time, they have a historical value'[35].

---

[35] Orwell, *La Catalogne libre (1936-1937)*, 8.

In Orwell's original intentions, these chapters represented an objective counterbalance to the extreme subjectivity of the narrative arising from the overlap, in *Homage to Catalonia*, of the author's voice with that of the narrator. With these two chapters in the body of the work, Orwell chose to interrupt the first-person narrative by reporting on a multitude of excerpts from contemporary newspaper articles with a bare and objective account to present real and historical events.

In doing so, Orwell initially proposed a potentially universal criterion of objective truth: that is, to take into consideration, in the dialectical agon of politics, the thoughts and reasons of every side, including the opposite side. What he proposed was a still inorganic kind of literary *pastiche*, to convey a reality that is not exclusively filtered by the kind of subjectivity that is conveyed by the diary-reportage form.

Orwell would later realize, perhaps because of the flop in sales of the first edition, that his initial choice to place the two chapters in the middle was not a winning one.

The solution of moving the two chapters to the Appendix, however, seemed to us to be motivated primarily by a concern for the expectations of the reading public, rather than by any specific intention of the author, and was a solution that Orwell would not see realized in his lifetime.

For us, it was necessary to compare this with the choices of previous translators, and our final choice was to reproduce Orwell's initial decision, as in the first edition.

We expected that we would be going against the choices of other translators who were working on the retranslation of the same work, and we knew that translators' choices in the past decades had been antithetical to ours, but we opted for a philological approach and reinserted those two chapters into the body of the work. We intended to reinforce the historiographical value of the work, despite the risk that our choice might have repercussions on its readability.

We also believed that, if we had removed the two chapters from the central part of the work by relegating them to the Appendix, such a choice would have overshadowed the subjective motivations that drove Orwell's personal and ideological development, which would lead to his later works.

We were convinced that the choice to break away from the tradition of previous translations would be congenial to a greater understanding of the author's subjectivity at the time of the writing of *Homage to Catalonia*. To re-read these two chapters today in the 'body' of the work, more than eighty years after the publication of the first English edition, and after the unveiling of 'Document Forty-Two'[36], meant bringing them out of the cage of their historical contingency, offering a universal reading of them, in an anti-totalitarian tone and as a symbol of justice and equality: as Orwell, according to our interpretation, would have wanted.

After much discussion, we concluded that our choice, namely, not to position Chapters V and XI in the Appendix, would also 'satisfy' some marketing and sales aspects of our translation, considering that several retranslations of *Homage to Catalonia* to be published in 2021 would have adopted the same choices as previous translators (perhaps to avoid too much 'risk-taking'). Perhaps we would not have strayed from the previous 'tradition of translations' of *Homage* if several retranslations had not been published in the same year: in other words, the concurrent retranslation and publication of several Italian editions allowed us to be more daring on one hand; on the other, our choice also served to diversify our translation from the others.

We were conscious that our solution might be met with hostility on the part of some readers, and it was interesting, in retrospect, to investigate how the audience received it.

A useful tool in this regard can be the online reviews of readers. In our case, these reflected exactly the doubts and the final choice we had adopted. On Amazon's site, only to give an example, alongside more enthusiastic reviews attributable to the language of the translation such as 'written in a pleasantly readable manner', there were reviews such as this: 'Good book...

36 In which the Bulgarian Prime Minister Georgi Dimitrov wrote to General Vorošilov, some two weeks before the May Days (which are discussed in Chapters V and XI), describing the non-communist fringe in the Spanish Republican Front as 'fascist or semi-fascist' and suggesting that a rapid government crisis in Spain should be urged, and even provoked.

until halfway through, when it strangles you in a... colossally boring discourse about communism in which I was ignominiously beached...'[37].

6. Translating Errors, Orality and Multilingualism

Dealing with errors is another aspect relevant to understanding how we worked collaboratively, taking previous translations into different languages into account, and investigating paratext to discover elements that could help us understand how much the author's subjective choice had had a bearing on this specific aspect.

Homage to Catalonia is a work originally full of errors, and mistakes involve choices for the translator that are often not automatic, difficult to normalise, and generally lead to little unseen experiments.

What does an error in the source text represent? For the translator, such errors are a headache he or she would gladly do without. For Translation Studies and translation didactics, it could represent an interesting area of reflection. Therefore, we believe, as Franco Nasi reminds us, that the analysis of the type of error is only one piece of the puzzle to be formed: 'così come non si traducono parole ma testi, allo stesso modo non si traducono errori ma testi che contengono eventuali errori'[38] [just as one does not translate words but texts, in the same way, one does not translate errors but texts that contain possible errors].

What kind of errors were we confronted with as translators of *Homage to Catalonia*? How had previous translators dealt with them? And above all, how should we deal with different kinds of errors, when Orwell himself on the last page of the work warns the reader, with rare intellectual honesty, 'Beware of my partisanship, my mistakes of fact'[39]? Orwell is referring mainly to his interpretation of reality, which he describes as inevitably subjective 'the distortion inevitably caused by my having seen only one corner of events'[40],

---

37 See <https://www.amazon.it/Omaggio-alla-Catalogna-Ediz-integrale/product-reviews/8822755766/ref=cm_cr_dp_d_show_all_btm?ie=UTF8&reviewerType=all_reviews>

38 Franco Nasi, *Tradurre l'errore. Laboratorio di pensiero critico e creativo* (Macerata: Edizioni Quodlibet, 2021), 11.

39 George Orwell, *Homage to Catalonia* (London: Secker and Warburg, 1938), 246.

40 Orwell, *Homage to Catalonia*, 247.

but there are other errors in the work that are relevant to our discourse as they relate to retranslation.

These were errors of different kinds: from spelling, dates relating to actual events, the names of cities, of police forces, to grammatical mistakes in the Spanish phrases that litter the text and errors concerning verifiable facts.

Faced with each error, we had to figure out whether they were errors intended by the author (for in our opinion there were such errors), errors made unknowingly (perhaps due to bad memory), or whether we were facing errors that could be traced back to the press and the publisher.

As the translator of *Homage to Catalonia*, Daniele Petruccioli acknowledges: 'the problem is that Orwell never really revised his entire book carefully'[41]. In fact, we only know of his revision of the first six chapters of the French translator's draft and of his directions on a copy of the original work sent to Rober Senhouse of Secker Warburg in 1948, a few months before his death and while he was working assiduously on 1984.

But let us examine some of these errors to better understand our point.

The French translator worked towards drastic corrections and her stance toward errors influenced many translators in later decades. As mentioned before, it is interesting that the English editions of *Homage to Catalonia* from a certain time onwards will consider the corrections published in the 1955 French translation and will integrate them in subsequent English editions.

Our choice in this regard was consistent with the philological approach of our retranslation. We felt that if there were spelling errors that had been intended as such by Orwell, others were unintentionally added, as in the case of dates or spellings of place names that he knew only from hearing about them.

But, faced with the occasional foreign word improperly written by Orwell, our difficult choice each time was to guess whether that one was the result of the author's decision or whether it was an unconscious mistake, a typo or a misprint. As a rule, we kept those errors we deemed to be functional to the understanding of the text and vice-versa, if we interpreted the error as not intended, we corrected it.

---

41 Daniele Petruccioli, 'L'omaggio alla Catalogna, come è nato, come – forse – ha cambiato noi', in George Orwell, *Omaggio alla Catalogna* (Milano: Rizzoli, 2021), 19–21.

But let us begin by reading some passages from *Homage to Catalonia*, to understand the peculiar approach to orality that Orwell enacts and to examine how we dealt with errors.

'In the Lenin Barracks in Barcelona, the day before I joined the militia, I saw an Italian militiaman standing in front of the officers' table'[42], thus begins *Homage to Catalonia*. That Italian man addresses Orwell directly, in the original text, in the following terms:

> '*Italiano?*'
> I answered in my bad Spanish: '*No, Ingles. Y tu?*'
> '*Italiano*'[43].

What happens on the first page of the book? An Italian militiaman addresses an English militiaman by speaking directly to him in Italian, the Englishman replies in Spanish (or rather, in pseudo-Spanish), and, seemingly unconcerned, the Italian militiaman answers in Italian as if speaking a *lingua franca* (all in the presence of other militiamen who are most likely speaking in Spanish, Catalan or English).

From the very beginning of the work, Orwell seeks to reproduce the peculiar heteroglossia between militiamen who came from all over the world and immediately introduces the hybrid and frank language of exchange which gives the novel its peculiar 'polyphonic' character: the characters express themselves through a multilingualism that was not generally, and surprisingly, reproduced by translators of the *Homage*.

In *Homage to Catalonia*, Orwell superimposes different writing styles and registers, revealing an aspect of communication among the militiamen that is often forgotten: the dimension of peculiar heteroglossia that characterises the post-babelic Popular Front.

As a keen observer of the accents of spoken language and spelling[44], Orwell reproduces the multiplicity of voices by resorting to deliberately improper accents and 'properly incorrect' transcriptions. *Homage to Catalonia* was for

---

[42] Orwell, *Homage to Catalonia*, 1.
[43] Orwell, *Homage to Catalonia*, 1.
[44] See Orwell, 1947 [1968], 304–307.

Orwell a laboratory of his political thought and writing as he began to search for an alternative narrative style. He recreated a 'modest' language, marked by linguistic economy and repetition, capable of speaking to everyone and in line with the ambition of socialist literature: an oral and 'demotic' language (as Orwell called it[45]), leaning towards colloquialism. In doing so, Orwell chose to recreate the chaotic dialogues and speeches to which he participated or that he had overheard, reproducing the linguistic *pastiche* in which he was immersed at the front.

Once the oral imprint of a literary text has been detected, to what extent is it up to the translator to recreate it in another language without exclusively privileging the written form? This is the question that we set before us in translating *Homage to Catalonia* (1938)[46], characterised as it is by a narrative based on orality and plurilingualism. 'C'est l'oralité qui est à traduire'[47] [It is orality that must be translated], as claimed in one of Meschonnic's famous translation maxims; but what happens when translators are confronted with the rendering of 'literary orality'? What are the most conventionally adopted approaches? Are there any general criteria that are useful when transposing the spoken language of a literary text into translation? How to render these peculiarly oral aspects in translation?

The choices of the past translators of *Homage to Catalonia* seemed to oscillate, revealing that the most widespread tendency had consisted in the 'ennobling' of the lexical and syntactical texture of the prototext, through the reduction of the very frequent lexical and syntactical repetitions that infuse the prose of the original with greater communicative effectiveness (and make it look closer to oral speech).

It is surprising that, with this 'ennobling' tendency towards the source text, both the earlier translators into different languages and those who retranslated the work into Italian in 2021, aimed at flattening Orwellian multilingualism and at correcting the fragmentation of direct speech.

---

45 See Orwell, 1944 [2001], 310–316.

46 The original reference edition, from which we quote textual excerpts here, is G. Orwell, *Homage to Catalonia*, Secker and Warburg, London, 1938.

47 Henri Meschonnic, *Poétique du traduire* (Lagrasse: Éditions Verdier, 1999), 29.

But let us proceed step by step and go back to the answer given by the protagonist to the Italian militiaman, '*No, Ingles. Y tu?*'[48]. This sentence highlights how Orwell expressed himself in a language that betrays a sense of communicative difficulty through its improper use of accentuation, spelling and punctuation.

Orwell spoke Spanish without knowing how to speak it, and like him, many of the militiamen at the front spoke languages other than their mother tongue, with an approximation that the writer tries to realistically reproduce on the page. The protagonist is aware of his difficulty in speaking Spanish, and makes the reader aware of it several times:

> All this time I was having the usual struggles with the Spanish language. Apart from myself, there was only one Englishman at the barracks, and nobody even among the officers spoke a word of French. Things were not made easier for me by the fact that when my companions spoke to one another they generally spoke in Catalan. The only way I could get along was to carry everywhere a small dictionary which I whipped out of my pocket in moments of crisis.[49]

Given the 'usual struggles with the Spanish language' that characterised Orwell's experience in Spain, the approximation of Orwell's response to the Italian militiaman ('*No, Ingles. Y tu?*'), along with its imprecise transcription on the page, conveys its own meaning and turns out to be anything but a typo. Here are some translations of the short dialogue mentioned above[50]:

> '*No, inglés*,' I replied in my bad Spanish. '*Y tú?*' (trans. by Giorgio Monicelli, 1948).
> '*No, Inglés. Y tu?*' (trans. by Yvonne Davet, 1955)
> '*No, Inglés. Y tú?*' (trans. by Riccardo Duranti, 1993)
> '*No, inglés. ¿Y tú?*' (trans. by Virus Editorial, 2003)

---

[48] Orwell, *Homage to Catalonia*, 1.

[49] Orwell, *Homage to Catalonia*, 10.

[50] The translations examined here are: *Omaggio alla Catalogna*, Italian trans. by Giorgio Monicelli; *Omaggio alla Catalogna*, Italian trans. by Riccardo Duranti; *La Catalogne libre*, French trans. by Yvonne Davet; *Homenaje a Cataluña*, Spanish trans. by Virus Editorial.

Only Yvonne Davet, who was in direct contact with Orwell, retains in her translation (1955) the original spelling of the clumsy Orwellian Spanish. In the other cases reported here, behaving as if faced with typos or errors, the translators retouch the sentence, correcting lower case, question marks and accents.

This is surprising because the impression one gets is that many translators missed Orwell's intentionality to report a fragment of orality with its peculiar inaccuracies, which are due to the poor command of the Spanish language of which the protagonist repeatedly complains.

It is even more surprising that, from a certain point on, such 'corrective' revision of the skewed spellings found in the original work would also be applied by publishers of the book in English (corollary: to what extent was this choice influenced by the translators' previous revisionary choices?)[51].

How should we behave in our retranslation when faced with such specific fragments of speech containing errors in the prototext? The answer did not seem obvious to us, considering that the tendency of previous translators over time had been to normalise what, in an initial blunder, had been interpreted as errors in the original author's handwriting or editorial typos.

Translators often question whether they should correct errors present in a source text. We are convinced that this is possible, but under one unavoidable condition: that the error be in fact an error; in the case of a literary work, this certainty that an error is an error is rarely easy to achieve.

As stated above, we first needed to understand whether the formal inaccuracies in the transcriptions (in this case speech fragments) were intentional or random and fortuitous. In the case of *Homage to Catalonia*, a closer reading of the original work revealed that the frequency of formal inaccuracies affecting the various transcriptions of speech fragments does not, except in rare cases, characterise the rest of the work; therefore, these inaccuracies cannot be blamed on the author's approximation or editorial typos, as has often been done.

A similar 'erroneous' transcription of speech can for instance be found when the protagonist, eager to learn the use of weapons before going to

51 See for example the 1977 Penguin edition republishing the first edition of *Homage to Catalonia*.

the front, addresses the lieutenant, pulling his Hugo dictionary out of his pocket, in these terms: 'I used to drag my Hugo's dictionary out of my pocket and start on him in my villainous Spanish: "*Yo se manejar fusil. No se manejar ametralladora. Quiero apprender ametralladora. Quando vamos apprender ametralladora?*"[52].

Orwell admits that his Spanish is 'villainous' (and as such, he brings it mimetically to the page). How is it possible then, that, even in this case, some English translators and publishers will opt for the rendering of a correct Spanish language that is, paradoxically, anything but 'villainous'?

Let us compare a few solutions:

> Yo sé manejar fusil. No sé manejar ametralladora. Quiero aprender ametralladora. Cuándo vamos aprender ametralladora?
> *(trans. by Yvonne Davet, 1955)*

> Yo sé manejar fusil. No sé manejar ametralladora. Quiero aprender ametralladora. Cuándo vamos aprender ametralladora?
> *(trans. by Riccardo Duranti, 1993)*

> Yo sé manejar fusil. No sé manejar ametralladora. Quiero aprender ametralladora. ¿Cuándo vamos aprender ametralladora?
> *(trans. by Virus Ed., 2003)*

> Yo sé manejar fusil. No sé manejar ametralladora. Quiero apprender ametralladora. Quándo vamos apprender ametralladora?'
> *(trans. by Penguin, 1977)*

This is an almost flawless Spanish language in which the verisimilitude of the source text completely vanishes. In another moment, as Orwell with his militia trudges through the night under direct fire from the fascists, the captain of the division, one Levinski, known to all as Benjamin ('by birth a Polish Jew but speaking French as his native language'[53]), addresses the protagonist

[52] Orwell, *Homage to Catalonia*, 10.
[53] Orwell, *Homage to Catalonia*, 9.

in these terms, 'To keep ze head down! To keep ze head down!'[54]. Once again, the language of communication between militiamen of different nationalities is a hybrid *lingua franca* that seems to characterise life on the frontline.

In the rendering of this portion of speech, translators' choices were different. If in the Italian rendering Duranti preferred to maintain the distorted spelling of the original 'To keep ze head down! To keep ze head down!'[55], Virus Editorial's Spanish translator opted for a more ethnocentric rendering by translating directly into Spanish, '¡Mantén la cabeza baja! ¡Mantén la cabeza baja!'[56] thus removing the patina of heteroglossia of Levinski's expression and having the captain even speak in Spanish. Translator Yvonne Davet will opt for a hybrid solution, bringing back the original 'To keep ze head down! To keep ze head down!'[57], followed by the French translation in parentheses ('Garde la tête baissée! Garde la tête baissée!'[58]).

The general tendency of the translators of *Homage to Catalonia* with regard to the rendering of the portions of the dialogue with errors and mispronunciations in the original work was thus generally to veer toward anomalous forms of hypercorrection, correcting what the translators interpreted as errors in the prototext, even when the error might have had a significant value in the author's intentions and as such should be retained (albeit possibly modified).

It appears difficult to interpret such adjustments as forms of ennobling the source text, since they cannot be justified, except by taking into account the subjective perception of the translator.

We believe, as a rule, that when it is possible to know that the error on the author's part was not intended, the translator should correct it. Where, on the other hand, the translator does not have maximum certainty that that error is unintended, he or she must retain it in the translation.

---

54 Orwell, *Homage to Catalonia*, 93.

55 George Orwell, *Omaggio alla Catalogna*, trans. by Riccardo Duranti (Milano: Oscar Mondadori, 1993), 93.

56 George Orwell, *Homenaje a Cataluña*, trans. by Virus Editorial (Madrid: Diario El País, 2003), 41.

57 George Orwell, *La Catalogne libre (1936-1937)*, trans. by Yvonne Davet (Paris : Gallimard, 1955), 94.

58 Orwell, *La Catalogne libre (1936-1937)*, trans. by Yvonne Davet, 94.

One possible tool for understanding the intentionality of an error, if the author is no longer alive and/or it is impossible to speak directly with him or her, is represented by the paratext (interviews, conversations, correspondence, diaries, etc.), which can help reconstruct the subjective and non-accidental components that may be behind an error.

Our choice, and a highly unconventional one if compared to previous translations, was to repropose the multilingual dimension of the work we were translating.

The solution we chose, and our 'one-way dialogue' with previous translators, is an example of how a team of retranslators can *react* to the subjective choices of those who translated before. In our case, and perhaps because of the shared responsibility that characterised our collaborative retranslation, it was possible to 'dare a little more' than a single translator would have done, breaking away from the translation tradition of a specific work and bringing to light some important authorial choices that had not yet emerged.

Conclusions

In conclusion, collaborative literary retranslations, like almost any literary translation, are inherently subjective; this can have both beneficial and detrimental effects, from creative and innovative interpretations of source texts to inconsistencies in the retranslation process.

The translators' subjectivities involved in collaborative retranslations ideally 'dialogue' with the original author's subjectivity, and even the subjective choices of previous translators can influence a collaborative retranslation by emulation or distancing.

The whole retranslation process can be managed through clear guidelines, communication and a commitment to achieving a consistent and accurate final translation. Translation Studies can be enriched by exploring the subjectivity of the translator (who transmits his or her subjectivity to the translated text), and of the translated text and author (style, linguistic marks of deictic and axiological subjectivity, personal reference[59]). Research on the link between collaborative translation and subjectivity may prove helpful to

---

[59] Schmidt-Melbye, 'Ambiguïtés et hybridité – de la subjectivité dans le domaine de la traduction', 31.

provide a better understanding of both the status of the translated text and the role of translators in the history of translation. On one hand, « plus le traducteur s'inscrit comme sujet dans la traduction, plus, paradoxalement, traduire peut *continuer* le texte »[60] [the more the translator inscribes himself as subject in the translation, the more, paradoxically, translating can *drive* the text] ; on the other hand, « le sujet traduisant, tout comme l'écrivain, est porteur des représentations symboliques de sa société »[61] [the translating subject, like the writer, is the bearer of the symbolic representations of his or her society].

As such, it is important, if not fundamental, to consider the implications of subjectivity in collaborative retranslations to ensure the continuing production of effective, accurate and new translations.

References

Barnstone, Willis, *The Poetics of Translation: History, Theory, Practice* (New Haven: Yale University Press, 1993).

Benveniste, Émile, *Problèmes de linguistique générale I* (Paris: Gallimard, 1966).

Benveniste, Émile, *Problèmes de linguistique générale II* (Paris: Gallimard, 1974).

Charaudeau, Patrick, and Dominique Maingueneau, *Dictionnaire d'Analyse du Discours* (Paris: Gallimard, 2002).

Chen, Ya-Mei, 'The Translator's Subjectivity and Its Constraints in News Transediting: A Perspective of Reception Aesthetics', *Meta* 56/1 (2011), 119–44.

Constantinescu, Muguraş, 'La traductologie que j'ai développée est une réflexion qui s'appuie essentiellement sur mon propre travail de traducteur – Entretien avec Jean-René Ladmiral', *Atelier de traduction* 14 (2010), 15–30.

Delisle, Jean, *Portraits de traductrices* (Ottawa: Les Presses de l'Université d'Ottawa/Artois Presses Université, 2002).

60 See Meschonnic, *Poétique du traduire*.

61 Jean Delisle, *Portraits de traductrices* (Ottawa: Les Presses de l'Université d'Ottawa/ Artois Presses Université, 2002), 2.

Greenall, Annjo Klungervik, 'Translators' voices in Norwegian retranslations of Bob Dylan's songs', *Target* 27/1 (2015), 40–57.

Henri, France, and Karin Lundgren-Cayrol, eds, *Apprentissage Collaboratif À Distance – Pour Comprendre Et Concevoir Les Environnements D'apprentissage Virtuels* (Québec : Presses de l'Université du Québec, 2001).

Huang, Shufen, 'A Study of the Translator's Subjectivity in Literary Translation – Exemplified by the English Version of The Border Town', *Open Journal of Social Sciences* 7/5 (2019), 99–108.

Jansen, Hanne, and Anna Wegener, 'Introduction', in Hanne Jansen, and Anna Wegener, eds, *Authorial and Editorial Voices in Translation 1 – Collaborative Relationships between Authors, Translators, and Performers* (Montréal: Éditions québécoises de l'oeuvre, 2013), 1-38.

Kerbrat-Orecchioni, Catherine, *L'énonciation : de la subjectivité dans le langage* (Paris: Armand Colin, 2002 [1980]).

Meschonnic, Henri, *Poétique du traduire* (Lagrasse: Éditions Verdier, 1999).

Mingjian, Zha, and Tian Yu, 'On the Subjectivity of the Translator', *Chinese Translators Journal* 24 (2003), 19–24.

Nasi, Franco, *Tradurre l'errore. Laboratorio di pensiero critico e creativo* (Macerata: Edizioni Quodlibet, 2021).

Orwell, George, *Down and out in Paris and London* (New York: Harper and Brothers, 1933).

Orwell, George, *Burmese Days* (New York: Harper & Brothers, 1934).

Orwell, George, *Homage to Catalonia* (London: Secker and Warburg, 1938).

Orwell, George, *Animal Farm* (London: Secker and Warburg, 1945).

Orwell, George, *Omaggio alla Catalogna*, trans. by Giorgio Monicelli (Verona: Arnoldo Mondadori Editore, 1948).

Orwell, George, *1984* (London: Secker & Warburg, 1949).

Orwell, George, *La Catalogne libre (1936-1937)*, trans. by Yvonne Davet (Paris: Gallimard, 1955).

Orwell, George, 'As I please (1947)', in Sonia Orwell, and Ian Angus, eds, *The Collected Essays, Journalism and Letters of George Orwell. In Front of Your Nose 1945-1950* (London: Secker & Warburg, 1968), 304–7.

Orwell, George, *Omaggio alla Catalogna*, trans. by Riccardo Duranti (Milano: Oscar Mondadori, 1993).

Orwell, George, *Hommage à la Catalogne*, trans. by Yvonne Davet (Paris: Éditions 10/18, 2000).
Orwell, George, 'Propaganda and Demotic Speech', in Peter Davison, ed., *The Complete Works of George Orwell: I Have Tried to Tell the Truth: 1943-1944* (London: Secker & Warburg, 2001), 310–6.
Orwell, George, *Homenaje a Cataluña*, trans. by Virus Editorial (Madrid: Diario El País, 2003).
Orwell, George, 'Letter to Yvonne Davet (July 29, 1946)', in Peter Davison, ed., *George Orwell: a Life in Letters* (New York / London: Liveright Publishing Corporation, 2013).
Orwell, George, *1984*, trans. by Enrico Terrinoni (Roma: Newton Compton Editori, 2021).
Orwell, George, *La fattoria degli animali*, trans. by Enrico Terrinoni (Roma: Newton Compton Editori, 2021).
Orwell, George, *Omaggio alla Catalogna*, trans. by Francesco Laurenti and Fabio Morotti (Roma: Newton Compton Editori, 2021).
Orwell, George, *Giorni in Birmania*, trans. by Andrea Binelli (Roma: Newton Compton Editori, 2022).
Orwell, George, *Senza un soldo a Parigi e a Londra*, trans. by Andrea Binelli (Roma: Newton Compton Editori, 2022).
Petruccioli, Daniele, 'L'omaggio alla Catalogna, come è nato, come – forse – ha cambiato noi', in George Orwell, *Omaggio alla Catalogna* (Milano: Rizzoli, 2021), 19–21.
Pym, Anthony, 'The Translator as Author: Two Quixotes', *Translation and Literature* 14/1 (2005), 71–81.
Reboul, Anne, and Jacques Moeschler, *Dictionnaire encyclopédique de pragmatique* (Paris : Éditions du Seuil, 1994).
Schmidt-Melbye, Inger Hesjevoll, 'Ambiguïtés et hybridité – de la subjectivité dans le domaine de la traduction', *Synergies Pays Scandinaves* 7 (2012), 31–41.
Skibinska, Elzbieta, 'La Retraduction, Manifestation De La Subjectivité Du Traducteur', *Doletiana* 1 (2010), <https://raco.cat/index.php/Doletiana/article/view/148423>, accessed 10 November 2023.
Venuti, Lawrence, 'Retranslations: The Creation of Value', *Bucknell Review* 47/1 (2004), 1–7.

Xiaohan, Guo, and Mohamed Abdou Moindjie, 'A Perspective on the Translator's Subjectivity and its Constraints in Literary Translation: A Critical Analysis', *Journal of Positive School Psychology* 6/4 (2022), 3118–3123.

2

Collaborative Translation: Product Quality Assurance and Practice Evaluation

Federica Villareale

Abstract

The study of Collaborative Translation has only in the last few years become part of Translation Studies, giving rise to a vast number of questions related to this practice, which in turn open up the analysis of an equally great number of issues. Among these are concerns regarding the evaluation and quality assurance of translations carried out collaboratively, a crucial issue especially when dealing with collaboration between semi-professionals and non-professionals. It is precisely this analysis that will be developed in this essay: in particular, we will analyze the answers to a questionnaire that was specifically created to evaluate the collaborative translation process and the final product, both in terms of the quality of the translated text and of the usefulness for the translators in terms of skills and from a personal point of view.

Introduction

Translation is undoubtedly a practice with ancient origins; there is also no doubt that the method favoured by translators since time immemorial was collaboration. Besides the collaborative translations of sacred texts starting from the third century b.C. (the famous *Septuaginta* translation of the Bible from Hebrew into Greek is worth mentioning in this respect, commissioned by Ptolemy II Philadelphus and produced by seventy-two scholars who knew both languages perfectly), collaboration between different translators working on a single text was a widespread practice in the Greco-Roman world[62] and during the Middle Ages. In the same periods, retranslations, compilations from different texts, and multilingual translations[63], i.e., texts where different languages coexisted on the same page, were also common. Several documents testify to the fact that translators sometimes worked from intermediate versions of a text, not necessarily in the source language; others employed different copies and versions of the same text, often in different languages. Such practices and textual products highlight how translation has always involved more than one producing actor and consequently more than one single interpretative stance.

Today more than ever, the practice of translating different kinds of editorial products (from books to comics, from videogames to audio-visual material) by making recourse to the work of others is widespread, and such collaborations take place in different ways. The act of translating is not restricted to professionals anymore, but, and also thanks to the World Wide Web and to the rapid dissemination of online tools developed to simplify translation, the field has opened to online users with an interest in translation. These users, driven by the challenge and by their desire to offer a valuable contribution to the dissemination of a specific product in their country, engage in the translation of works they love, and in so doing explore new ways of translating collaboratively[64].

Despite all this, only recently have scholars begun to investigate the history of collaboration in the field of translation, and their analyses have found their rightful place within the discipline of Translation Studies. Among the many points that have been examined, this essay analyses the concerns

---

62 Francesco Laurenti, 'Introduzione. Oltre la monade: tradurre collaborativamente', in Francesco Laurenti, ed., *La traduzione collaborativa. Tra didattica e mercato globale delle lingue* (Roma: Aracne, 2022), 17.

63 Rainier Grutman, 'Multilingualism', in Mona Baker, and Gabriela Saldanha, eds, *Routledge Encyclopedia of Translation Studies*, 2nd edition (London: Routledge, 1998), 182.

64 Consider for instance crowdsourcing and community translation (see Alberto Fernández Costales, 'Collaborative Translation Revisited: Exploring the Rationale and the Motivation for Volunteer Translation', *Revue internationale d'interprétation et de traduction / International Journal of Interpretation and Translation* 10 (2012), 115–42.

raised by the evaluation and quality assurance of translations produced collaboratively, a key issue that especially concerns collaborations with or between semi- and non-professional translators. In particular, this essay will show how it is possible to measure both the quality of the final collaborative product (the translated text) and of the process. The results have been obtained via a questionnaire designed specifically to answer these questions, i.e. to evaluate the process of collaborative translation (CT) and of the final product in terms of the accuracy of the translated text and of the benefit to the translators involved, both in terms of an improvement in their skills and of their personal experience.

1. Quality Assurance in Collaborative Translation

Laurenti writes:

> gli approcci del mercato oggi, parallelamente alla diffusione della traduzione automatica, del crowdsourcing e della traduzione collaborativa, iniziano a essere orientati verso una prospettiva "dinamica" in cui tutti i partecipanti coinvolti nel processo traduttivo (clienti, manager, traduttori, utenti e lettori) possono decidere congiuntamente quale può essere il livello sufficientemente buono di una traduzione, ovvero la sua "adeguatezza allo scopo" [65].
>
> [Currently, market approaches, due to the dissemination of automatic translation, crowdsourcing, and collaborative translation, are oriented towards a more 'dynamic' view, where all participants in the translation process (customers, managers, translators, users, and readers) contribute to judging a translation as sufficiently good, or 'suitable for purpose'. (Our translation)]

The development of translation practices and the evolution of the aims of translation itself have made current research models on the quality of translation more dynamic and realistic and have encouraged researchers to account for constraints in time and resources.[66] Thus, quality is no more

[65] Laurenti, 'Introduzione. Oltre la monade: tradurre collaborativamente', in Laurenti, ed., *La traduzione collaborativa. Tra didattica e mercato globale delle lingue*, 33.

[66] Miguel A. Jiménez-Crespo, *Crowdsourcing and Online Collaborative Translations: expanding the limits of Translation Studies* (Amsterdam/Philadelphia: John Benjamins Publishing Company, 2017), 120.

being perceived in absolute terms as the ideal to achieve, since maximum quality is neither attainable nor desirable in many situations. On the other hand, professional as well as non-professional translators attach great value to the 'quality' of the final product, although most do not agree on how to measure it.

Based on the results of our questionnaire, we can affirm that it is possible to guarantee that the final translation will have a higher quality if, before work on the translation is even started, a unified work method is agreed upon by all participants in the project, along with the tools that will be employed. Submitting a self-evaluation questionnaire to aspiring translators also helps ensuring better quality, as will be shown below.

1.1 Working method

There are different methods that can be employed to organise collaborative translation work, and they vary according to the number of actors involved, the customer's requests, available time and resources, etc. The method that has shown itself to be the most efficient is based on an organisational model in two steps[67] that can be adapted to translate almost any text.

Specifically, the first stage is dedicated to an initial evaluation of the features of the job, including clarifying the objectives, target, customer's requests and deadlines, evaluating specific challenges in the source text, and estimating the amount of effort that will be required from translators during the time that it takes to finish the job, so as to avoid any difficulties during the translation process that may affect the quality of the finished product.

---

67 An organisational pattern, or design pattern, is a solution to a design problem. The idea was introduced by architect Christopher Alexander and was later adapted to various other disciplines, particularly software engineering. Each pattern takes a picture of a continuously repeating problem (in our case, the organisation of a collaborative translation) and describes the core of a solution in a way that the pattern itself can be replicated indefinitely, without the actions performed necessarily being the same (see: <https://www.pps.org/article/calexander>, accessed 10 June 2024).

Table 2.1 Organizational model for collaborative translation works

	Organising Work in Collaborative Translation
Context	This model can be employed to simplify the work of a translation team working collaboratively on a project, regardless of the number of participants.
Problem	Although translating a text collaboratively presents several challenges, one of the issues that can majorly affect the quality of the product is represented by organisational problems. This is because collaborative translation requires a high degree of coordination, especially when teams are sufficiently numerous, as the final product must comply with specific standards regarding its overall quality, coherence, and cohesion. This model aims at offering a series of guidelines for organising collaborative translation work in an efficient way.
Solution	The work can be organised in two stages: Stage 1: Preparation In this stage, the features of the prospective work are evaluated. Specifically: • Understanding the aim of the job (what is most important for the customer – accuracy in terminology, speed, meeting a deadline, etc.), the target, and the date for delivery of the final product. • Evaluating the challenges of the source text, to establish intermediate review deadlines and taking into account the amount of work that is required from translators. • Ensuring all involved translators understand what kind of effort is required of THEM and clarifying what their expectations are, in terms of effort and compensation, so that these details are clear from the start. Stage 2: Organising the work Based on the evaluations carried out in Stage 1, this stage is dedicated to organising translation work by: • Creating smaller or bigger teams, which can include translators and other professionals (editors, reviewers, etc.). • Clearly defining the work method that each team will have to follow (whether translated texts have to be revised in real-time, what is the maximum time that can elapse between comments and responses, etc.). • If more than one team is present, determining how textual coherence will be guaranteed (by translators, by reviewers, by both, etc.). • If required, naming a referee for the team to liaise with the customer. • Choosing the right tools to perform the job of translating and revising, which will have to be used by all participants in the same ways. • Individuating strategies to create and preserve backup copies in ways that are appropriate to the nature of the team. • Planning intermediate deadlines to monitor the advancement of work.

Organising Work in Collaborative Translation	
Examples	*Il Teatro Fantasma*[68] is a good example of a translation performed by two people, while the volume *Tutte le guerre di Putin. Dalla Cecenia all'Ucraina*[69] has been translated collaboratively by about thirty people.

The second stage deals with the organisation of the work itself, to be carried out based on the results of the previous stage. Among other things, this stage sees the creation of working teams, with the definition of ways to ensure consistency and textual coherence within the team and among different teams and the choice of tools to be employed by all members of the project, according to the type of translation.

1.2 Tools[70]

Today, there are many tools available that can be suited for collaborative translation, and it can be hard to choose one or more of them as the best and most efficient. Thus, we thought aspiring translators could make use of a comprehensive classification that takes into account not only the kind of translation support these tools offer, but also their main function (communication, coordination, or collaboration) and the criteria they must satisfy to be considered suitable for collaborative work. In particular, the communicative function is typical of those services that allow people to exchange information on their actions; the coordinating function is fulfilled by those services that allow participants to identify their respective role in the work process, acquire information about its advancement, see clearly the collaborative task of the team, and be notified of new elements or changes in the process; the productive or collaborative function is fulfilled by those services that allow translators to share 'work objects' that may be further developed according to individual and collective contributions.

68 Mat Osman, *Il teatro fantasma,* transl. Paola Olivetto and Mirko Zilahy (Roma: Blu Atlantide, 2023).

69 Mark Galeotti, *Tutte le guerre di Putin. Dalla Cecenia all'Ucraina*, Francesco Laurenti and Ludovica Maggi, eds (Milano: Gremese editore, 2022).

70 On this topic, see Francesco Laurenti, and Federica Villareale, 'Traduzione, ambienti virtuali e nuove tecnologie: strumenti informatici per la collaborazione', *Testo a Fronte. Teoria e pratica della traduzione, 69(2), 201-220, 2023.*

Table 2.2 Types of tools based on their function and on the kind of support they offer

Communication Tools	Help information circulating among participants. Function: **Communication**
Coordination Tools	They are project management and monitoring tools that synchronise, control and accelerate interactions between collaborators. Function: **Coordination**
Sharing Tools	They allow a group to work together on the same document using the same application, offering the possibility of working online and remotely. They make it possible to create a document accessible to anyone, anywhere, anytime that several people can manipulate at the same time. Function: **Coordination and Collaboration**
Information Management Tools	Allow users to upload on the web new information related to the content they are working on, or to obtain general information useful for the objective. Function: **Collaboration**

1.3 Self-evaluation questionnaire

Translators working on collaborative projects – especially in crowdsourcing – often do not undergo a previous selection and, due to this, the quality of the final product may sometimes be low. Moreover, the variation between professionals and semi-professionals with different backgrounds can drive sceptics to think that this necessarily lowers the quality of the final product. Regarding this, a questionnaire submitted to participants that evaluates their background, previous experience, and their familiarity with other projects based on collaborative translation would work both as a tool for self-evaluation and as a tool to filter out inexperienced translators, since it would alert translators to which aspects of their skill set have to be improved and which others are instead already acquired. If and when the results are shared, they would allow other translators to know in advance which aspects of their colleagues' translations warrant a more careful approach, and which specific sections in the texts translated by their colleagues should be looked at more closely.

2. Questionnaire for evaluating collaborative translation[71]

2.1 Origins and Aims

It is possible to give different answers to many questions regarding CT (How can it be defined? Does a univocal definition exist? What is the minimum number of participants to be able to speak of CT? Do we consider only translators as participants or are also reviewers and experts working on the different stages of a translation included?), all of which cannot really be disputed as the answers depend on the personal perceptions of the people involved. On the contrary, questions about the convenience and quality of CT can find univocal answers based on quantitative data and on the experiences of professionals, regardless of the size of the team.

To perform such an analysis, it is necessary to pose specific questions to the translators involved in the process of collaborative translation, the answers to which provide pertinent quantitative and qualitative data that is easily interpreted, so that a clear conclusion can be reached. In this perspective, we have designed a questionnaire to answer six fundamental interrogatives in the analysis of collaborative translation. These questions can be traced back to the main interrogation regarding CT:[72] is it a convenient practice and if so, does it deserve to be promoted, as it saves time and raises the quality of the final product, regardless of whether the participants are professionals or not?

---

71 The research team is grateful for the collaboration of Giuseppe Sofo and Yanick Hamon (Venice, Università Ca' Foscari) on this project.

72 1. Understanding how translators 'thought' about translation before CT and studying how this changed once the project was finished; 2. Understanding how translators evaluate the change in the perception of their own translations after CT; 3. Understanding how translators evaluate CT in general; 4. Studying the perceived usefulness of CT; 5. Understanding whether the quality of a collaboratively translated text is higher than that of a text translated by a single translator; 6. Understanding, according to the translators involved in the project, which are the benefits of CT, what are its the problems, and whether translators would recommend its implementation in degree programmes.

2.2 Structure

The research took place in an academic environment and the questionnaire was submitted to semi-professional translators (i.e.: students in their second year of the MA degree in Specialised Translation) who took part in the collaborative translation of the volume *Putin's Wars* by Mark Galeotti from English into Italian, at the end of their work. The definitive form of the questionnaire consisted of thirty-six questions grouped in five macro-areas, each of them probing one fundamental issue in our research and allowing us to evaluate both the quality of the final product and the process of collaborative translation. Results have also allowed us to evaluate the usefulness of the process as far as translators and the text are concerned, based on the work of internal (translators) and external observers (the researchers analysing the results).

2.2.1 Questions concerning the background of the translator (questions 1-8)

The questionnaire has been devised to be completely anonymous, so that subjects would be free to answer questions sincerely and without fear of judgement; however, we have added eight questions that allow us to classify participants in the study and consequently analyse the data with more awareness of their different characteristics. Specifically, differences in age, gender and in the other known language(s) may determine the nature of answers connected to translation methods and previous work experiences, among others.

Since we first submitted our questionnaire in an academic setting, we have made the decision to probe participants on their previous studies (in this case, their choice of BA degree), to understand if they had studied translation before and to what extent, and whether different BA choices may influence how the students approach translation, organise their work and manage communications with their colleagues. Moreover, we have decided to ask participants whether they had practiced translation before, and in which contexts, to understand the answer to the following questions in the light of their previous translation experience.

2.2.2 Questions evaluating perceived change (questions 9-17)

One of the major aims of our questionnaire was to investigate whether the implementation of collaborative translation practices implied changes in the translation methods and in the translators' perception of their own ability to translate a text, review it, liaise with collaborators and organise their own work, but also in relation to translators' confidence in their own language and revision skills, both in the case of approaching a text individually and with several collaborators, regardless of whether these collaborators have the same or more experience.

Questions in this section are divided into two groups. The first one considers translators' experiences previous to the start of the project (introduced by the sentence 'Before taking part in this project'); the second group of questions is aimed at highlighting the changes that are a result of taking part in a collaborative translation project (introduced by the sentence 'After taking part in this project'). Moreover, we have added question no. 17 to investigate whether collaborative translation work had produced some kind of change in the translation skills of participants as they perceived them.

2.2.3 Questions evaluating quality and perceived utility (questions 18-30)

Another significant aim of the study was to understand whether collaborative translation is actually useful for translators and whether it contributes to the production of higher-quality texts compared to texts that are individually translated.

This section is the longest since all questions are different; most questions allow participants to choose between two or more choices (some requiring responders to motivate their answer), while no. 19 requires participants to indicate their agreement with fourteen different claims, based on a five-point Likert rating scale.[73] Questions no. 20, 21, and 22 are decisive since the analysis of the answers to these questions has provided a clear and immediate answer to two of the main interrogatives that have generated this study (i.e. interrogatives about quality and the saving of time).

[73] Rensis Likert was a social psychologist, who developed a rating scale that allows participants to choose between more than two responses, rating, for example, the level of satisfaction, quality, happiness, difficulty, likelihood or agreement (see: <https://www.ispring.it/blog/scala-likert>, accessed 22 March 2023).

2.2.4 Questions evaluating tools (questions 31 and 32)

In our digital age, it is no longer possible to think of translators as people who work alone in their study, poring over encyclopaedias and dictionaries. Today, the Web allows translators to use a series of tools devised to facilitate their work, both from the point of view of language (online dictionaries, translation software, etc.) and from that of content (online pages dedicated to specific topics and online press). These, when used with some awareness of their potential pitfalls, can make translation more accurate and save time.

For this reason, we felt that it was important to understand which tools are preferred by participants and whether there is a relationship between the tools and the perceived changes in the production of translated text.

2.2.5 Open-ended questions for the overall evaluation of collaborative translation (questions 33-36)

The final part of the questionnaire consists of four open-ended questions that allow respondents to express their opinion about the main strengths and weaknesses of the CT project they participated in, and to explain whether they would advise others to implement CT practices in their degree courses in Translation.

2.3 Analysis of the results

2.3.1 Quantitative analysis

At the time of the study, 76.5 per cent of participants were less than 25 years old, while 17.6 per cent were aged between 25 and 35; one single participant was over 35. Although 47.1 per cent of participants had attended the BA in Interpreting and Translation (IULM) and the remaining percentage had similar backgrounds in languages and language mediation, only 64.7 per cent of them had any form of professional training in the field of translation, while 11.8 per cent of them had never studied it. However, all participants had practiced translation during their BA, with different aims and in different contexts; 88.2 per cent did so only for academic/educational purposes. For what concerns collaborative translation, 88.2 per cent had not practiced it before.

a. Translation

The first data to deserve some commentary are those concerning the changes that participants perceived took place regarding their translation skills and their ability to organise translation work. 64.7 per cent of responders maintains that their ability to produce a translation is better after participating in the project; similarly, Figure 2.1 and 2.2 show perceived improvements in participant's ability to organise their work and to relate with colleagues. It is certain that collaborative work contributed to the improvement of such soft skills, today indispensable in any field of work, but especially useful in a field such as translation, which implies the ability to compromise.

In general, we can claim that collaborative practices appear to have helped participants improve their linguistic skills in both working languages *via* continual comparison (41.2 per cent agrees with the claim 'My skills in my second language have improved', while 35.3 per cent agrees with the same claim also in the case of their native language). It is worth noticing how 82.3

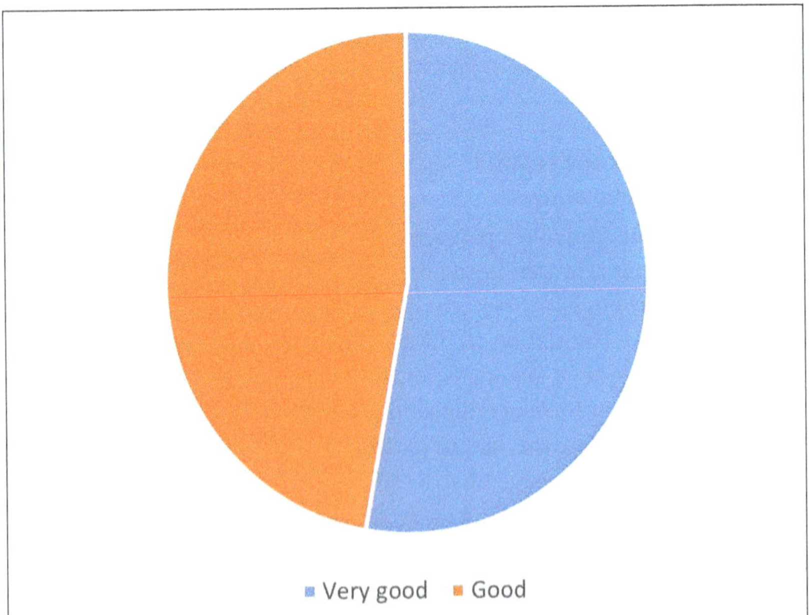

Figure 2.1 Participants' perception of their abilities to organise translation work **before** the study

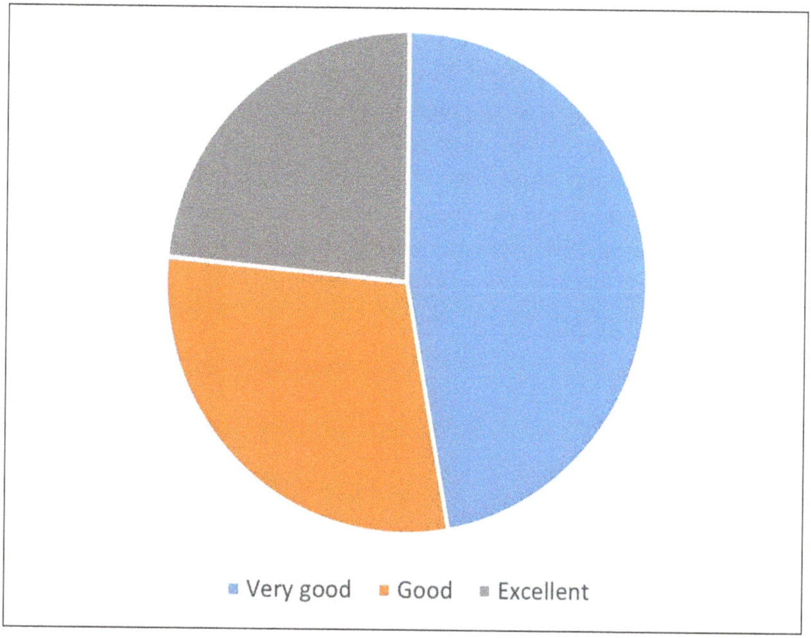

Figure 2.2 Participants' perception of their abilities to organise translation work after the study

per cent of responders chose to 'agree' or 'strongly agree' with the claim 'My perception of professional translation has improved'. This highlights how implementing collaborative practices would respond to the requests of those students who feel they lack real-world work experience to prepare them to face the challenges of the modern workplace with more confidence, which are ever more varied and very different from what is generally presented in an academic setting (cf. Table 2.3).

b. Personal experience and relationships with colleagues

Another merit that should be recognised to CT is its contribution to an improvement in translators' confidence in their abilities. Before taking part in the project, 58.8 per cent of responders were worried that they would offend their collaborators with their corrections and 47.1 per cent felt insecure regarding their abilities to evaluate or comment on others' translation choices. After the project was concluded, these numbers were significantly diminished: to

35.3 per cent in the case of the first claim and to an impressive 5.9 per cent in the case of the second claim. Similarly, translators' confidence in their ability to detect strong or weak points in a translation has doubled since before the project, from 29.4 per cent to 58.8 per cent. As has been previously mentioned, CT allows translators to collaborate with colleagues with very different backgrounds and experiences, which can contribute to a sense of inferiority in younger and less experienced professionals who are in the position of correcting a senior or more knowledgeable colleague. In the case of

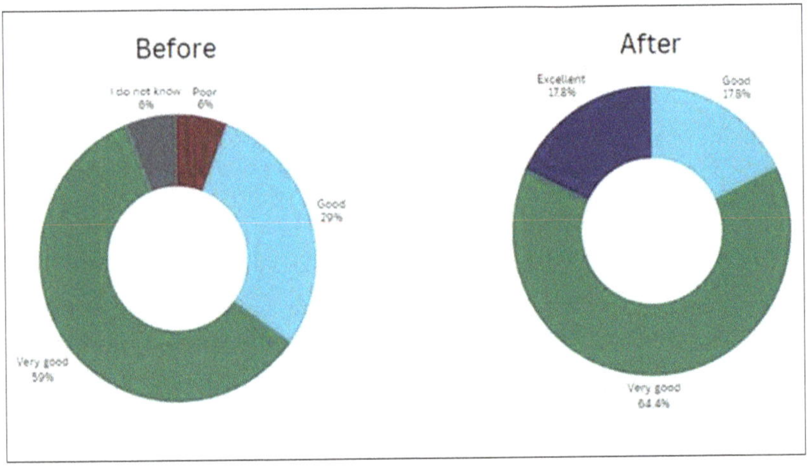

Figure 2.3 Changes in ability to liaise with colleagues

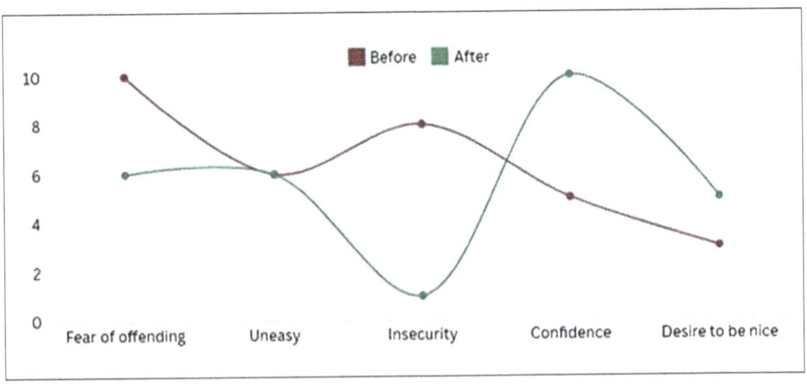

Figure 2.4 Changes in the relationship with colleagues

this project, some of the participants (35.3 per cent) perceived this claim as real, however after taking part in the CT project and experiencing productive collaboration with colleagues, this percentage dropped to 23.5 per cent.

c. Some thoughts on time

One of the most important questions concerning CT is also one of the most difficult to answer and concerns the time necessary to complete a translation. We have asked participants their opinion ('Do you think that, by adopting a collaborative approach to translation, there has been a reduction in the time that was necessary to hand in the final version of the translated text?'), and their answers have highlighted a 'definition' problem: what is really meant

Table 2.3 Percentages of answers to positive questions

	Strongly Disagree	Disagree	Neither agree nor disagree	Agree	Strongly agree
The quality of my translations has improved	0	11.8	41.2	29.4	17.6
My skills in my second language have improved	0	23.5	29.4	41.2	5.9
My skills in my first language have improved	5.9	23.5	29.4	35.3	5.9
My perception of the complexity of professional translation has improved	5.9	5.9	5.9	52.9	29.4
My translation skills have improved	0	17.6	29.4	29.4	23.5

when we talk about 'a reduction in time'? 29.4 per cent of interviewed answered 'Do not know'. In fact, without more explanation, answers can be less informative, as each translator may refer arbitrarily to one of three scenarios: 1. The customer receives the text translated collaboratively sooner, this being a reduction in overall production time; 2. The amount of text on which a single translator has to work is smaller, therefore taking up less of their time; 3. If it is indeed true that the time commitment of each translator is reduced, it is also true that time to ensure coherence and to dedicate to collaborative revision is very much increased and thus we should not be talking about 'a reduction in time' in this case.

Here, it is worth dedicating some words to the ideas of self- and other revision. A text translated by a single person certainly requires more time, since the translator must approach the whole text alone, study the topic and sometimes disambiguate terminology and phrasing. However, once the translation is done, the revision of the text on the part of the translator (self-revision) is generally a much faster process: the translator has already internalised the meaning of the text and consequently will not modify it much when reviewing, even after several readings. Moreover, they probably will not change much either in the style or in the chosen terminology, as these features represent peculiarities of their own approach. If the customer does not invest more time and resources to have the text reviewed by someone else (which would then constitute an instance of other revision), they risk having a text that is ready for publication, the quality of which cannot be however guaranteed. On the contrary, those translators who, after having translated a much smaller portion of the text, discuss with others the entire translated text (other revision) will undoubtedly spend more time revising the text, but will be able to guarantee a higher quality of the finished product. This is due to several factors: (a) the meaning that an individual translator gave to the portion of text they were assigned can change more easily following discussion with colleagues who are thinking about the text *ex novo* in the light of the finished work; (b) the discussion allows for terminological choices that have been long debated and considered (e.g.: 'We spent hours discussing a single word among the team'). Moreover, style is also similarly changed and amended to create a text that is as coherent as possible; (c) another pair of eyes not used to the text (both source and target) can more easily perceive mistakes that have gone unnoticed by the initial translator and suggest ideas that are more suitable to the context or to the target language.

Therefore, and before choosing either self- or other-revision, customers should clarify which exactly are their priorities (cf. Section 1.1) and specify the amount of effort required. This is because, as shown by the answers to our questionnaire, translators who are not used to work in CT are often left unfavourably surprised at the amount of revision work, jeopardising the evaluation of this practice and consequently translators' inclination to take part in similar projects (one of the comments regarding the issue of time commitment reads: 'The times for revising and discussing the work should be shorter, as 5-6 hours a week to revise the portion of text that was assigned to the team were too much').

2.3.2 Qualitative analysis

The comments of participants in answer to the last four questions (cf. Section 2.2.5) have thrown light onto significant issues in the context of CT and underlined important aspects regarding the best way of implementing CT processes. These answers have allowed researchers to claim with absolute certainty (all responders gave the same answer) that collaborative translation should be implemented in the syllabus of degree courses in translation. Despite many still looking at CT with a mixture of suspicion and mistrust and despite the general lack of scholarly work on the subject, collaborative translation as a practice is nowadays widespread in the work environment, and it is therefore necessary to familiarise students with the kind of teamwork that is required in CT and with the amount of effort this work entails. Moreover, implementing CT would provide students with work experience in the real world, helping them to better face the challenges of the workplace and answer its demands more confidently.

Conclusions

Some insight may be gained from the study presented here, regarding the usefulness, quality and capillary presence of collaborative translation in the digital world. Since we live in a world that is increasingly interconnected and where information is transferred increasingly faster between actors, translation cannot afford not to be collaborative. Therefore, theorists of translation should spend more time investigating the nuances of this practice, since collaboration is not limited to professionals or semi-professionals but, as mentioned before, increasingly involves amateur translators; these in turn are represented by a series of different figures who enact different translation practices, each with their own set of peculiarities that should ideally be described in detail if we want to reach a more stable and exhaustive definition of collaborative translation. To do so, our investigative modes have to evolve and focus more on the analysis of the practices enacted by the actual participants in such collaborative projects, on their opinions and, more significantly, on the final products, to avoid the mistake of substituting theory for practice.

Moreover, and given that CT is in a continual state of development and flux – also thanks to its close connection to technical progress – studies on this topic cannot be deemed 'conclusive' or 'concluded' but are intrinsically *in fieri*. In an experimental perspective, we hope that study of the practices and evaluation of CT will be expanded by more partners and enriched by their experience. Collaborative translation is an ever-evolving practice, and any tool to study it and evaluate it must be similarly open to new developments. After all, it is not only translation that is a collaborative act: everything that concerns translation is inherently collaborative.

Appendix 1. Questionnaire for the evaluation of collaborative translation

1. Sex: M F
2. Age: ____________________
3. BA degree: ____
4. How many years have you been studying English as a second language?

   ____
5. Third language: _________________

N.B. In this questionnaire, the word 'translation' refers to the entire translation process, from first draft in the target language to the last revision to the final draft.

6. Have you studied translation during BA?
   a. Yes, but did not have professional training
   b. Yes, and had professional training
   c. No

7. Did you practice translation during BA?
   a. Yes, but only for academic/educational purposes
   b. Yes, at a professional level (with or without being compensated)
   c. No

8. Before this experience, had you ever taken part in collaborative translation projects?
   a. Yes
   b. No
   c. Yes, however I do not know if my experience can be described as 'collaborative'

The following questions should be read only in relation to the specific collaborative translation project that this questionnaire is built on.

9. Before taking part in this project, and if you have studied translation during BA, which method did you employ to translate?
   a. I would read the entire text, then proceed with the translation
   b. I would read a portion of the text and translate it, then repeat the same process for all sections
   c. I would start translating right away

10. Before taking part in this project, and if you have studied translation during BA, which method did you employ to revise translated text?
    a. I would revise my translation against the source text for accuracy and would pay less attention to the cohesion and coherence of the translation and to the usability of the text in Italian
    b. Initially, I would check my translation against the source text for accuracy; then I would focus on the cohesion and coherence of the translation and on the usability of the text in Italian
    c. I would revise my translation considering its cohesion and coherence and the usability of the text in Italian, without looking at the source text
    d. Some combination of the above
    e. Other: ____ ________

11. Before taking part in this project:

	Poor	Good	Very Good	Excellent	Do not know
How did you evaluate your translation skills?					
How did you evaluate your ability to organise translation work?					
How did you evaluate your ability to liaise with potential collaborators?					

12. Before taking part in this project, which emotions would you have felt if you had to evaluate/comment the translation choices of a colleague *together* with them? (Choose all that apply)
    a. I would have been worried to give offence
    b. I would have tried to use nice words to gratify them
    c. I would have been confident in my ability to evaluate the strengths/weaknesses of a translation
    d. I would have felt insecure regarding my ability to evaluate my colleague's translation choices
    e. I would have felt uneasy suggesting emendations to more experienced colleagues

13. AFTER taking part in this project, has your translation method undergone any changes?
    a. No
    b. Yes

14. AFTER taking part in this project, what method do you employ to revise translated text?
    a. I revise my translation against the source text for accuracy and pay less attention to the cohesion and coherence of the translation and to the usability of the text in Italian.
    b. Initially, I check my translation against the source text for accuracy; then I focus on the cohesion and coherence of the translation and on the usability of the text in Italian.
    c. I revise my translation considering its cohesion and coherence and the usability of the text in Italian, without looking at the source text
    d. Some combination of the above.
    e. Other: ____

15. AFTER taking part in this project:

	Poor	Good	Very Good	Excellent	Do not know
How do you evaluate your translation skills?					
How do you evaluate your ability to organise translation work?					
How do you evaluate your ability to liaise with potential collaborators?					

16. AFTER taking part in this project, which emotions would you feel if you had to evaluate/comment the translation choices of a colleague *together* with them?
    (Choose all that apply)
    a. I would be worried to give offence
    b. I would try to use nice words to gratify them
    c. I would be confident in my ability to evaluate the strengths/weaknesses of a translation
    d. I would feel insecure regarding my ability to evaluate my colleague's translation choices
    e. I would feel uneasy suggesting emendations to more experienced colleagues

17. AFTER taking part in this project, do you think your abilities to produce a translation have improved?
    a. Yes
    b. No

18. AFTER taking part in this project, would you say that collaborative translation: (Choose all that apply):
    a. Increases people skills and discussion skills
    b. Allows team members to better understand the source text
    c. Reinforces the bond between the members of the team
    d. Increases the motivation to take part in discussions
    e. Facilitates the exchange of ideas between participants

f. Allows everyone to correct the mistakes of other team members, ensuring a qualitatively better result
g. Allows 'everyone and always' to improve even when we are faced with less experienced collaborators
h. Highlights the difference in skills among collaborators

19. Answer the following questions based on your experience of collaborative translation

	Strongly Disagree	Disagree	Neither Agree nor Disagree	Agree	Strongly Agree
The quality of my translations has improved					
My skills in my second language have improved					
My skills in my first language have improved					
I prefer my work to be evaluated and corrected by my peers rather than a teacher					
I liked group work (3 or more people)					
I prefer working alone					
I prefer working in small groups (2 people)					
I liked taking part in discussions on translation					
I find it useless to have my work revised by my peers, as they do not have enough competence					

	Strongly Disagree	Disagree	Neither Agree nor Disagree	Agree	Strongly Agree
The work of revising others' translations was boring					
My perception of the complexity of professional translation has improved					
My translation skills have improved					
A good group environment was created					
All participants put the same effort in all stages of the project					

20. Do you think that the quality of the final translation benefitted from the collaborative approach?
    a. Yes
    b. No

21. Do you think that, by adopting a collaborative approach to translation, there has been a reduction in the time that was necessary to hand in the final version of the translated text?
    a. Yes
    b. No
    c. Do not know

22. Has this project helped you in seeing what your most common translation mistakes are and how you can improve?
    a. Yes
    b. No

23. During the revision of the whole final text together with your colleagues, which aspects have you collectively focused on? (Choose all that apply)
    a. Formal aspects (syntax, lexicon, assonances, alliteration, etc.)
    b. Accuracy and fidelity to the source text
    c. Respect of communicative intentions of the text
    d. Usability in Italian

24. Do you trust the comments of your colleagues regarding your translation?
    a. Yes
    b. No
    c. Not completely
    Why?____
    ____
    ____
    ____

25. As a translator receiving feedback on their translation by their peers, do you think that feedback was useful?
    a. Yes
    b. No

26. As a reviewer who gives feedback on the translation of a colleague, do you think that giving feedback was useful to you?
    a. Yes
    b. No

27. As a reviewer who gives feedback on the translation of a colleague, do you think that feedback was useful to them?
    a. Yes
    b. No

28. As a translator, do you think that knowing the identity of your reviewer has influenced your judgement regarding their feedback?
    a. Yes
    b. No
    Why?____
    ____
    ____

29. As a reviewer, do you think that knowing the identity of translators has influenced your judgement?
    a. Yes
    b. No
    Why?____
    ____
    ____

30. What part of the project has been more formative/educational/professionalising? (Choose all that apply)
    a. Giving feedback to my colleagues
    b. Receiving feedback on my translations
    c. Reviewing others' work has suggested solutions I did not consider
    d. All of the above
    e. None of the above
    f. Other:____

31. During this collaborative translation project, which non-digital tools have you employed?
    a. Monolingual dictionaries (hard copy)
    b. Bilingual dictionaries (hard copy)
    c. Thesaurus (hard copy)
    d. Encyclopaedia
    e. Own knowledge
    f. Other:____

32. While translating, which online tools did you employ?
    a. Monolingual dictionaries (online)
    b. Bilingual dictionaries (online)
    c. Thesaurus (online)
    d. Webpages
    e. Online magazines and blogs
    f. Translation software that favours guided learning on the part of the user (e.g.: *Reverso context*) or automatic translation (specify which):
    ____
    ____
    ____
    g. Other:______________________________

33. What would make this experience better in your opinion? What worked best?
    ____
    ____
    ____
    ____
    ____
    ____

34. According to your experience, what are the main issues with collaborative translation?
    ____
    ____
    ____
    ____
    ____
    ____

35. After this project, do you think that collaborative translation as a practice should be implemented in degree courses in Translation? Motivate your answer.

____
____
____
____
____
____

36. Any other observations, suggestions or comments?

____
____
____
____
____
____

References

Alexander, Christofer, and Sara Ishikawa, Murray Silverstein, *A Pattern Language. Towns, Buildings, Construction* (Oxford: Oxford University Press, 1977).

Bistué, Belén, 'Introduction: Collaborative Practices, Multi-Version Texts, and the Difficulty of Thinking Translation', in Belén Bistué, ed., *Collaborative Translation and Multi-Version Texts in Early Modern Europe* (Farnham: Ashgate Publishing Limited, 2013), 11–18.

Bistué, Belén, 'On the Incorrect Way to translate: The Absence of Collaborative Translation from Leonardo Bruni's *De Interpretatione Recta*', in Anthony Cordingley, and Céline Frigau Manning, eds, *Collaborative Translation. From the Renaissance to the Digital Age* (New York: Bloomsbury Publishing, 2017), 33–48.

D'Alverny, Marie-Thérèse, "Les traductions à deux interprètes: d'arabe en langue vernaculaire et de langue vernaculaire en latin", in Geneviève Contamine, ed., *Traduction et traducteurs au Moyen Âge: actes du colloque internationale du Centre National de la Recherche Scientifique* (Paris: CNRS, 1989), 193–206.

Désilets, Alain, and Jaap van der Meer, 'Co-creating a repository of best practices for collaborative translation', *Linguistica Antverpiensia* 10 (2011), 27–45.

Estellés-Arolas, Enrique, and Fernando González-Ladrón-de-Guevara, 'Towards an integrated crowdsourcing definition', *Journal of Information Science* 38/2 (2012), 189–200.

Fernández Costales, Alberto, *Traducción, localización e internacionalización: el caso de las páginas web universitarias / Translation, Localization, and Internationalisation: the Case of University Websites*, Doctoral Thesis (Universidad de Oviedo, 2010).

Fernández Costales, Alberto, 'Collaborative Translation Revisited: Exploring the Rationale and the Motivation for Volunteer Translation', *Revue internationale d'interprétation et de traduction / International Journal of Interpretation and Translation* 10 (2012), 115–42.

Fernández Costales, Alberto, 'Crowdsourcing and Collaborative Translation: Mass Phenomena or Silent Threat to Translation Studies?', *Hermeneus* 15 (2013), 85–110.

Fuks, Hugo, and Alberto Raposo, Marco Aurelio Gerosa, Carlos Lucena, 'The 3C Collaboration Model', in Ned Kock, ed., *Encyclopedia of E-Collaboration* (New York: Information Science Reference, 2007), 637–44.

Galeotti, Mark, *Putin's Wars. From Chechnya to Ukraine* (Great Britain: Osprey Publishing, 2022).

Galeotti, Mark, *Tutte le guerre di Putin. Dalla Cecenia all'Ucraina*, Francesco Laurenti and Ludovica Maggi, eds (Milano: Gremese editore, 2022).

Gréselle-Zaïbet, Olfa, 'Vers l'intelligence collective des équipes de travail: une étude de cas', *Management & Avenir* 4/14 (2007), 41–59.

Grutman, Rainier. 'Multilingualism', in Mona Baker, and Gabriela Saldanha, eds, *Routledge Encyclopedia of Translation Studies,* 2nd edition (London: Routledge, 1998), 182–85.

Henri, France, and Karin Lundgren-Cayrol, eds, *Apprentissage Collaboratif À Distance - Pour Comprendre Et Concevoir Les Environnements D'apprentissage Virtuels* (Quebec: Presses de l'Université du Québec, 2001).

Huss, Joanna Trzeciak, 'Collaborative translation', in Kelly Washbourne, and Ben van Wyke, eds, *The Routledge Handbook of Literary Translation* (London: Routledge, 2018), 389–405.

Jiménez-Crespo, Miguel A., *Crowdsourcing and Online Collaborative Translations: expanding the limits of Translation Studies* (Amsterdam/Philadelphia: John Benjamins Publishing Company, 2017).

Kozar, Olga, 'Towards Better Group Work: Seeing the Difference between Cooperation and Collaboration', *English Teaching Forum* 2 (2010), 16–23.

Ladmiral, Jean-René, 'La traduction au pluriel', in Enrico Monti, and Peter Schnyder, eds, *Traduire à plusieurs – Collaborative Translation* (Paris: Orizons, 2018), 19–35.

Larsonneur, Claire, 'Crowd and Cloud: ce que le numérique change à la traduction', in Enrico Monti, and Peter Schnyder, eds, *Traduire à plusieurs – Collaborative Translation* (Paris: Orizons, 2018), 375–387.

Laurenti, Francesco, 'Introduzione. Oltre la monade: tradurre collaborativamente', in Francesco Laurenti, ed., *La traduzione collaborativa. Tra didattica e mercato globale delle lingue* (Roma: Aracne, 2022), 11–45.

Laurenti, Francesco, *La traduzione collaborativa. Tra didattica e mercato globale delle lingue* (Roma: Aracne, 2022).

Laurenti, Francesco, and Federica Villareale, 'Traduzione, ambienti virtuali e nuove tecnologie: strumenti informatici per la collaborazione', *Testo a fronte, Teoria e pratica della traduzione, 69(2)*, 2023, 201–220.

Lévy, Pierre, *L'intelligence collective: pour une anthropologie du cyberspace* (Paris: La Découverte, 1994).

Mack, Manfred, *Pleine valeur: pour que l'entreprise génère un nouvel épanouissement économique et humain* (Neuilly-sur-Seine: Julhiet Editions, 2003).

Miller, Rob, *Crowd Computing*, talk for Research Microsoft (2013), <https://www.microsoft.com/en-us/research/video/crowd-computing/>, accessed 23 June 2023.

Morin–Hernández, Katell, *La révision comme clé de la gestion de la qualité des traductions en contexte professionnel*, Doctoral thesis (Université Rennes 2, 2009), <https://theses.hal.science/tel-00383266/document>, accessed 22 March 2023.

Munday, Jeremy, *Introducing Translation Studies. Theories and applications*, 3rd edition (London/New York: Routledge, 2012).
O'Brien, Sharon, 'Collaborative translation', in Yves Gambier, and Luc van Doorslaer, eds, *Handbook of translation studies* (Amsterdam/ Philadelphia: John Benjamins Publishing Company, 2012), vol. 2, 17–20.
Osman, Mat, *Il teatro fantasma*, transl. Paola Olivetto and Mirko Zilahy (Roma: Blu Atlantide, 2023).
Piotto, Valentina, *Traduire à plusieurs: une nouvelle approche à la traduction entre pluralité et collaboration*, MA thesis (Venezia: Università Ca' Foscari, 2021).
Piotto, Valentina, and Giuseppe Sofo, 'Collaborazione e strumenti digitali nel campo della traduzione', in Francesco Laurenti, ed., *La traduzione collaborativa. Tra didattica e mercato globale delle lingue* (Roma: Aracne, 2022), 223–246.
Piquet, Alexandre, *Guide pratique du travail collaboratif: Théories, méthodes et outils au service de la collaboration* (Brest: Télécom Bretagne, 2009).
Pym, Antony, *Exploring translation theories*, 2nd edition (London/New York: Routledge, 2014).
Pym, Antony, ed., *Translation Research Projects 3* (Tarragona: Intercultural Studies Group, 2011).
Roskelly, Hephzibah, 'The Risky Business of Group Work', in Gary Tate, et al., eds, *The Writing Teacher's Sourcebook*, 4th edition (New York: Oxford University Press, 2000) 123–28.
Sofo, Giuseppe, and Yannick Hamon, 'La traduction collaborative à l'ère numérique: pratiques collaboratives et numériques de révision en traduction', in Francesco Laurenti, ed., *La traduzione collaborativa. Tra didattica e mercato globale delle lingue* (Roma: Aracne, 2022), 49–80.
Stewart, John, Wencke Orbán, and Joachim Kornelius, 'Cooperative Translation in the Paradigm of Problem-Based Learning', *T21N – Translation in Transition* 1 (2010), 10–18.
Wang, Jun-song, 'Translation Quality Assessment: Bridge the Gap between Theory and Practice', *Journal of Literature and Art Studies* 7/10 (2017), 1701–1706.
Zainudin, Intan Safinaz, and Norsimah Mat Awal, 'Translation techniques: problems and solutions', *Procedia – Social and Behavioral Sciences* 59 (2012), 328–34.

3

It takes (at least) two: exploring the collaborative dimensions of extreme translations and transcreation

Lara Delle Foglie

Abstract

Texts which escape conventional translation rules (i.e. poems, experimental prose, proverbs, tongue-twisters, songs, audiovisual content and marketing copy) have always been a controversial subject in Translation Studies. They raise questions concerning what it means to translate, and whether translation is supposed to involve change. Consequently, extreme translations and transcreation are two yet-to-be-acknowledged phenomena. This essay attempts at defining them and distinguishing between the two, while analysing their inherently collaborative nature. This leads to a reflection on current practices in collaborative translation: namely, the ways translators interact with each other, as well as with authors, revisors, clients and even with machines.

Introduction

The history of translation harks back to more than 2,000 years ago. However, it was not until the publication of James Holmes' 'The Name and Nature of Translation Studies' that scholars interested in the subject started seeking a common framework. In 1972, Holmes wrote:

> At first glance, the [...] situation today would appear to be one of great confusion, with no consensus regarding the types of models to be tested, the kinds of methods to be applied, the varieties of terminology to be used. More than that, there is not even like-mindedness about the contours of the field, the problem set, the

> discipline as such. Indeed, scholars are not so much as agreed on the very name for the new field[74].

Reading these words today, we are struck by the realisation that we are still far from the *like-mindedness* Holmes aimed for. Naturally, significant progress has been made thanks to the many, crucial contributions that have followed this fundamental essay, and Translation Studies have reached academic recognition, developing in different directions. Yet, there is still no unanimity concerning the extension of the discipline. Recurrent questions surrounding the topic include what qualifies as a translation, what it means to translate, what the task of the translator is and how translations should be evaluated. Somewhat ironically, researchers in this field cannot seem to find an agreement on the official terminology to define what a translation is.

If we look up the etymology of the verb *translate*, we find that it comes from the Latin *traducĕre*, which literally means 'to carry [something] across'. As a result, according to most definitions, to translate is to transfer information from a source language to a target language. One may assume that this act of carrying across has no influence on the object being transferred. What changes is the language, while the information must remain the same. The translation must be literal, transparent, in order to be deemed faithful. The concept behind this definition is that translation should guarantee nothing gets left behind and nothing is added to the original meaning.

For literal translation to be an ideal approach, though, all languages should assign meaning to concepts in similar ways and number of words. Since this is demonstrably not true, and every language has, in fact, its own peculiar structure, interlingual communication is not as straightforward as it may seem. As brilliantly explained by Lawrence Venuti, 'Meaning is a plural and contingent relation, not an unchanging unified essence, and therefore a translation cannot be judged according to mathematics-based concepts of semantic equivalence or one-to-one correspondence'[75]. A similar sentiment

74 James S. Holmes, 'The Name and Nature of Translation Studies', in Lawrence Venuti, ed., *The Translation Studies Reader* (London / New York: Routledge, 2004), 173.

75 Lawrence Venuti, *The Translator's Invisibility: A History of Translation*, 2nd edition (London / New York: Routledge, 2008), 13.

has also famously been summarised by George Steiner: 'Fidelity is not literalism or any technical device for rendering "spirit"'[76]. If a literal translation cannot guarantee fidelity, suddenly, all translation supposedly becomes an act of betrayal. '*Traduttore traditore*' [the translator is a traitor], says a well-known Italian adage.

The issue of fidelity becomes more and more pressing when we look at unconventional texts, such as poems, experimental prose, proverbs, tongue-twisters, songs, comics, audiovisual content or marketing copy. In these cases, it becomes clear that the meaning of a sentence is not just the meaning of its words[77]. When tasked with the translation of a tongue-twister, for instance, we cannot simply focus on the meaning of words, since we would not end up with a tongue-twister in the target language. At the same time, a new tongue-twister mimicking the sound of the source language could show little to no resemblance to the original in terms of what the text says. Thus, contemplating what fidelity is brings forth a more fundamental, existential question surrounding identity. If translating is 'saying almost the same thing'[78], Umberto Eco posits:

> Abbiamo molti problemi a stabilire che cosa significhi "dire la *stessa* cosa". [...] davanti a un testo da tradurre, non sappiamo quale sia *la cosa*. [...] in certi casi, è persino dubbio che cosa voglia dire *dire*.[79]
>
> [We find it very difficult to establish what it means to "say almost the *same* thing". [...] when faced with a text to translate, we do not know what *the thing* is. [...] in some cases, one may even question what it means to *say* at all].[80]

Subsequently, such unconventional texts are deemed controversial. Despite having been observed by several researchers and scholars throughout history,

---

76 George Steiner, 'The Hermeneutic Motion', in Lawrence Venuti, ed., *The Translation Studies Reader* (London / New York: Routledge, 2004), 190.

77 David Bellos, *Is That a Fish in Your Ear? Translation and the Meaning of Everything* (New York: Faber and Faber, 2011).

78 Umberto Eco, *Dire quasi la stessa cosa: Esperienze di traduzione* (Milano: Bompiani, 2019), 9.

79 Eco, *Dire quasi la stessa cosa: Esperienze di traduzione*, 9.

80 All translations are my own unless otherwise noted.

these texts still hold no specific space within Translation Studies and are often referred to as untranslatable. In fact, there are many examples of seemingly 'untranslatable texts' being rendered into several languages. Said renditions have sometimes been defined as something other than translation – rewriting, recreation, inspiration, or worse, plagiarism. Therefore, it may be useful to study these texts within a proper research framework, in order to demonstrate that there can be no translation without change.

Namely, the translation of unconventional texts has been the object of two interesting, lesser-known phenomena: extreme translations and transcreation.

1. On extreme translations

One of the most important contributions on extreme translations can be found in the work of Franco Nasi, who describes extreme translations as the translations of texts that were originally written under linguistic constraint, including songs, nursery rhymes, poems, experimental prose and advertisements[81]. Nasi's crucial text on the subject, *Traduzioni Estreme* [*Extreme Translations*] (2015), highlights the importance of 'stabilire una relazione ritmica con quel testo'[82] [establishing a rhythmic relationship with the text]. His approach breaks away from literalism and reminds us of Saussure's and Pierce's theories on linguistic signs, nudging us to remember that words are, in fact, not just the names of things[83]. Sound is an element which contributes to conveying the sense of the text just as much as (if not more than) the meaning of the words that compose it. As explained by Daniele Petruccioli, Italian translator of extreme texts such as Mark Dunn's *Ella Minnow Pea: A Progressively Lipogrammatic Epistolary Fable*[84] (2001): 'Tradurre referenti non è tradurre'[85] [Translating referents is not what translating is].

As a result, we may define extreme translations as the translations of texts in which the relationship between meaning and sound cannot be ignored or

---

[81] Franco Nasi, *Traduzioni estreme* (Macerata: Edizioni Quodlibet, 2015).

[82] Nasi, *Traduzioni estreme*, 26.

[83] Bellos, *Is That a Fish in Your Ear? Translation and the Meaning of Everything.*

[84] Mark Dunn, *Ella Minnow Pea: A Progressively Lipogrammatic Epistolary Fable* (San Francisco: MacAdam/Cage Publishing, 2001).

[85] Daniele Petruccioli, *Le pagine nere: appunti sulla traduzione dei romanzi* (Roma: La Lepre Edizioni, 2017), 57.

understated. Without recreating the same kind of relationship in the target language, the text loses any meaning and simply cannot be translated. We speak of extreme translations – as in plural – due to the fact that these texts can be visualised on a continuum, where either sound or word meaning can be slightly more or less of an immediate priority for the translator. For example, both James Joyce's *Finnegans Wake*[86] (1939) and Raymond Queneau's *Exercices de style*[87] [*Exercises in Style*] (1947) are notoriously hard texts to translate, albeit for different reasons.

Joyce's *Finnegans Wake* has been described as a major example of an *open work*[88], a piece of literature which seems to have no definite interpretation. This layering of multiple possible meanings was built up through the invention of a new, plurilingual language, later named *Finneganian*, which looks like English and sounds like it belongs to several different languages, when read aloud. In this case, the translator is free to create their own version of *Finneganian*, their own neologisms. The real challenge lies in maintaining the polysemous nature of the text. Meaning is the priority, as the translator must 'carry across' all the messages and references they can find within the original text. At the same time, it is also important to note the new version of *Finneganian* should look like the target language, in order to be approachable for its target audience. Past attempts at translating *Finnegans Wake* without keeping both elements in check, such as Charles K. Ogden's version in Basic English[89] (1932), have failed to successfully convey the meaning of the text at large. Another famous work of prose which could be included within this category is *Alice's Adventures in Wonderland*[90] by Lewis Carroll (1865).

On the other hand, Queneau's *Exercices de style* retells the same story ninety-nine times, each in a different style. Queneau experiments with different textual genres, punctuation, rhetorical devices, jargon and slang. Most of the book falls under the category of *constrained writing*, as it includes lipograms,

---

86 James Joyce, *Finnegans Wake* (Oxford: Oxford University Press, 2012).

87 Raymond Queneau, *Exercices de style* (Paris: Gallimard, 1947).

88 Umberto Eco, *Opera aperta. Forma e indeterminazione nelle poetiche contemporanee*, 4th edition (Milano: Bompiani, 1962).

89 James Joyce, *Anna Livia Plurabelle. Nella traduzione di Samuel Beckett e altri*, trans. by James Joyce and others (Torino: Einaudi, 1996).

90 Lewis Carroll, *Alice's Adventures in Wonderland* (London: MacMillan, 1865).

anagrams, homeoteleutons, onomatopoeias and more. Here, the translator's immediate priority is sound. If the original text is lipogrammatic, the translation must be too. If the linguistic constraint is not respected, the exercise is pointless. Of course, the same story should be told all ninety-nine times, but literalism cannot be pursued, as vowels and consonants logically do not appear with the same frequency in different languages. Most Oulipian works, if translated, may fall within this category.

Umberto Eco analysed both Joyce's and Queneau's works in *Dire quasi la stessa cosa: Esperienze di traduzione* [*Saying Almost the Same Thing: Experiences in Translation*] (2003), in his account of *rifacimenti radicali* [radical rewritings][91]. Specifically, he focused on the Italian *Anna Livia Plurabelle* (Book I, chapter 8 of *Finnegans Wake*), which is a self-translation by James Joyce[92], and the Italian *Esercizi di stile* [*Exercises in Style*], which was translated by Umberto Eco himself[93].

According to Eco, such challenging texts cannot be truly translated, but only rewritten. Radical rewritings, he claims, break away from literalism through a series of licenses which prevent backtranslation into the original text. In other words, a proper translation must stay within the confines of a so-called *reversibility threshold*[94], to always guarantee one's ability to recognise (and eventually go back to) the original text.

Nevertheless, when commenting upon Joyce's self-translation, Eco writes:

> Il Joyce italiano non è certamente un esempio di traduzione "fedele". Eppure leggendo questa sua traduzione, vedendo il testo completamente ripensato in un'altra lingua, se ne comprendono i meccanismi profondi, il tipo di partita che si intende giocare [...] al di là della fedeltà a questo o a quel rimando citazionistico. Joyce, in qualche modo, rimane entro i confini della traduzione propriamente detta e non si disperde nella palude delle libere interpretazioni[95].

---

[91] Eco, *Dire quasi la stessa cosa: Esperienze di traduzione*, 299.

[92] Joyce, *Anna Livia Plurabelle. Nella traduzione di Samuel Beckett e altri*. It is worth noting that Joyce's self-translation first appeared in 1940 under the title of *Anna Livia Plurabella* and the names of Nino Frank and Ettore Settanni.

[93] Raymond Queneau, *Esercizi di stile*, trans. by Umberto Eco (Torino: Einaudi, 1983).

[94] Eco, *Dire quasi la stessa cosa: Esperienze di traduzione*, 299.

[95] Eco, *Dire quasi la stessa cosa: Esperienze di traduzione*, 312.

[Certainly, the Italian Joyce is not an example of a "faithful" translation. Yet, when we read his translation and we see the text completely reimagined in another language, we can understand its deepest mechanisms, the kind of game one wants to play [...] regardless of fidelity to this or that reference. Joyce somehow manages to stay within the confines of proper translation without getting swamped with free interpretations.]

On a similar note, in the preface of *Esercizi di stile*, he comments:

Si trattava [...] di decidere cosa significasse, per un libro del genere, essere fedeli. Ciò che era chiaro è che non voleva dire essere letterali. [...] Fedeltà significava capire le regole del gioco, rispettarle, e poi giocare una nuova partita con lo stesso numero di mosse[96].

[The point was [...] establishing what it meant, for a book of this kind, to be faithful. What was clear is that it did not mean being literal. [...] Fidelity was about understanding the rules of the game, respecting them, and then playing a new round in the same number of moves.]

It would certainly be bold to suggest Joyce's Italian translation could be unfaithful to the author's intentions. Likewise, Eco's commentary of his own translation of *Exercices de style* shows the extent of his commitment to understand what the text *said*, with the end goal in mind to let the Italian readers join in on the game Queneau originally played with the French. In order to translate, we must first understand. This is why, following Heidegger's studies on understanding, Steiner asserts that 'Comprehension, as its etymology shows, "comprehends" not only cognitively but by encirclement and ingestion. [...] We "break" a code: decipherment is dissective, leaving the shell smashed and the vital layers stripped'[97].

In *Experiences in Translation*, Eco claims: 'I would tend to exclude rewriting from the ranks of translations because there is no doubt that it is an anomalous case of translation proper, which falls into the category of intrasystemic

96 Umberto Eco, 'Introduzione', in Queneau, *Esercizi di stile*, XX.
97 Steiner, 'The Hermeneutic Motion', in Venuti, ed., *The Translation Studies Reader*, 187.

interpretations'[98]. Yet, his hypothesis surrounding radical rewritings falters on the fact that it fails to distinguish between what translation is and what it is not. It is hard to set an exact threshold beyond which a text ceases to be itself, when translated. This is because translation is a process of understanding, which requires *cracking the text open*, as suggested above. Change inevitably occurs throughout the entirety of the translation process. The concept has been remarked by Enrico Terrinoni (who translated the latest Italian version of *Finnegans Wake* together with colleague Fabio Pedone[99]):

> To translate a text means to change it in many ways, not only to change its language. The process implies a change of scenarios, in that both the source space from which the text arises and the target space where it ends up being re-read are subject to external forces (the translator's choices, the market's expectations, the publisher's demands) that utterly change its nature. Moreover, what changes is not just the text itself, its "before" and "after", but also the perception of its location in the history of culture[100].

In conclusion, knowing literalism is not a viable option, since the sense of the text is embedded in the relationship between sound and meaning which is fixated in the time and the space of the original, we can either give up on translating altogether, or embrace what Steiner calls a *fourfold hermenia*: 'a hermeneutic of trust (*élancement*), of penetration, of embodiment, and of restitution'[101].

---

98 Umberto Eco, *Experiences in translation*, trans. by Alastair McEwen (Toronto / Buffalo / London: University of Toronto Press, 2001), 106.

99 Their translation came out in two instalments. James Joyce, *Finnegans Wake, libro III, capitoli 1 e 2*, trans. by Enrico Terrinoni and Fabio Pedone (Milano: Mondadori, 2017). James Joyce, *Finnegans Wake, libro III, capitoli 3 e 4, libro IV*, trans. by Enrico Terrinoni and Fabio Pedone (Milano: Mondadori, 2019).

100 Enrico Terrinoni, 'Who's Afraid of Translating Ulysses?', *Translation and Literature* 22/2 (2013), 244.

101 Steiner, 'The Hermeneutic Motion', in Venuti, ed., *The Translation Studies Reader*, 190.

2. On transcreation

As already stated, languages do not exist in a vacuum; therefore, matters of sound, connotation, contextual information, culture and medium make up a significant part of what a sentence actually means. After taking all these elements into account, it becomes clear that literal approaches to translation create a harmful assumption that translating is simply converting words from one language to another. This stereotype is detrimental not only to the practice itself, but to professional translators as well.

Whenever literal translation fails, we may get the idea that translation is, by definition, impossible. Most importantly, this leads us to fall under the impression that translators should be invisible. A translator can even be seen as someone who 'invades, extracts, and brings home'[102], a disturbing image which suggests translation stands for theft and cultural appropriation, rather than being an occasion for mutual enrichment, knowledge dissemination and fruitful communication. Invisibility as a concept is contradictory, as the translator cannot but interpret what is in front of their eyes, just like any other reader. Furthermore, as once again pointed out by Venuti, invisibility does not imply fidelity, to the point that it can lull the reader into an *illusion of transparency*, resulting from the adoption of an ethnocentric, target oriented approach 'reducing if not simply excluding the very differences that translation is called on to convey'[103].

The translator's invisibility policy has prompted a series of practices which have soon proved detrimental to the profession. Such practices range from the infamous per-word rates, to unrealistic deadlines, to the systematic exclusion of the translator from discussions of the project at large. Often, literary translators cannot even find their names on the cover of the books they translated – a glaring example of the little recognition the category gets. If we add to this the overwhelming increase in the use of machine translation (MT) and artificial intelligence (AI) regardless of the complexity of the text, it is to no one's surprise that several translators are looking for ways to make their work stand out. Perhaps the most interesting strategy some translators have adopted is transcreation.

---

102 Steiner, 'The Hermeneutic Motion', in Venuti, ed., *The Translation Studies Reader*, 187.
103 Venuti, *The Translator's Invisibility*, 16.

As with extreme translations, the notion of transcreation does not currently have a universally shared definition, to the point that the word cannot be found in any of the main English dictionaries. Originally brought up by literary translator Purushottama Lal[104] as early as 1957, the term 'transcreation' has since been used to describe several different practices. In the second edition of the *Routledge Encyclopedia of Translation Studies* (2009), Ira Torresi writes:

> The crosslinguistic and cross-cultural transfer of multimodal promotional texts is often termed localization, adaptation or (less frequently) transcreation or rewriting. The latter set of terms suggests a kind of transfer which is less concerned with issues of "faithfulness" and more, perhaps, with functional equivalence and adequacy. These terms, rather than "translation", may therefore appear more appropriate for use in connection with advertising, where the quality of the "translated" text is usually assessed according to functionalist criteria[105].

Once again, what springs to mind is the 'great confusion'[106] Holmes complained about in his essay. As we have already noticed when discussing the topic of extreme translations, trying to define fidelity is not as simple as it may seem. In addition, suggesting that localisation, adaptation, transcreation and rewriting stand for the same practice may bring up further misunderstandings. The association between transcreation and rewriting reminds us of the reasoning Eco adopted in *Dire quasi la stessa cosa*, which demonstrably fails to distinguish between what translation is and what it is not. Similarly, 'the concept of adaptation requires recognition of translation as non-adaptation, a somehow more constrained mode of transfer'[107]. The definition is, admittedly, quite fuzzy.

---

104 Purushottama Lal, *Great Sanskrit Plays in Modern Translation* (New York: New Directions Publishing, 1964).

105 Ira Torresi, 'Advertising', in Mona Baker, and Gabriela Saldanha, eds, *Routledge Encyclopedia of Translation Studies*, 2nd edition (London and New York: Routledge, 1998), 7.

106 Holmes, 'The Name and Nature of Translation Studies', in Venuti, ed., *The Translation Studies Reader*, 173.

107 Georges L. Bastin, 'Adaptation', in Baker, and Saldanha, eds, *Routledge Encyclopedia of Translation Studies*, 3.

Transcreation has been reclaimed by professionals from different domains – especially in the literary, audiovisual and marketing fields. It has been used to describe the plurilingualism in Joyce's works[108], to refer to intersemiotic translation[109], or even to indicate 'a hybrid practice/service halfway between translation and copywriting'[110]. Unfortunately, there seems to be no consensus on what transcreation actually entails.

'What's in a name?', one might consider. What makes the term transcreation so controversial, and not just a matter of linguistic intricacies, is that this practice is becoming popular on the market as *more* than translation. This claim presumably originates as an attempt to differentiate one's services from machine translation or amateur translation[111]. Transcreation often denotes a service which is inherently creative, and transcreators stand out as professionals who can be trusted as more than simple 'language experts', bringing to the table cultural awareness and understanding of the target market. This encourages and justifies a broader involvement of the translator in the project at large, while allowing the professional to set their own deadlines and their own rates. As pointed out by Jeremy Munday, though, 'the term "translation" becomes disadvantaged if added value is given to roles bearing other labels'[112].

When Claudia Benetello observes that 'the transcreation professional [...] is not "just the translator" and is "listened to" rather than simply "used"'[113], one cannot help but see this as one of the consequences of the so-called 'translator's invisibility'. Many translators could provide the same sort of service as transcreators, if popular belief did not classify this professional figure as one that should remain in the shadows. This is true for all domains of translation,

---

108 Rosa Maria Bollettieri Bosinelli, 'Transcreative Joyce', *Scientia Traductionis* 8 (2010).

109 David Katan, 'Introduction', in David Katan, and Cinzia Spinzi, eds, *Transcreation and the Professions* (Bologna: Iconesoft Edizioni - Gruppo Radivo Holding, 2014), 17.

110 Claudia Benetello, 'When translation is not enough: Transcreation as a convention defying practice. A practitioner's perspective', *The Journal of Specialised Translation* 29 (2018), 29.

111 Katan, 'Introduction', in Katan, and Spinzi, eds, *Transcreation and the Professions*, 17.

112 Katan, and Spinzi, eds, *Transcreation and the Professions*, 22.

113 Claudia Benetello, 'Hybridisation adds value in translation and interpreting', in David Katan, and Cinzia Spinzi, eds, *Translation plus: The added value of the translator* (Bologna: Iconesoft Edizioni - Gruppo Radivo Holding, 2021), 113.

even the most technical ones, because translation is not simply converting words from one language to another. Knowing a language in depth requires cultural awareness, and cultural awareness implies understanding of the target market, if the translator's job ultimately is to sell what they are translating.

From a marketing perspective, the term 'transcreation' proves particularly useful to sell translation services – no wonder it is mostly used by translators who work within advertising. However, if we look at what the term actually stands for from the viewpoint of a translation scholar, transcreation may be nothing short of a buzzword. The current use of the word as more than a translation might eventually backfire, causing disruption both on the market and in academic domains. In the words of Yves Gambier: 'It might destabilize Translation Studies (TS): what is then its object of investigation?'[114].

What follows is a suggestion. Perhaps, we could look at transcreation as a translation approach which must prioritise consideration of the physicality of the target text. This means transcreation may, indeed, concern several domains, such as literature, advertising, audiovisual content and more. While this does not imply transcreation is *more* than translation, the term might be useful in order to explore an element of translation which is often overlooked: the need to keep in mind that different languages stretch across time and space in different ways. This definition could be useful when observing time- and space-related restraints in audiovisual translation, such as the need to stay within the so-called *safe area* for captioning and the need to respect lip sync in dubbing. When considering literary translation, it may refer to issues related to displaying the text on the page (such as in comics or in poetry). Finally, in marketing translation, it may indicate the need to take into account the shape and size of packaging or billboards, so that the translation can fit within the given space, as well as time restraints in translating jingles meant for TV spots or online content.

While extreme translations concern linguistics (specifically, the complex relationship between sound and meaning which is unique to each language), transcreation could refer to the way different languages establish a different

[114] Katan, and Spinzi, eds, *Transcreation and the Professions*, 21.

relationship with the same medium, resulting in substantial translation changes.

It should be noted that transcreation, on this basis, would not be a synonym for adaptation. Adaptation implies the passage from one medium into another (such as a novel being adapted into a movie), and often concerns intralingual translation – staying within the same language. The medium changes, but the language can remain the same. On the other hand, we may talk of transcreation whenever the medium is unchanged, but major differences between the source and the target language cause the translator to move away from a literal translation, which would not physically fit due to the specific time or space restraints of that medium. For instance, if a TV spot must be translated, it will not become a different kind of advertisement, or be displayed on a different medium, but the voice(s) in it will speak a different language.

In other words, all transcreation is translation, but not all translations require transcreation skills.

3. On collaborative translation

As we have demonstrated, extreme translations and transcreation are two different types of translation. However, they share several common elements, which confirm their status as translation practices. Conversely, exclusion of these two practices from Translation Studies would cause great difficulty in defining what translation actually is.

The controversy surrounding extreme translations and transcreation partly concerns their inherently collaborative nature, which challenges stereotypes revolving around the translator. While common, outdated depictions of the profession show the translator working alone, perhaps in the middle of the night, locked away in an ivory tower, translation has, in fact, always been a collaborative practice[115]. Collaboration is at the heart of all translation, since the translator's task is to enable communication between authors and readers, a position which requires mediation, empathy, cultural awareness and linguistic knowledge.

---

[115] Francesco Laurenti, *La traduzione collaborativa. Tra didattica e mercato globale delle lingue* (Roma: Aracne, 2022).

Extreme translations and transcreation bring the translator to visibility, as both practices showcase the value of the translator's interpretation, their effort towards understanding the mechanisms that make the message work in the source language, and towards recreating similar conditions in the target language.

Notably, extreme translations often require the translator to gather as much as possible information on the intricacies of the source text; this entails getting in touch with the author (if possible) or carrying out research on their works at large and sometimes even their personal biography (as it is common in poetry translation). For instance, in Georges Perec's lipogrammatic novel *La Disparition*[116] [*A Void*] (1969), writing without ever using the letter 'e' is not just a linguistic choice, but rather, a reference to the author's personal life, which should not be overlooked.

Coming back to *Finnegans Wake* (a novel where different languages literally 'collaborate' on the page, to create *Finneganian*), several groups of scholars worldwide have been reading, studying and analysing the book for decades to reveal its many meanings – no professional translator would ever dive into the translation without taking advantage of this mine of information. When reading translations of *Finnegans Wake*, one is reminded of how much research is needed to translate.

Furthermore, the history of its translations is dotted with even closer collaborations between the author and the translator (as in the case of the French and Italian translations which Joyce himself worked on[117]) or between translators (such as the aforementioned Italian translation by Terrinoni and Pedone[118]). When the text openly suggests multiple interpretations, trying to translate it in a way that only allows one is in all respects a disservice to the reader and the text itself. As a result, collaborative translation is the smartest approach to ensure the text keeps its interpretative multiplicity. Similarly, retranslation proves to be a valid way to explore further interpretations from different viewpoints, which creates, in the end, a collaborative translation.

---

116 Georges Perec, *La Disparition* (Paris: Gallimard, 1969).

117 Joyce, *Anna Livia Plurabelle. Nella traduzione di Samuel Beckett e altri.*

118 Joyce, *Finnegans Wake, libro III, capitoli 1 e 2*. Joyce, *Finnegans Wake, libro III, capitoli 3 e 4, libro IV.*

If there is no such thing as a perfect translation, it goes without saying that translation is inherently meant to be collaborative, to be infinite[119]. Otherwise, retranslation would cease to exist.

Many definitions of transcreation also tend to implicitly underline its collaborative nature. As we have seen, the term is often used nowadays to sell a service where the translator is always available to the client, even beyond simple linguistic conversion tasks. The transcreator is visible in their work (which substantially distances itself from the original text) and is also an active participant in the project at large. A transcreator cannot be invisible, because they cannot hide behind their work, and are expected to give a *rationale* of their choices, if questioned. This visibility exists because the transcreator is seen as an invaluable collaborator, as a subject who interprets and guides successful communication (turning words into sales). In fact, one may argue that all translators should rise to the same visibility, as they, too, collaborate with several professional figures. Depending on their area of expertise, they may collaborate with other translators, as well as with authors, revisors, publishers, voice actors, illustrators, game developers, language service providers and clients.

The rise in the use of MT and AI has brought up questions surrounding the added value of the translator. Translation experiences such as transcreation and extreme translations play a fundamental role in showcasing the collaborative nature of all translation. When we talk about fidelity, we must ask ourselves: who or what should the translator be faithful to? The author, the readers, the text itself? Translation builds bridges from one culture to another; this is a space of collaboration, which thrives off communicative intent. As explained by computational linguist Emily M. Bender, 'a system trained only on form has *a priori* no way to learn meaning'[120]; as a result, all technological advances in translation should not aim to remove translators from the translation process. While machines

[119] Terrinoni, 'Who's Afraid of Translating Ulysses?', 241.

[120] Emily M. Bender, and Alexander Koller, 'Climbing towards NLU: On Meaning, Form, and Understanding in the Age of Data', Proceedings of the 58th Annual Meeting of the Association for Computational Linguistics, *Association for Computational Linguistics* (2020), 5185.

can certainly be a valuable tool for the translator, and their use should be encouraged and further researched, we must remember that translation is, at the bottom, a communicative act, which algorithms can only mimic without real understanding.

References

Baker, Mona, and Gabriela Saldanha, eds, *Routledge Encyclopedia of Translation Studies*, 2nd edition (London / New York: Routledge, 1998).

Bastin, Georges L., 'Adaptation', in Mona Baker, and Gabriela Saldanha, eds, *Routledge Encyclopedia of Translation Studies*, 2nd edition (London / New York: Routledge, 1998), 3–6.

Bellos, David, *Is That a Fish in Your Ear? Translation and the Meaning of Everything* (New York: Faber and Faber, 2011).

Bender, Emily M., and Alexander Koller, 'Climbing towards NLU: On Meaning, Form, and Understanding in the Age of Data', Proceedings of the 58th Annual Meeting of the Association for Computational Linguistics, *Association for Computational Linguistics* (2020), 5185–98.

Benetello, Claudia, 'Hybridisation adds value in translation and interpreting', in David Katan, and Cinzia Spinzi, eds, *Translation plus: The added value of the translator* (Bologna: Iconesoft Edizioni - Gruppo Radivo Holding, 2021), 100–23.

Benetello, Claudia, 'When translation is not enough: Transcreation as a convention defying practice. A practitioner's perspective', *The Journal of Specialised Translation* 29 (2018), 28–44.

Bollettieri Bosinelli, Rosa Maria, 'Transcreative Joyce', *Scientia Traductionis* 8 (2010), 190–3.

Carroll, Lewis, *Alice's Adventures in Wonderland* (London: MacMillan, 1865).

Dunn, Mark, *Ella Minnow Pea: A Progressively Lipogrammatic Epistolary Fable* (San Francisco: MacAdam/Cage Publishing, 2001).

Eco, Umberto, *Dire quasi la stessa cosa: Esperienze di traduzione* (Milano: Bompiani, 2019).

Eco, Umberto, *Experiences in translation*, trans. by Alastair McEwen (Toronto / Buffalo / London: University of Toronto Press, 2001).

Eco, Umberto, 'Introduzione', in Raymond Queneau, *Esercizi di stile* (Torino: Einaudi, 1983), V–XX.
Eco, Umberto, *Opera aperta. Forma e indeterminazione nelle poetiche contemporanee*, 4th edition (Milano: Bompiani, 1962).
Holmes, James S., 'The Name and Nature of Translation Studies', in Lawrence Venuti, ed., *The Translation Studies Reader* (London / New York: Routledge, 2004), 172–85.
Joyce, James, *Anna Livia Plurabelle. Nella traduzione di Samuel Beckett e altri*, trans. by James Joyce and others (Torino: Einaudi, 1996).
Joyce, James, *Finnegans Wake* (Oxford: Oxford University Press, 2012).
Joyce, James, *Finnegans Wake, libro III, capitoli 1 e 2*, trans. by Enrico Terrinoni and Fabio Pedone (Milano: Mondadori, 2017).
Joyce, James, *Finnegans Wake, libro III, capitoli 3 e 4, libro IV*, trans. by Enrico Terrinoni and Fabio Pedone (Milano: Mondadori, 2019).
Katan, David, 'Introduction', in David Katan, and Cinzia Spinzi, eds, *Transcreation and the Professions* (Bologna: Iconesoft Edizioni - Gruppo Radivo Holding, 2014), 10–19.
Katan, David, and Cinzia Spinzi, eds, *Transcreation and the Professions* (Bologna: Iconesoft Edizioni - Gruppo Radivo Holding, 2014).
Katan, David, and Cinzia Spinzi, eds, *Translation plus: The added value of the translator* (Bologna: Iconesoft Edizioni - Gruppo Radivo Holding, 2021).
Lal, Purushottama, *Great Sanskrit Plays in Modern Translation* (New York: New Directions Publishing, 1964).
Laurenti, Francesco, *La traduzione collaborativa. Tra didattica e mercato globale delle lingue* (Roma: Aracne, 2022).
Nasi, Franco, *Traduzioni estreme* (Macerata: Edizioni Quodlibet, 2015).
Perec, Georges, *La Disparition* (Paris: Gallimard, 1969).
Petruccioli, Daniele, *Le pagine nere: appunti sulla traduzione dei romanzi* (Roma: La Lepre Edizioni, 2017).
Queneau, Raymond, *Esercizi di stile*, trans. by Umberto Eco (Torino: Einaudi, 1983).
Queneau, Raymond, *Exercices de style* (Paris: Gallimard, 1947).

Steiner, George, 'The Hermeneutic Motion', in Lawrence Venuti, ed., *The Translation Studies Reader* (London / New York: Routledge, 2004), 186–91.

Terrinoni, Enrico, 'Who's Afraid of Translating Ulysses?', *Translation and Literature* 22/2 (2013), 240–8.

Torresi, Ira, 'Advertising', in Mona Baker, and Gabriela Saldanha, eds, *Routledge Encyclopedia of Translation Studies*, 2nd edition (London and New York: Routledge, 1998), 6–10.

Venuti, Lawrence, *The Translator's Invisibility: A History of Translation*, 2nd edition (London / New York: Routledge, 2008).

4

Teamwork and the Art of Audio Description – Collaborative Intersemiotic Translation at the Service of Blind and Low-vision Audiences

Laura Giordani

Abstract

Audio description, commonly referred to as "AD", guarantees accessibility to visual content for blind or partially sighted individuals. This article explores the importance of teamwork, highlighting the benefits of collaboration between writers, voice-over artists, and experts in recording and mixing. It illustrates the potential, modalities, and challenges arising from the interaction between professionals from different fields and with diverse sensitivities. Equally relevant, if not central, is the cooperation with blind and visually impaired people in creating, testing, and refining ADs. The analysis demonstrates the transformative impact of synergy between different skill sets, which improves the quality of ADs and promotes a more complete and inclusive user experience.

Introduction: The Role of the Audio Description and Audio Describers

Everyone has the right to access culture and entertainment, regardless of their ability or disability, in the spirit of full social inclusion[121]. Audio descriptions transform visual information into auditory content, allowing blind and partially sighted people to access films, plays, sporting events, photographic

[121] On the issue of the right to access culture, see also Laura Giordani, 'Diritto di esserci anche al cinema', *Diari di Cineclub* 86, Cineclub Roma (2020), 20, <https://www.cineclubroma.it/diari-di-cineclub-roma/raccolte/anno-2020/884-diari-di-cineclub-n-86-settembre-2020>, accessed 10 September 2024.

exhibitions, museum exhibitions, and much more. Recently, not only the visually impaired but also people suffering from cognitive disabilities have benefitted from audio descriptions[122]. Additionally, language teachers have chosen to use ADs with their international students. Recreational use of audio descriptions is widespread and, to a certain extent, resembles radio broadcasts narrating stories in serial form (i.e. radio theatre).

The *audio describer* or *describer* is the author responsible for composing these original, creative texts. They are highly trained professionals who objectively describe what happens on screen, translating actions, body language, facial expressions, setting, and clothing into words. This must be done with full respect to blind and low-vision end-users, abiding by the European and Italian guidelines, as well as the original content and dialogues[123]. Their work should be as objective, precise, simple, and clear as possible without leaving room for subjective interpretations. Finally, the atmosphere of the product must also be maintained intact, especially in the case of audiovisuals[124].

2. Analysis

2.1 AD in the context of audiovisual translation

Together with subtitling, audio description is a form of translation that guarantees accessibility to audiovisual products for people with sensory disabilities. The practice is rooted in *intermodal mediation*, which 'translates' visual images into verbal descriptions. Categorising and placing AD in the field of translation, particularly in audiovisual translation, has long been controversial and debated. To resolve the issue, specialists in the field have relied on Roman Jakobson[125] and his definition of the three types of translation: *intralingual*, *interlingual* and *intersemiotic*. In summary,

---

[122] See Joel Snyder, *The Visual Made Verbal: A Comprehensive Training Manual and Guide to the History and Applications of Audio Description* (American Council of the Blind, 2007), 82-3.

[123] For a complete overview of the European Guidelines, please refer to the website: <https://www.ofcom.org.uk>.

[124] See Snyder, *The Visual Made Verbal: A Comprehensive Training Manual and Guide to the History and Applications of Audio Description*, 158, 217.

[125] Roman Jakobson, 'On Linguistic Aspects of Translation', in Reuben Arthur Brower, ed., *On Translation* (Cambridge, MA: Harvard University Press, 1959).

> intralingual translation, or *rewording*, is the interpretation of verbal signs by means of other signs of the same language. [...] Interlingual translation, or translation proper, is an interpretation of verbal signs by means of some other language. [...] Intersemiotic translation, or *transmutation*, is an interpretation of verbal signs by means of signs of nonverbal sign systems.[126]

Audio description is argued to be an intersemiotic translation as it 'translates' visual images into *sound images*. It differs from Jackobson's definition of intersemiotic translation in that it does not start from interpreting verbal signs. Notably, Joel Snyder emphasises that 'Audio Description is a literary art form in itself. It is a type of poetry [...]. It provides an oral version of the visual – the visual is made verbal, aural [...] and oral'[127]. Given the specific traits of each of the three modes, it is apparent that audiovisual translation incorporates heterogeneous semiotic components[128]. Overall, these practices fall into two primary modalities: isosemiotic and diasemiotic. Isosemiotic translation maintains the sign system of the original content, while diasemiotic transposes it, in the case of audiovisuals, from visual to written, as in subtitling. Interestingly, because it is a textual procedure aimed at voice-over narration and auditory use by the public, AD involves both moments. On the one hand, it transfers visual content into written and oral form. On the other, through spoken words, it conveys audio-descriptive information that

---

126 See in this regard Jakobson, 'On Linguistic Aspects of Translation', in Brower, ed., *On Translation*, 232-3. Also see Julian Bourne and Catalina Jiménez Hurtado, 'From the Visual to the Verbal in Two Languages: a Contrastive Analysis of the Audio Description of The Hours in English and Spanish.' in Jorge Díaz Cintas, Pilar Orero, and Aline Remael, eds, *Media for All. Subtitling for the Deaf, Audio Description, and Sign Language*, Series: Approaches to Translation Studies, Volume 30 (Leiden: Brill, 2007), 175-87; Anna Jankowska, and Agnieszka Szarkowska, '*Text-to-speech Audio Description of Voiced-over Films. A case study of audio described Volver in Polish*', in Elisa Perego, *Emerging topics in translation: Audio description* (Trieste: EUT Edizioni Università di Trieste, 2012), 81-94.

127 Snyder, *The Visual Made Verbal: A Comprehensive Training Manual and Guide to the History and Applications of Audio Description*, 75.

128 For an in-depth study of audiovisual translation practices and rootedness in the defining concept of *screen translation*, see Mara Logaldo, *Teoria e tecnica della traduzione audiovisiva. Tradurre, adattare, sottotitolare per lo schermo* (Roma: Dino Audino Editore, 2021), 11-15.

reaches the user along with the dialogues of the cultural product aurally experienced by the blind and visually impaired user.

Lastly, the AD script is accompanied by specific cues that guide the narrator's interpretation, for instance, distinguishing narrated parts from read parts (as in the case of on-screen signs and subtitles or clips that must be read faster or modified during mixing for space reasons)[129].

2.2 AD as an original creative text. Differences between AD and interlingual translation

Of particular note is Snyder's use of the term 'Arte' ['Art'][130]. In the Italian Encyclopedia Treccani, in the corresponding entry, the following is reported:

> In senso lato, ogni capacità di agire o di produrre, basata su un particolare complesso di regole e di esperienze conoscitive e tecniche, quindi anche l'insieme delle regole e dei procedimenti per svolgere un'attività umana in vista di determinati risultati. Il concetto di arte come *tèchne*, complesso di regole ed esperienze elaborate dall'uomo per produrre oggetti o rappresentare immagini tratte dalla realtà o dalla fantasia, si evolve solo attraverso un passaggio critico nel concetto di arte come espressione originale di un artista, per giungere alla definizione di un oggetto come opera d'arte.[131]
>
> [In a broad sense, any ability to act or produce based on a particular set of rules and cognitive and technical experiences, therefore also the set of rules and procedures to carry out a human activity in view of certain results. The concept of art as *techne*, a complex of rules and experiences elaborated by humanity to produce objects or represent images taken from reality or fantasy, evolves only through a critical passage into the concept of art as an original expression of an artist, to reach the definition of an object as a work of art.]

---

129 For an in-depth discussion on the descriptive script, please refer to chapter *AD as a descriptive text*.

130 See Snyder, *The Visual Made Verbal: A Comprehensive Training Manual and Guide to the History and Applications of Audio Description*.

131 See the entry 'Arte' in Italian Encyclopedia Treccani, Institute of the Italian Encyclopedia, founded by Giovanni Treccani, <https://www.treccani.it/enciclopedia/arte/?search=arte%2F>, accessed 10 September 2024. Unless otherwise indicated, this paper's translator has provided all translations of Italian quotations.

Again in the Encyclopedia Treccani, in the entry 'Creatività' ['Creativity'], one may read:

> In psicologia, processo intellettuale divergente rispetto al normale processo logico astratto. Secondo J.P. Guilford, iniziatore degli studi sull'intelligenza creativa,[132] la creatività sarebbe caratterizzata da nove fattori principali: particolare sensibilità ai problemi, capacità di produrre idee, flessibilità di principi, originalità nell'ideare, capacità di sintesi, capacità di analisi, capacità di definire e strutturare in modo nuovo le proprie esperienze e conoscenze, ampiezza del settore ideativo, capacità di valutazione.[133]
>
> [In psychology, an intellectual process divergent from the normal abstract logical process. According to J.P. Guilford, initiator of creative intelligence studies, creativity is characterised by nine main factors: particular sensitivity to problems, ability to produce ideas, flexibility of principles, originality in devising, ability to synthesise, ability to analyse, ability to define and structure one's experiences and knowledge in a new way, breadth of the ideational sector, ability to evaluate.]

From these two definitions and following Snyder, it is possible to derive the specificities of AD and the differences between it and interlingual translation. As *an original creative work of art*, audio description can be defined as an activity inspired by lexical, stylistic and prosodic guidelines to represent the audiovisual and diegetic aspects of cultural and entertainment products. Equally important is the describer's experience, understood not only as accumulated professional expertise but also as an empirical stratification of the experience of a perceiving subject. Combining the elements above, the artistry of the audio-descriptive act emerges as an original, unprecedented and unrepeatable *unicum*. The subjective component is further elucidated by the nine factors mentioned in the second definition of the Encyclopedia

[132] Joy Paul Guildford, *Creative Talents: their Nature, Use and Development* (Buffalo, NY: Bearly Ltd, 1986).

[133] See the entry 'Creatività' in Italian Encyclopedia Treccani, Institute of the Italian Encyclopedia, founded by Giovanni Treccani, <https://www.treccani.it/enciclopedia/creativita/?search=creativit%C3%A0%2F>, accessed 10 September 2024.

Treccani, which perfectly summarises the skills each describer applies in carrying out their work.

In addition to being original and creative, audio descriptions are functional works whose *raison d'être* describes what happens onstage as an aid to blind and visually impaired people. This is another fundamental difference between ADs on the one hand and interlingual translation and narrative texts on the other. The audio describer's creative work consists of formulating an original text from an audiovisual medium. In doing so, they should observe the principles of objectivity, clarity, and simplicity while expressing their empirical subjectivity. To respect the work in its original form, the describer must try to keep the atmosphere of the product intact, preserving its rhythm and adapting to the genre and style in question. ADs must give the impression of being part of one single audiovisual product, making the various pre- and post-production steps indistinguishable. Therefore, ADs should be neither heavy nor tiring for the user, neither too detailed nor too scanty, given the audience's heterogeneity and each user's different level of blindness and visual memory.

On the other hand, interlingual translation is faced with the question of *equivalence*. In fact, there is 'ordinarily no equivalence between the code-units, while messages may serve as adequate interpretations of alien code-units or messages'[134]. In this regard, as Jakobson specifies

> translation from one language into another substitutes messages in one language not for separate code-units but for entire messages in some other language. Such a translation is a reported speech; the translator *recodes* and *transmits* a message received from another source. Thus, translation involves two equivalent messages in two different codes[135].

Focusing on the three concepts of equivalence, recoding, and transmission, it is possible to outline the differences and similarities between interlingual and intersemiotic translation. By definition, interlingual translation and intersemiotic translation mediate between sign systems. Interlingual translation

---

[134] Jakobson, 'On Linguistic Aspects of Translation', in Brower, ed., *On Translation*, 233.
[135] Jakobson, 'On Linguistic Aspects of Translation', in Brower, ed., *On Translation*, 233.

does that isosemiotically, while intersemiotic translation acts diasemiotically. Furthermore, both interlingual and intersemiotic translators interpret starting sign systems for users who cannot access them. However, equivalence, considered in the above terms, appears to be an interlingual problem, as the intersemiotic describer does not have to transpose a complex of beliefs and verbal representations from one linguistic and cultural system to another. Instead, intersemiotic description is a work of *subsumption* that associates the seemingly chaotic diversity of an audiovisual narrative's sensory and diegetic data with linguistic modes conforming to the conceptual schemes of the ideational processes of blind and visually impaired people.

Given these preliminary differences, both professional figures, the interlingual translator and the intersemiotic translator, have the task of recoding and transmitting the initial content. Nevertheless, it should be noted that, on the interlingual side, sign interpretation involves specific attention to the grammatical, lexical, and cultural (non-) bijection of the works being translated. Conversely, the intersemiotic translator operates in a context closer to interlinguistics, where the question of an intercultural rendering is not present in a narrow sense, nor will there be any problems related to calques, neologisms, and metalinguistic operations[136]. Unfortunately, including people with sensory disabilities in the education system represents a very recent achievement.

That said, in all its forms, translation profoundly influences the reception of audiovisual products by readers, viewers and users. It fulfils the task of making accessible content whose source language is often unknown to the end user. Thus, it necessarily interferes with the semiotic and expressive meaning of the source text and has to counterbalance this inherent trend through different strategies and methods[137].

Both intersemiotic and interlingual translations aim to maintain the tone and style of the work they translate. However, one further difference arises from the way the translation is rendered. The interlingual translator must adequately recode the work's nuances in its source language. Conversely, the

136 Jakobson, 'On Linguistic Aspects of Translation', in Brower, ed., *On Translation*, 233.
137 In this regard, see Logaldo, *Teoria e tecnica della traduzione audiovisiva. Tradurre, adattare, sottotitolare per lo schermo*, 9.

describer must translate and recompose perceptive information, considering the users' ideational and sensory capabilities. Also, the directors' and actors' diegetic intentions should be considered. This profoundly influences the language used when creating an audio description. In contrast, the care that the interlingual translator owes their user is of a different kind: they must ensure that the message of the source language is accurately rendered in both its content and the expressive forms chosen by the original author. The interlingual translator must then adapt the work to the target language by making cross-cultural renditions capable of transmitting the original intention in understandable or familiar ways to the target culture. It is worth emphasising that the description of colour in ADs for children, technical terms without a visual counterpart, and specific cues from film and television productions cannot be strictly considered cultural mediation operations.

A final consideration goes to the idiolects, which derive from and reflect perceptual differences inherent to our condition as sentient beings. From an epistemological point of view, determining whether language gives form to reality or reality forms language is beyond this study's scope. Still, superimposing idiolectic and perceptual differences to the cultural features that come with each linguistic system is problematic. An example would be an Italian publisher wishing to have a famous Japanese novel translated into Italian. If the publisher gave their translator a pre-existing English translation of the novel on which to work, the quality of the final result would be poor.

These brief considerations are intended to bring the academic community's attention to legitimacy. To what extent can original, creative intersemiotic translations be translated interlingually?[138] All theoretical issues set aside, interlingually translating audio descriptions appears doomed to fail since the differences between each country's guidelines originate from specific cultural and linguistic peculiarities.

---

138 In this regard, please refer to Anna Jankowska, *Translating Audio Description Scripts. Translation as a New Strategy of Creating Audio Description*, Elżbieta Chrzanowska-Kluczewska, and Wladyslaw Witalisz, eds (Berlin: Peter Lang Edition, 2015).

2.3 AD as a descriptive text

From a textual standpoint, audio description consists of a script whose content describes the characters, their actions, body language, facial expressions, clothing, and the setting within which they move. In most cases, the *space* available in the soundtrack of an audiovisual product (i.e., the time intervals that do not contain substantial dialogues or sounds) is barely sufficient to describe protagonists, antagonists, and co-protagonists[139]. Sometimes, however, directors and screenwriters who extensively resort to fast-paced dialogue make this task impossible. For the success of their descriptive, illustrative, and evocative intent, ADs must never overlap with the dialogues of the audiovisual work or with noises, sounds, or musical pieces whose significance contributes crucially to the unravelling of its plot[140].

A *descriptive text* is an intersemiotic translation. Therefore, its primary purpose is to translate graphic and audiovisual elements into signals that can be recorded on an audio channel. Subsequently, *voice-over artists* interpret the text in a recording studio while a sound engineer adjusts the microphones' volume and cues the soundtrack at the points indicated[141]. Once the recording is completed, the audio engineer passes the soundtrack (or track) to the synchroniser or the mix engineer, who cleans it from any clicks and background noise and synchronises it to the video by *pulling up* (i.e., anticipating) or *stretching* (modifying the extension in the space available) the *clips* (the individual writing units, read and recorded separately in the studio) that make up the provided recording.

Thus denoised and synchronised, the audio track is mixed with the film, the Music and Effects track (M&E), and the Voice-over track (VO) or Production Sound. Therefore, the VO track and Production Sound differ from the mixed track containing the AD. This is why the closing credits that the describer attaches to each AD always include the names of the describer, the voice-over

---

139 See, in this regard, John Patrick Udo, and Deborah I. Fels, 'Suit the Action to the Word, the Word to the Action. An Unconventional approach to Describing Shakespeare's *Hamlet*', *Journal of Visual Impairment & Blindness*, 103/3 (2009),178-83.

140 For compliance with the end user and the original work within the framework of the Ofcom Guidelines, please refer to the website: <www.ofcom.org.uk>.

141 See Laura Giordani, and Valerio Ailo Baronti, *Audiodescrizione. Il Signore degli anelli. La compagnia dell'AD* (Roma: HOPPY farm, 2023), 18-19.

artist, and the mix engineer. The coordination between these highly specialised professionals is, therefore, crucial for successful post-production work. To ensure this, the clips in the AD's script are accompanied by three types of additional information: *time codes*, *technical and illustrative cues*, and *pronunciations*. Pronunciations include terms and proper names that do not belong to the target language of the audio-described work.

The time code, often indicated by the acronym 'TC', consists of four numerical pairs that show hours, minutes, seconds, and frames per second. In most cases, descriptive texts require hours, minutes, and seconds, or just minutes and seconds, for works whose duration does not exceed 60 minutes. However, during recording and mixing, the audiovisual processing, production, and post-production software currently used for synchronisation requires the insertion of all four pairs of digits. Moreover, depending on the client's requirements, the TCs in the script's clips may include both *in* and *out* cues that specify the exact moment the recording begins and ends. The technical and illustrative cues also assist the recording studio's audio engineer and voice-over artist. These include the cues for the actors' or dubbers' lines marking the beginning of the clips, the noises on which the clips will have to *overlap*, the reading indications to aid the voice-over artists, and the pauses that separate clips not interspersed with dialogue. Finally, the pronunciations in the descriptive text, which also facilitate the voice-over artist's work, show not only the correct phonetic transcription of the words but also an inevitable adaptation to the phonological rules of the target language.

2.4 Collaborative AD in the Writing Phase

The production of audio descriptions involves professionals with different skills, including writing and cinematic language experts, narrators, sound technicians and, ideally, blind and visually impaired people who can provide direct feedback. ADs, therefore, belong to an industry that fits within the broader sector of film and television editing and post-production. This preliminary listing offers valuable insight into the inherently collaborative nature of audio description. However, the authentic value of such cooperation, or *collaboration*, is expressed above all in several creative minds' synergic drafting of a single text.

This paper will focus on the describers whose task is to draft a descriptive text. Nowadays, authorship is considered an individual type of work. This is substantiated by the intrinsic difficulty of producing two identical descriptions of the same audiovisual work. Moreover, AD was initially conceived as a creative act by authors whose work occurred privately and independently. Nonetheless, this paper suggests that outlining a series of guidelines and indications of good practice for a new collaborative approach can generate an enhanced, faster, and more effective method of composition that helps the end user. Furthermore, alongside this first conceptual and cultural challenge, it must be added that it is not always possible to collaborate 'equally'. The edited product must be internally consistent in style and content and meet formal criteria determining its paratextual elements' length, shape, and structure. From this perspective, the *coordinator*'s figure represents a sound synthesis between authorship's inevitable individuality and the potential of writing jointly.

Ultimately, the coordinator is a leader: they determine the guidelines to proceed collaboratively. Depending on the duration of the work to be described, which must always be previewed, the coordinator will select the team members and distribute the work following its duration and narrative structure. Regarding this distribution's logic, it should be noted that the *structured paradigm* (i.e., the dramatic and diegetic blueprint for the visual narrative known as a *script*) presents a threefold partition that does not always consist of acts of equal extent. Consequently, the coordinator should try to assign portions of the work while keeping in mind the coherent unfolding of each narrative act. Concurrently, they must choose how to organise the headlines and end credits, especially when describing episodes that refer to serial narratives. They will also need to interact with the client to understand their needs.

Whenever the audiovisual work presents a sufficiently extensive sequence of headlines, the coordinator will decide whether to include a descriptive *introduction* that serves as a preliminary context for the viewer. Nevertheless, introductions should be employed sparingly, as they carry the risk of revealing elements that would be presented at later points in the narrative. In this sense, narration as such is hugely different from what AD can and should aim to achieve in its creative purpose. Therefore, authors must limit themselves to writing introductions for products in which a prologue can functionally integrate with the initial work as a whole. This is the case for children's programmes, for which including a prologue is not discretionary but strongly recommended where possible. The function of a prologue in such contexts is not only to convey information of educational value but also *to connote, place* and *colour*[142] characters whose presentation is often made impossible by the overabundance of dialogues.

The coordinator should also write a summary of the selected guidelines and organise periodic meetings in which the team can discuss their interpretations and compositional choices.

Finally, it is essential that each describer carefully review the work of their colleagues so that the iterative connotations provided for the various elements of the narrative do not present contradictions or inconsistencies. This synergy between team members has the potential to drive innovation. Different ideas can be shared and developed, leading to creative solutions that may not emerge otherwise in an individual working context. However, as in any collaborative environment, conflicts may arise due to differences in opinions or methods. Following set procedures to manage and resolve frictions is decisive.

It may be helpful to remember that what matters is not the beauty of the text but its usefulness. Describers must not 'become attached' because what they write is not a narrative or a translation but an aid for blind and visually impaired users. The concept of 'authorship' must be abandoned for the users' sake so that they may access cultural and entertainment media through audiovisual material.

Describing, not explaining, in a limited time is challenging for anyone who lacks solid preparation and substantial professional experience[143]. Also,

142 For an in-depth definition of the audio-descriptive concepts of placement, connotation and colouring, please refer to the study carried out in Giordani, and Baronti, *Audiodescrizione. Il Signore degli anelli. La compagnia dell'AD*, 42.

143 A more in-depth analysis of the challenges and capabilities of the figure of the audio describer is also carried out in Laura Giordani, 'Cinema e TV: veicoli culturali', *Diari di Cineclub* 89, Cineclub Roma (2020), 4, <https://www.cineclubroma.it/diari-di-cineclub-roma/raccolte/anno-2020/1139-diari-di-cineclub-n-89-dicembre-2020>, accessed 10 September 2024.

it should be remembered that the ultimate scope of the descriptive text is listening, not reading. This combination of spoken and written language is particularly valuable when colleagues review each other's work as a team. An individual describer would never be able to detect all the nuances, textual references and intersemiotic references resulting from coordinated teamwork.

The effectiveness of an audio description, and therefore of a team's work, lies in keeping the describer's idiolectal style consistent with the overall syntactic constructs and lexical choices made in the creative phase. Choosing exact verbs and nouns must be preferred over periphrases. Nevertheless, language offers many figures of speech capable of producing the same vivid impressions while occupying less space. Ekphrasis[144] and hypotyposis are two clear examples of how an intersemiotic translation faithful to the audiovisual content combines with adding emotional nuances consistent with the narrative intent of an audiovisual work[145]. Therefore, the coordinator's critical selection is the final step towards a perfect intersemiotic adhesion between the descriptive signifier and the audiovisual signified.

In the case of audiovisual products inspired by literary works, the coordinator and descriptive team should read the reference texts and discuss them collectively to outline connotative procedures in keeping with the adjectives and figures of speech used. The order in which the descriptive information is presented expresses stylistic intent. Therefore, it must be discussed and chosen carefully. The same applies to both illustrative and non-illustrative descriptions. Dedicating attention to the oral destination of the text is also of primary importance. The script must guarantee a euphony and prosodic pleasantness for the voice-over artist to read in all its parts. Sound figures such as alliterations, rhymes, and cacophonies should be avoided if the script's lines are to be well articulated, smooth and easy to understand.

---

144 For a more in-depth analysis of the use of ekphrasis in relation to audiovisual works, see also Laura Giordani, 'L'audiodescrizione: i musei in TV e al cinema', *Diari di Cineclub* 88, Cineclub Roma (2020), 29, ≤https://www.cineclubroma.it/diari-di-cineclub-roma/raccolte/anno-2020/1052-diari-di-cineclub-n-88-novembre-2020≥, accessed 10 September 2024.

145 See Giordani, and Baronti, *Audiodescrizione. Il Signore degli anelli. La compagnia dell'AD*, 19-20.

3. Collaborative revision

Once the creative phase is concluded, 'tying' the parts written by each describer requires a first collective revision in which the team tries to amalgamate and harmonise the text sections to smoothen any prosodic, lexical, or stylistic inconsistencies. Recurring expressions such as 'It's daytime', 'A new day breaks', and 'They go to' will be examined and compared with the corresponding formulations used by the other colleagues. It is worth emphasising that the different expressions chosen should not reveal that the audio description was written by more than one author. In addition, the team must ensure that the parts of the audio-described product containing more extended spaces include more non-illustrative descriptions.

During the revision process, agreeing on a procedural criterion for checking spelling mistakes is necessary. The same applies to all glossary nomenclatures, together with the related time codes. The last chapter on the apparatuses attached to the descriptive text will extensively discuss the detection of nomenclatures, character names, and related pronunciations.

Furthermore, checking for repetitions, alliterations, assonances, and cacophonies can be treacherous. Verifying the describers' lexical accuracy is probably the riskiest phase in terms of discord and conflict. It involves researching and choosing terms that should not be too technical. At this point, opinions tend to vary significantly among team members. Therefore, the coordinator will be responsible for considering each person's skills and specialities. Finally, the coordinator's and the team's scrutiny must focus on the adequacy of the register and the terms used. For these to be appropriate to the film genre and target audience, the team must review the film analysis carried out by its members, correcting any lack of details and ensuring that diegetically relevant aspects have not been overlooked or misunderstood.

3.1 The users' feedback and collaboration

As Udo and Fels (2009) note, audio description is an *ex post facto* adaptive strategy designed to guarantee the participation of blind and visually impaired people in a culture eminently based on visual entertainment[146]. For ADs to be effective, it is recommended that they

> [do] not present users who are blind or have low vision with an experience that is equal or equivalent to that of sighted persons, since it focuses on the description of what is seen—the set, actors' movements, and lighting—rather than on what is meant to be seen—the director's vision. Concentrating exclusively on the visual pieces, rather than on the entertainment experience as a whole, description may impede users from suspending their disbelief, constantly reinforcing the lack of access to and dependence on visual stimuli.[147]

In this regard, Gerber argues for collaboration with the blind and visually impaired public[148]. To what extent descriptions should deviate from objectivity in favour of an interpretative method is still debated. Hence, referring to other, more specific studies is strongly suggested.

The emotions that an audiovisual work can transmit vary from viewer to viewer (better still, from user to user), sighted, blind, or visually impaired as they may be. The sighted person receives their emotional stimulus from viewing content with images. On the other hand, hearing is essential for blind or visually impaired users as it allows them to perceive audiovisual sounds and noises. Thus, their emotions derive from their personal life experience, which varies depending on whether they were blind from birth or have become so. However, the soundtrack's sounds and noises are not sufficient to convey these emotions. A careful description of the scenes without dialogue

---

[146] See Udo, and Fels, 'Suit the Action to the Word, the Word to the Action. An Unconventional Approach to Describing Shakespeare's *Hamlet*', *Journal of Visual Impairment & Blindness*, 103/3.

[147] For a critical discussion of the issue, see Udo, and Fels, 'Suit the Action to the Word, the Word to the Action. An Unconventional Approach to Describing Shakespeare's *Hamlet*', *Journal of Visual Impairment & Blindness*, 103/3, 178-83.

[148] See Elaine Gerber, 'Seeing isn't Believing: Blindness, Race, and Cultural Literacy', *The Senses and Society* 2/1 (2007), 27-40. It is also worth highlighting the research carried out by Joel Snyder. In this regard, see the Italian edition of Snyder, *The Visual Made Verbal: A Comprehensive Training Manual and Guide to the History and Applications of Audio Description*.

is also necessary for this to happen. It is hard for the sighted viewer and the inadequately trained describer to understand the essential elements of film narration without redundancies or periphrases and technicalities that impede clarity and coherence[149]. The language of the sighted tends to tell, not describe. On the contrary, the ideal for an effective audio description is well summarised by the famous principle of '*show, don't tell*'.

One last critical expedient is cooperating, whenever possible, with people with congenital and acquired blindness and low vision. This difference becomes significant concerning the issue of colour since congenital blindness implies that the user (and reviewer) has never experienced it. As mentioned in this paper, the established practice in audiovisuals for minors is to associate colours with objects that users can experience through alternative sensory pathways. For example, green will be associated with grass by similarity or metaphor, and yellow with the sun. The case of audiovisual products for adults and the general public is partly different. In this type of description, colour must be considered carefully. It should be included only when relevant to the film narration. Again, all the team members should be involved at this stage of the decision-making process.

3.2 Apparatuses attached to the descriptive text

Glossaries are essential for audio descriptions to maintain adequate consistency of style and content. Overall, two types can be identified: the list of pronunciations detected while viewing the audiovisual product and the notes regarding the characters' names, stage objects, diegetic places and spaces and more. During the viewing and detection phase, the relevant pronunciations concern the characters' names and, more generally, those foreign terms that occasionally appear in the audio descriptive clips. A TC must accompany each note to indicate the point at which a name or term first appears in the dialogue. Anticipating functional elements would alter the development of the film's narrative. Describers must not mention a character's name before it has been mentioned by other characters in the audiovisual product. The

---

[149] For an in-depth discussion of the collaboration with blind and visually impaired users, refer to the work of Louise Fryer, *An Introduction to Audio Description: A Practical Guide* (Routledge, 2016), chapter 14.

blind and low-vision user only knows as much as the screenwriters want them to know at any given time.

The characters' connotations must help the user identify them immediately. For this reason, all denotative and connotative attributes must be consistent with what the audience has already learned about the storyline, the characters' relationships within the narrative context, and the protagonists' evolution throughout the plot. In most cases, during collaborative writing, the detection process falls almost entirely on the describer to whom the initial part of an audiovisual product is assigned. However, serial products inspired by literary works require several team members to draft a glossary at the outset. This is especially useful with film franchises that will employ new writing teams to audio describe the chapters to come.

Finally, the information entered in the glossary must be shared online. Each describer should refer to it when connoting the characters, places and objects in their portion of the assigned work. Also, sharing photographs of the characters connoted by other team members may help make them easily identifiable.

4. Conclusion

ADs are intrinsically original, creative, and artistic intellectual works. They serve blind and visually impaired users, guaranteeing their right to access audiovisual products that are either cultural or for entertainment. A comparison with interlingual translation has shown what problems may arise in the transference of audio-descriptive works from one language to another due to linguistic, epistemological, cultural, and prescriptive reasons. An analysis of the synergic creation and revision process, with the collaboration of blind and visually impaired professionals and users, has revealed functional procedures to enhance the audio-descriptive work by optimising time, increasing expressive alternatives, verifying the sources, and preparing useful devices to coordinate future descriptions.

References

'Arte', Enciclopedia Treccani, Istituto della Enciclopedia Italiana fondata da Giovanni Treccani, <https://www.treccani.it/enciclopedia/arte/?search=arte%2F>, accessed 10 September 2024.

Bourne, Julian, and Jiménez Hurtado, Catalina, 'From the Visual to the Verbal in Two Languages: a Contrastive Analysis of the Audio Description of *The Hours* in English and Spanish.', in Jorge Díaz Cintas, Pilar Orero, and Aline Remael, eds, *Media for All. Subtitling for the Deaf, Audio Description, and Sign Language*, Series: Approaches to Translation Studies, Volume 30 (Leiden: Brill, 2007), 175-87.

Enciclopedia Treccani, Istituto della Enciclopedia Italiana fondata da Giovanni Treccani. 'Arte', <https://www.treccani.it/enciclopedia/arte/?search=arte%2F>, accessed 10 September 2024.

Enciclopedia Treccani, Istituto della Enciclopedia Italiana fondata da Giovanni Treccani, <https://www.treccani.it/enciclopedia/creativita/?search=creativit%C3%A0%2F>, accessed 10 September 2024.

Fryer, Louise, *An Introduction to Audio Description: A Practical Guide* (London/New York: Routledge, 2016).

Gerber, Elaine, 'Seeing isn't Believing: Blindness, Race, and Cultural Literacy', *The Senses and Society* 2/1 (2007), 27–40.

Giordani, Laura, 'Diritto di esserci anche al cinema' *Diari di Cineclub*86, Cineclub Roma (2020), 20, <https://www.cineclubroma.it/diari-di-cineclub-roma/raccolte/anno-2020/884-diari-di-cineclub-n-86-settembre-2020>, accessed 10 September 2024.

Giordani, Laura, 'L'audiodescrizione: i musei in tv e al cinema', *Diari di Cineclub* 88, Cineclub Roma (2020), 29, <https://www.cineclubroma.it/diari-di-cineclub-roma/raccolte/anno-2020/1052-diari-di-cineclub-n-88-novembre-2020>, accessed 10 September 2024.

Giordani, Laura, 'Cinema e tv: veicoli culturali', *Diari di Cineclub* 89, Cineclub Roma (2020), 4, <https://www.cineclubroma.it/diari-di-cineclub-roma/raccolte/anno-2020/1139-diari-di-cineclub-n-89-dicembre-2020>, accessed 10 September 2024.

Giordani, Laura, 'Quando l'audiodescrizione incontra il grande cinema fantasy', *Diari di Cineclub* 90, Cineclub Roma (2021), 35, <https://www.cineclubroma.it/diari-di-cineclub-roma/raccolte/anno-2021/1208-diari-di-cineclub-n-90-gennaio-2021>, accessed 10 September 2024.

Giordani, Laura, and Valerio Ailo Baronti, *Audiodescrizione. Il Signore degli anelli. La compagnia dell'AD* (Roma: HOPPY farm, 2023).

Guildford, Joy Paul, *Creative Talents: their Nature, Use and Development* (Buffalo, NY: Bearly Ltd, 1986).

Jakobson, Roman, 'On Linguistic Aspects of Translation', in Reuben Arthur Brower, ed., *On Translation* (Cambridge, MA: Harvard University Press, 1959), 232–39.

Jakobson, Roman, *Saggi di linguistica generale*, Heilmann, Luigi, ed. (Milano: Feltrinelli Editore, 2002).

Jankowska, Anna, *Translating Audio Description Scripts. Translation as a New Strategy of Creating Audio Description*, Elżbieta Chrzanowska-Kluczewska, and Wladyslaw Witalisz, eds (Berlin: Peter Lang Edition, 2015).

Jankowska, Anna, and Agnieszka Szarkowska, '*Text-to-speech Audio Description of Voiced-over Films. A case study of audio described Volver in Polish*', in Elisa Perego, ed., *Emerging topics in translation: Audio description* (Trieste: EUT Edizioni Università di Trieste, 2012), 81–98.

Logaldo, Mara, *Teoria e tecnica della traduzione audiovisiva. Tradurre, adattare, sottotitolare per lo schermo* (Roma: Dino Audino Editore, 2021).

Snyder, Joel, *The Visual Made Verbal: A Comprehensive Training Manual and Guide to the History and Applications of Audio Description* (New York: American Council of the Blind, 2007).

Snyder, Joel, *Immagini in parole. Manuale di formazione e guida complete alla storia e alle applicazioni dell'Audiodescrizione* (San Diego: AE Academic Publishing, 2023).

Udo, John Patrick, and Deborah I. Fels, 'Suit the Action to the Word, the Word to the Action. An Unconventional Approach to Describing Shakespeare's *Hamlet*', *Journal of Visual Impairment & Blindness* 103/3 (2009), 178–83.

PART II

Collaborative Translation and Human-Machine Interaction

5

Generative AI and the correlation of text and image in the intersemiotic translation of literary works

Fabio Morotti

Abstract

This paper investigates the intersection of generative AI, intersemiotic translation and collaborative translation, focusing on the creation of an audiovisual version of Virgil's *Aeneid* through human-AI collaboration. The video project, which employs text-to-image (T2I) and image-to-video (I2V) generative models to reinterpret *The Aeneid*, highlights the significance of textual prompts in shaping AI outputs. By examining the framework for the collaboration between the researchers and AI tools, the paper elucidates the challenges and opportunities inherent in integrating AI into creative practices. It emphasises that the adaptation process necessitates a careful translation of literary language into prompts that AI can interpret and addresses the limitations of current generative technologies. The findings indicate that AI can facilitate innovative adaptations, but achieving fidelity to the source material requires a nuanced understanding of both the literary text and the capabilities of generative AI. This paper contributes to the emergent discourse on AI in Translation Studies and computational creativity, advocating for a multidisciplinary approach that draws from adaptation studies, generative culture and prompt engineering. The proposed collaborative model, which can serve as a framework for future explorations of AI in storytelling, underscores the essential role of human oversight and creative input in the generative process. Funded by the European Union – Next Generation EU, Mission 4 Component 1 CUP H46E22000000006.

Every stage in the history of computer media
offers its own aesthetic opportunities,
as well as its own imagination of the future:
in short, its own 'research paradigm'[150].

Introduction

The rise of artificial intelligence (AI) has inaugurated a new method of content creation resulting from machine-human cooperation. In the field of computational creativity and, on which this paper draws, new technologies such as machine learning, natural language processing, visual perception and pattern recognition are increasing human-AI interaction and reorienting the scope and possibilities of theoretical and research methods[151]. New tools, software and platforms are continually launched and updated, resulting in 'a relationship in which both the human agent and the machine contribute to the decision-making process'[152]. This interaction between users and machines has been characterised as a form of 'collaboration' between computational and human agents or 'co-creation'[153].

This paper reflects on collaboration in intersemiotic translation using AI generative software. In particular, it focuses on the adaptation of literary texts to video and the role played by textual prompts in the visual synthesis produced by AI. In this context, I will analyse AI*neid, Virgil's* Aeneid *in the*

---

150 Lev Manovich, *The Language of New Media* (Cambridge, Massachusetts; London, England: The MIT Press, 2001), 34.

151 See Kaifang Fan, and Chunlei Wang, 'Translation Studies in the Era of AI: Characteristics, Fields and Significance', *International Journal of Translation and Interpretation Studies*, 3/4 (2023), 68–77, <https://al-kindipublisher.com/index.php/ijtis/article/view/6349>, accessed 28 August 2024.

152 Ardavan Bidgoli, Eunsu Kang, and Daniel Cardoso Llach, 'Machinic Surrogates: Human-Machine Relationships in Computational Creativity', arXiv (New York: Cornell University, 2019), <https://arxiv.org/abs/1908.01133>, accessed 26 August 2024.

153 See Jichen Chu, Antonios Liapis, Sebastian Risi, Rafael Bidarra, and G. Michael Youngblood, 'Explainable AI for Designers: A Human-Centered Perspective on Mixed-Initiative Co-Creation', 2018 IEEE Conference on Computational Intelligence and Games (CIG) (Maastricht, 2018), 1–8, <https://ieeexplore.ieee.org/document/8490433/>, accessed 9 September 2024.

Age of AI (3' 20"). This audiovisual version of Virgil's *Aeneid*, a classic of Latin literature, was adapted via two of the most prominent applications of generative AI, text-to-image (T2I) and image-to-video (I2V) technology. The ad hoc work model, developed to integrate the generative software used in the project with the professionals involved in its realisation, is taken into consideration.

This video project[154] was born from a partnership between the International Center for Research on Collaborative Translation (IULM University, Milan) and Karma Lab (Koç University, Istanbul), with support from the Aeneas Route Association and funding from NextGenerationEU. It is the result of a significant collaborative effort involving approximately ten professionals in a variety of fields: literary translation, film adaptation, generative culture, film-making and visual storytelling, heritage studies, interactive media design, editing, post-processing and subtitling.

As Translation Studies take their first steps in this vast new field of research, we can rely on a nascent literature on Translation Studies and AI[155]. Given the interdisciplinary nature of the project, this paper also draws upon a range of additional sources from the fields of computational

[154] The author of this paper participated in the research as part of a doctoral programme in Visual and Media Studies (IULM University) in the context of a visiting period (Koç University). Dr Asım Evren Yantaç (Co-Director of the Karma Lab, Koç University) assumed the role of Scientific Advisor. Dr Francesco Laurenti, Director of the International Center for Research on Collaborative Translation (IULM), an academic with expertise in the field of collaborative translation, acted as the Scientific Advisor and Coordinator. Sumru Deniz, a graphic designer from the Karma Lab at Koç University, was responsible for the script development and interaction, as well as the image development utilising generative AI software. Laura Arcangeli, a ComfyUI animator, provided advice and assistance with the post-production phase. Eleonora Gatto and Federica Villareale, Research Collaborators at the International Center for Research on Collaborative Translation (IULM), were responsible for subtitling and provided assistance with the project. Dr Marta Muscariello, a linguist and member of the Euresis Center for Diagnosis, Intervention, DSA Research Center (IULM), was responsible for developing an audio description for the visually impaired.

[155] See Kaifang, and Wang, 79–94; John A. Barnden, 'Metaphor and Artificial Intelligence: Why They Matter to Each Other', in Raymond W. Gibbs Jr., ed., *The Cambridge Handbook of Metaphor and Thought* (London: Cambridge University Press, 2008), 311–38.

creativity[156], intersemiotic translation[157], prompt engineering[158] and adaptation studies[159]. In addition, I have drawn on contributions from generative culture[160] and cinema AI[161].

1. A *literary* intersemiotic translation with AI generative synthesis

Intersemiotic translation is a vast area of research that engages with a multitude of disciplines and a diverse array of semiotic phenomena, including

---

[156] See Maria Teresa Llano, Mark D'Inverno, Matthew Yee-King, Alon McCormack, Jon Ilsar, Alison Pease and others, 'Explainable Computational Creativity', arXiv (New York: Cornell University: 2022), <https://arxiv.org/abs/2205.05682>, accessed 5 September 2024; Tony Veale, and F. Amílcar Cardoso, eds, *Computational creativity: The philosophy and engineering of autonomously creative systems* (Cham: Springer, 2019); Tony Veale, and Rafael Pérez Y Pérez, 'Leaps and Bounds: An Introduction to the Field of Computational Creativity', *New Generation Computing* 38/4 (2020), 551–63, <http://link.springer.com/10.1007/s00354-020-00116-w>, accessed 18 September 2024.

[157] See Nicola Dusi, 'Intersemiotic Translation: Theories, Problems, Analysis', Semiotica,2015/206 (2015), 181–205, <https://www .degruyter .com /document /doi /10 .1515 /sem-2015-0018/html>, accessed 19 August 2024; Roman Jakobson, *On Linguistic Aspects of Translation* (Harvard University Press eBooks, 1959), <https://doi.org/10.4159 /harvard.9780674731615.c18>, accessed 27 August 2024.

[158] See Yaru Hao, Zewen Chi, Li Dong, and Furu Wei, 'Optimizing Prompts for Text-to-Image Generation', arXiv (New York: Cornell University, 2022) <https://arxiv.org/abs /2212.09611>, accessed 21 August 2024; Jonas Oppenlaender, 'A Taxonomy of Prompt Modifiers for Text-to-Image Generation', *Behaviour & Information Technology* (2023), 1–14 <https://www.tandfonline.com/doi/full/10.1080/0144929X.2023.2286532>, accessed 11 August 2024.

[159] See Linda Costanzo Cahir, *Literature into film: Theory and practical approaches* (Jefferson: McFarland, 2006); John M. Desmond, and Peter Hawkes, *Adaptation: Studying Film and Literature*, (Michigan: McGraw-Hill, 2005); Linda Hutcheon, *A Theory of Adaptation* (New York: Routledge, 2006).

[160] See Francesco D'Isa, *La rivoluzione algoritmica. Arte e intelligenza artificiale* (Bologna: Luca Sossella Editore, 2024); Lev Manovich, 'AI image and generative media: Notes on ongoing revolution', in Lev Manovich and Emanuele Arielli, eds, *Artificial aesthetic: A Critical Guide to AI, Media and Design* (2023), <http://manovich. net /index. php / projects /artificial-aesthetics -book>, accessed 2 September 2024.

[161] See Marcel Danesi, *'AI-Generated Cinema', in Marcel Danesi, ed., AI-Generated Popular Culture*, (Springer Nature Switzerland, 2024), 45–65, <https://link .springer .com /10 .1007/978 -3 -031 -54752 -2_3>, accessed 22 August 2024.

literature, cinema and video production. Jakobson, in his renowned work *On Linguistic Aspects of Translation*, proposed a three-part classification of translation. He defined *intersemiotic translation* or '*transmutation*' as 'an interpretation of verbal signs by means of signs of nonverbal sign systems'[162]. Such an operation encompasses many of the processes occurring in film adaptation, which can be described as 'the transfer of a printed text in a literary genre to film'[163].

Film adaptation involves the translation of a text from one semiotic system to another, with the two systems retaining a significant degree of autonomy[164] in their expressive capabilities. Film-makers and video creators must navigate an intricate process when translating narratives, themes and artistic vision from one medium to the other; they must decide which elements of the source material to focus on, such as themes, specific scenes and characters[165], balance fidelity and creativity and employ fundamental processes such as amplification and condensation of the source-text narrative. In this context, adaptation can be classified as 'close, loose, or intermediate'[166] or 'literal, traditional, or radical'[167], contingent on the degree of liberty exercised in the treatment of the source text.

The advent of generative culture is having a transformative impact on the creative industry and film-making, reinvigorating the discourse that has been briefly introduced here. T2I and T2V models represent a burgeoning category of artificial intelligence systems that enable users to interact with the AI generation process to create videos and images through natural language text, specifically via textual prompting[168]. Two aspects merit particular attention.

---

162 Jakobson, *On Linguistic Aspects of Translation*, 261.
163 Desmond and Hawkes, *Adaptation: Studying Film and Literature*, 1.
164 Dusi, *'Intersemiotic Translation: Theories, Problems, Analysis'*, 186–188.
165 See Gamze Nil Arkan, 'Cinema Literary Adaptations as a Narrative Form', Contemporary Issues of Communication, 2/2 (2023), 50–58, <https://dergipark .org .tr /tr /pub /conicom /issue /80112 /1351082>, accessed 6 September 2024.
166 Desmond and Hawkes, *Adaptation: Studying Film and Literature, 3.*
167 Cahir, *Literature into film: Theory and practical approaches*, 17.
168 See Imran Shafiq Ahmad, Nazia Siddiqui and Boubakeur Boufama, 'A Comparative Study of Text-to-Image Generative Models', in 2024 IEEE 12th International Symposium on Signal, Image, Video and Communications (ISIVC) (Marrakech: Morocco, 2024), 1–6, <https://ieeexplore.ieee.org/document/10577779/>, accessed 3 September 2024;

Firstly, at present, the majority of software and generative functionalities utilising AI for figuration have only English-language user interfaces. Given that English functions as the mother language for most of AI video generators, interlingual translation is an intrinsic aspect of any creative process involving these tools.

Secondly, in the context of the filmic adaptation process, this type of generative synthesis, which relies mainly on natural (English) language, introduces a new level of interaction between text and video, with the potential for a direct correlation between the source text and its figuration (for instance, through reuse of words, descriptions and adjectives from a literary source). As a result, the text is no longer confined to the world of the written word but rather can be fully or partially integrated with the visual world, with the representation and 'interpretation' being dependent on the machine's data training and other parameters provided to it.

As a text-prompting approach offers the possibility of binding the figurative results to the source text, it has the potential to stimulate a reframing of controversial and fundamental aspects of adaptation studies, including the concepts of literary dimension and faithfulness[169]. However, the complete and autonomous utilisation of the source text as a prompt is infeasible, given

---

Ming Ding, Zhuoyi Yang, Wenyi Hong, Wendi Zheng, Chang Zhou, Da Yin, and others, 'CogView: Mastering Text-to-Image Generation via Transformers', *arXiv* (New York: Cornell University, 2021), <https://arxiv.org/abs/2105.13290>, accessed 29 August 2024; Patrick Esser, Johnathan Chiu, Parmida Atighehchian, Jonathan Granskog, and Anastasis Germanidis, 'Structure and Content-Guided Video Synthesis with DiffusionModels', in 2023 IEEE/CVF International Conference on Computer Vision (ICCV) (Paris, 2023), 7312–22, <https://ieeexplore .ieee .org /document /10377444/>, accessed 30 August2024; Oran Gafni, Adam Polyak, Oron Ashual, Shelly Sheynin, Devi Parikh, and Yaniv Taigman, 'Make-A-Scene: Scene-Based Text-to-Image Generation with Human Priors', in Shai Avidan, Gabriel Brostow, Moustapha Cissé, Giovanni Maria Farinella, and Tal Hassner, eds, Computer Vision – ECCV 2022, (Springer Nature Switzerland, 2022), 89–106, <https:// link .springer .com /10 .1007 /978 -3 -031 -19784 -0_6>, accessed 23 August 2024.

169 In film adaptation studies, the concept and idea of fidelity is particularly problematic, if not 'inappropriate [...] for either understanding or judgement' of a transposition. See Brian McFarlane, 'Novel to film: an introduction to the theory of adaptation', *Choice Reviews Online* 34/06 (1997), 34–3224, <http://choicereviews.org/review/10.5860/CHOICE.34-3224>, accessed 2 September 2024.

the current state of development of generative AI, with its potential for bias, constraints and hallucinations[170]. While it is possible to conceive of and implement a direct transition from literary text to figuration, the results, as those who work with generative AI tools are aware, can be inaccurate or implausible, as shown below.

In fact, the utilisation of both literal and literary sources in a prompt, without the involvement of a human interpreter, can produce curious and anomalous outcomes like the demons shown in the output below. This is because AI generative software often cannot comprehend poetic language, metaphor and metonymy:

> **Source text: 'And now Lucifer was rising above the heights of Ida,** bringing the dawn' (Virgil, 2015, II, 796-804)
> **Prompt: Lucifer was rising on Mount Ida, dawn, cinematic, very realistic, 1080 p, --ar 16:09 (Software used: Midjourney)**

Literary text is especially hard for AI generative platforms to understand, and each transition from text to image or text to video has to be complemented by several refinements of the textual prompts to ensure the plausibility and coherence of the results. As highlighted by Barnden[171], literary text often includes metonymies, metaphorical and poetic language, idioms, rhetorical questions and sarcasm, and AI often lacks the deep contextual and emotional

---

170 See Andrew L. Smith, Felix Greaves, and Trishan Panch, 'Hallucination or Confabulation? Neuroanatomy as Metaphor in Large Language Models', *PLOS Digital Health* 2/11 (2023), <https://dx.plos.org/10.1371/journal.pdig.0000388>, accessed 3 September 2024; Peiqi Sui, Eamon Duede, Sophie Wu, and Richard So, 'Confabulation: The Surprising Value of Large Language Model Hallucinations', in Lun-Wei Ku, Andre Martins, and Vivek Srikumar, eds, Proceedings of the 62nd Annual Meeting of the Association for Computational Linguistics 1, (Thailand: Bangkok, 2024), 14274–84, <https://aclanthology.org/2024.acl-long.770>, accessed 9 September 2024. The authors of the very interesting *Confabulation: The surprising value of large language model hallucinations* suggest that hallucinations or 'confabulation' can be a valuable and creative resource.

171 See John A. Barnden, 'Metaphor and Context: A Perspective from Artificial Intelligence', in Andreas Musolff and Jörg Zinken, eds, *Metaphor and Discourse* (London: Palgrave Macmillan, 2009), 79–94; Barnden, 'Metaphor and Artificial Intelligence: Why They Matter to Each Other', 311–38.

Figure 5.1. Output

knowledge that humans possess. This means that the literary source text has to be carefully translated into less poetic or metaphoric language to be *grasped* by the machine and produce an accurate output.

The process of designing prompts or inputs in a manner that elicits valuable outputs is referred to as prompt engineering. The ability to interact with AI efficiently represents a fundamental form of media literacy[172] and facilitates 'collaborativeness' between humans and machines.

2. Towards a *literal* and literary video adaptation of *The Aeneid*

The intuition of a new possible relationship between text and figuration yielded the paradoxical conclusion that the choice of attempting a *faithful* adaptation of the source text would be experimental rather than conservative. This consideration led the research team involved in the project AI*neid, Virgil's* Aeneid *in the Age of AI* to adopt a strategy of *literal* and literary video adaptation of *The Aeneid*, even though AI video generative software is currently limited by a lack of consistency in movement and human expressions.

T2V models are still in the early stages[173] and seem unsuitable at present for complex narratives, such as that of *The Aeneid*, that involve multitudinous shots, recurring characters and locations, and scene transitions. For this reason, a double translation using T2I, followed by I2V, was employed, although this method entailed a general loss of quality in the clips that were generated and a significant increase in the typical visual disturbances that characterise AI cinematic figuration (mainly low stability and loss of photo-definition).

The Aeneid[174], a literary masterpiece written between 29 and 19 BC by the Roman poet Virgil, has been a source of fascination for centuries and

[172] See Vivian Liu, and Lydia B. Chilton, 'Design Guidelines for Prompt Engineering Text-to-Image Generative Models', *CHI Conference on Human Factors in Computing Systems* (2022), 1–23, <https://doi.org/10.1145/3491102.3501825>, accessed 26 August 2024.

[173] Roberto Gozalo-Brizuela, and Eduardo C. Garrido-Merchán, 'A Survey of Generative AI Applications', arXiv (New York: Cornell University, 2023), 8, <https://arxiv.org/abs/2306.02781>, accessed 30 August 2024.

[174] See William Anthony Camps, *An introduction to Virgil's «Aeneid»* (London: Oxford University Press, 1969).

inspired many literary and artistic adaptations in diverse forms.[175] It has left an indelible mark on numerous later poets and writers, influencing iconography throughout the history of art[176].

The Aeneid narrates the adventures of the semi-god Aeneas, son of Venus, a Trojan hero who survives the fall of Troy and embarks on a journey to the shores of Italy, where he lays the foundations of Rome. Virgil's *Aeneid* presents the story as a myth, narrating the 're-foundation' of Roman history[177] to celebrate Octavian Augustus[178] and his descendants and justify his imperial claims.

The Aeneid is a lengthy and complex poem, so accommodating it within the constraints of the short video format selected necessitated significant condensation and streamlining of the plot and characters. The adaptation process was guided by the following programmatic guidelines:

- The video was conceived as a single episode of a prospective series designed to enhance and promote a cultural itinerary, the Aeneas Route (Aeneas Route - Cultural Routes, s.d.)[179], mainly via social media and online platforms.
- The audiovisual narration was limited to the three episodes of the poem relating to the Turkish sites of Troy, Antandros and Enez. Consequently,

175 See Giuliana Calcani, *Dal Mito alla Storia. La Rappresentazione della leggenda di Enea tra adattamenti e varianti* (Roma: Edizioni Efesto, 2017); Tommaso Casini, 'Tra lessico pittorico e iconografia: Annibal Caro e la fortuna della traduzione dell'Eneide', *Gli dèi a corte - letteratura e immagini nella Ferrara estense* (Firenze: Istituto di Studi Rinascimentali, 2009), 115-134.

176 See Daniele Fortuna, 'The iconography of Aeneas' escape from Troy in the European figurative culture', in Sandra Gatti, ed., *Aeneas in the Troas and Latium Regions. Mythology and Archaeology, Proceedings of the International Symposium Edremit 26 October 2021* (Roma: Edizioni Ponte Sisto, 2022), 223–245.

177 Sergio Madonna, Stefania Nisio, Maria Fenelli, Alessandro Jaia, and Laura Ebanista, 'Enea and Turno; the landscape of myth between geology and archaeology', *Memorie Descrittive della Carta Geologica d'Italia*, 109 (2022), 124.

178 See Makya Williamson, 'Virgil's Aeneid: The cornerstone of Roman identity', *Tenor of Our Times*, 8 (2019), 159–171.

179 'Aeneas Route – Cultural Routes – www.coe.int', Cultural Routes, <https://www.coe.int/en/web/cultural-routes/aeneas-route-4>, accessed 2 September 2024.

only the second and third chapters of *The Aeneid* were included in the film narration.

- The video was created without the use of cameras[180]. This was done to direct attention towards the generative process associated with textual prompts and highlight the limitations and figurative potential of commercially available T2I and I2T software based on AI.
- The textual component was given particular emphasis, with descriptions, words and adjectives provided by *The Aeneid* used to generate the locations, characters and dialogues of the video through textual input.
- Virgil's text (in its English translation[181]) was employed as the narrating voice of the video.

The decision to utilise extradiegetic narration in the video was driven by the perception that it was the technique most closely aligned with a literary mode of narrating through images[182]; hence, it accorded with our general research strategy of fidelity to the text. Additionally, in the specific case of *The Aeneid*, the narrator's voice made it possible to minimise dialogue between characters and thus the use of lip-sync – a tool not yet fully satisfactory in many AI applications[183]. Lastly, the use of a narrating voice was intended to facilitate the transposition, given the time constraints imposed by Runway Gen-2, the software used for generating video clips, which allowed for a maximum of eight seconds at the time of production.

The researchers were presented with two distinct stylistic and narrative options. They could either simulate the conventions of traditional cinema or draw

[180] An exception to this was an aerial photograph, which was included in the generative process from image to video with the aim of promoting the cultural itinerary Aeneas' Route. This was done to provide consistency between the real and legendary landscapes described in *The Aeneid*.

[181] Virgil, and A.S. Kline, *The Aeneid* (Roman Roads Media, 2015).

[182] See Dusi, 'Intersemiotic Translation: Theories, Problems, Analysis', 196.

[183] As highlighted by Lev Manovich, this is a very challenging area 'because human verbal communication is certainly a very strict 'genre' – if a speaker makes a gesture or facial expression that does not correspond to what he or she is saying, we will notice this immediately.' See Lev Manovich, 'What is Digital Cinema?', in Shane Denson, and Julya Leyda, eds, *Post-Cinema. Theorizing 21st-Century Film* (Falmer: REFRAME Books 2016), 20–50, <https://doi.org/10.25969/mediarep/13459>, accessed 10 September 2024.

inspiration from more unconventional forms of video production. One possible line of exploration was to utilise the flaws of AI expressively and creatively by, for instance, emphasising interpolation, thus treating the low stability that characterises AI video generation as an aesthetic form[184]. Although researchers were aware that the freer and more associative conventions of experimental video would have proved an easier path to implement, especially at a stage where AI video generation is taking its first steps, a conventional and naturalistic narrative, marked by photorealism and simulation, was chosen instead, with the intention of highlighting the structural limits of AI film-making. Indeed, this approach would ensure that users, researchers and viewers would immediately notice all mistakes that AI made. This was particularly important given the archaeological and historically situated context of the narrative, despite its status as a legendary tale penned by Virgil over a millennium after the purported events[185].

3. Defining and customising a 'collaborative' research model

The preceding sections introduced the reflections and main guidelines that guided the project and provided an idea of the levels of interaction between storytelling, man-machine collaboration and the professions involved in this intersemiotic translation. The research team also reflected on the optimal framework for arranging and coordinating the contributions of each professional and considered the peculiar nature of the AI generative process.

Stories represent a fundamental mode of cultural expression, and innovative forms and methodologies within the domain of storytelling have always evolved in response to the advent of new media and technology. New tools are not 'aseptic' and thus transform the artist's conception[186]; thus the advent

184 See the works presented at the AI Film Festival. See Runway AI Film Festival, <https://aiff.runwayml.com>, accessed 18 August 2024.

185 Should we consider the narratives of Aeneas's adventures to be connected to a historical event, then we must posit that Aeneas and the Trojan exiles arrived in Italy around the twelfth century BC as the majority of scholars place the fall of Troy around 1200 B.C. See Barry Strauss, *The Trojan War: A new history* (New York: Simon & Schuster, 2007).

186 Paolo Gallina, *La protoarte dei robot: Quando l'arte, la robotica e l'intelligenza artificiale si intrecciano* (Mimesis: Milano, 2023), 16.

of AI has resulted in a paradigm shift in the way creativity is perceived and approached. This shift, as observed by Cristóbal Valenzuela, CEO of Runway, one of the leading platforms in the field of video generation, entails a transition 'from render pixels to generate pixels':

> Now the moment we're going to start switching from render pixels to generate pixels, you might never have to export anything again because you're just generating them hopefully at some point in real time. And so the narrative possibilities there radically change the form of idea of creating content linearly and having that being distributed in the same way to everyone might change[187].

The other distinctive feature of the generative process, as emphasised by the academic Lev Manovich[188], is that it is a 'predictive medium'. This implies that the results of the process cannot be fully controlled, leading to the need to devise and implement working models that can adapt to the predictive and largely random nature of the distinctive visual synthesis produced by AI.

To translate such discourse into the context of AI*neid, Virgil's* Aeneid *in the Age of AI*, the team had to develop a functional work model for the intersemiotic translation process that would enable the professionals involved in the project to be fully engaged at each stage, contribute their input, monitor the results because of the predictiveness of the generative process and reiterate or refine their attempts if necessary. In essence, the aim was to provide a multidisciplinary working space in which human agents could engage with AI-enabled tools in a variety of ways and assume different roles at various stages of the project's life cycle.

This objective was achieved by utilising mainstream digital collaborative platforms, such as MIRO[189] and file-hosting services, including Google Drive[190], for sharing, communication and interaction among the researchers, AI users

---

[187] Curiosity Podcast, 'The Future of Generative AI Video with Cristóbal Valenzuela, CEO and Co-Founder of Runway', Founders in Arms Podcast (2023), <https://foundersinarms.substack.com/p/the-future-of-generative-ai-video>, accessed 29 August 2024.

[188] Lev Manovich, 'AI image and generative media: Notes on ongoing revolution', 5.

[189] MIRO | The Innovation Workspace, <https://miro.com/>, accessed 01 September 2024.

[190] Personal Cloud Storage & File Sharing Platform – Google, <https://www.google.com/drive/>, accessed 25 August 2024.

and technicians. The AI generative platforms employed for the production of the video included ComfyUI[191], Midjourney[192], and Runway[193], which were selected following a survey and evaluation[194] of the software available on the market. The researchers were also tasked with creating a new format for analysing and organising the literary source text, given the different ways the literary source text would be used in the context of the adaptation.

The team proceeded to develop a working model comprising five key phases, taking into account the aforementioned premises, the tools and interface of the software, the research objectives and the stylistic adaptation strategy. The key phases in the working model encompass the steps of the creative process that run

- from the literary text to the multi-column adaptation worksheet (Stage 1)
- from the multi-column adaptation worksheet to drafting the textual prompts (Stage 2)
- from the textual prompts to the images (T2I with Midjourney V6; Stage 3)
- from the images to the video clips (I2V with Runway Gen-2; Stage 4)
- from the video clips to editing (Stage 5)

The contribution and level of automation that AI can provide at each of these five stages may vary according to the specific needs of the users and creators. In the context of this research project, steps 1 and 2 were primarily the result of human work but, in their structure and conceptualisation, took into consideration the AI-driven generative process that predominated in steps 3 and 4. Step 5 was completed without the use of AI, involving only the use of conventional editing software.

---

191 comfyanonymous, 'Github.Com-Comfyanonymous-ComfyUI_-_2023-12-04_17-57-46', (2023), <http://archive.org/details/github.com-comfyanonymous-ComfyUI_-_2023-12-04_17-57-46>, accessed 3 September 2024.

192 Midjourney, <https://www.midjourney.com/home/>, accessed 5 September 2024.

193 Runway | Tools for Human Imagination, <https://runwayml.com/>, accessed 13 August 2024.

194 See Gozalo-Brizuela and Garrido-Merchán, 'A Survey of Generative AI Applications'.

In the initial stage, the researchers selected one of the numerous existing English translations of *The Aeneid*[195] as English was the only language that the AI software they employed was programmed to understand. They then focused on the second and third chapters, identifying characters and episodes that could be used to construct a narrative that would be comprehensible even to an audience lacking prior knowledge of the story[196]. Next, the two chapters were subjected to analysis and breakdown, with particular attention paid to the textual elements pertinent to the narrator's voice, the dialogue to be transferred to the video and the drafting of the textual prompts for the creation of the images. This resulted in the formulation of a multi-column adaptation worksheet, in which each column served to visually delineate the nature of the operation and the relevant field to facilitate the identification of the task and the professional who was involved.

Based on the worksheet produced in Stage 1, a series of textual prompts was developed for the subsequent passage from T2I. These prompts were derived from information and descriptions provided by the literary source, human interpretations of that source and metadata specific to the software (Midjourney).

---

[195] English verse translations include: Virgil, *The Aeneid,* trans. by Patric Dickinson (New York: New American Library, 1961); Virgil, *The Aeneid,* trans. by David Ferry (Chicago: University of Chicago Press, 2017); Virgil, *The Aeneid,* trans. by A.S. Kline (Moscow, Idaho: Roman Roads Media, 2015); Virgil, *The Aeneid of Virgil,* trans. by Allen Mandelbaum (New York: Bantam Classics, 1981); Virgil, *Aeneid,* trans. by Len Krisak (Philadelphia, PA: University of Pennsylvania Press, 2020); Virgil, *The Aeneid,* trans. and edited by Barry Powell (Oxford: Oxford University Press, 2015); Virgil, *The Aeneid,* trans. and edited by David West (London: Penguin Classics, 1990).

[196] The audiovisual narration opens with the appearance of Creusa's ghost to Aeneas, accompanied by the burning of Troy. Subsequently, the Trojan refugees congregate at Antandros, at the foot of Mount Ida, where they construct a fleet and embark on the sea, ultimately establishing the city of Aeneadae. However, following the macabre vicissitudes of Polydorus, which are portents of ill omen, the fleet sets sail once more into the unknown, which forms the conclusion of the video.

Table 5.1 The multi-column adaptation worksheet, developed and employed throughout the adaptation process, defined the textual prompts and voice-over and indicated specific filmic aspects, including the duration of the scenes and the type of shots

SCENE N° 1 Troy, 'among the city roofs'	**For text prompts**	**Voice-over**	**Duration**	**Camera**
1.1 The ghost of Creusa appears to Aeneas	Among the city roofs, the unhappy ghost and true shadow of Creusa appeared. The ghost of Creusa speaks: 'Oh ENEAS, sweet husband, what use is it to indulge in such mad grief? This has not happened without the divine will: neither its laws nor the ruler of great Olympus. Yours is long exile, you must plough a vast reach of sea: and you will come to Hesperia's land. There, happiness, kingship and a royal wife will be yours. Banish these tears for your beloved Creusa. I, a Trojan woman, shall never go as slave to some Greek wife: instead the great mother of the gods keeps me on this shore. Now farewell, and preserve your love for the son we share.' Creusa fades into thin air.	Among the city roofs The unhappy ghost and true shadow of Creusa appeared before my eyes. I was dumbfounded, my hair stood on end and my voice stuck in my throat.	20''	head and shoulder

In Stage 3, the textual prompts that were elaborated in Stage 2 were fed to Midjourney[197], enabling the generation and selection of images based on the results. Stages 3 and 2 were inextricably linked: depending on the outputs, the textual prompts could be completely reworked or partially refined to improve consistency and provide iconic enhancement of the images that were generated. The generated images were used at this stage to create a reference storyboard, a useful tool that allows the definition of scenes, shots and video effects.

In the fourth stage, which involved I2V, the images that were produced were fed as input to Runway Gen-2. The video clips that were generated resulted from human interactions with the various settings and tools, which reproduced cinematic language and the movement of objects and characters and adjusted the intensity of the generative process. In this manner, a multitude of discrete video segments were generated, each representing a distinct narrative element.

In the last stage, the video clips were edited. During the postproduction process, the audio, narrative voice-over, music and subtitles were added to create the final audiovisual product. This editing process integrated all of the components to ensure narrative coherence and aesthetic quality, thus concluding the intersemiotic translation process.

Conclusion

The rise of AI generative culture is expanding the theoretical frameworks surrounding intersemiotic translation. In the next years, much work needs to be done in this direction. Among the creative potentialities of generative

[197] The creative process with Midjourney can be outlined as follows. After inputting the command '/imagine' and a series of keywords (known as prompts), the user is presented with four preliminary images derived from those inputs. If any of the images are of interest, they can be upscaled, developed further, or used to create additional variants. If the initial drafts fail to meet the user's expectations, the user may repeat the process with the same keywords or reformulate the prompt to obtain different results. See Anna Jaruga-Rozdolska, 'Artificial Intelligence as Part of Future Practices in the Architect's Work: Midjourney Generative Tool as Part of a Process of Creating an Architectural Form', *Architectus* 3/71 (2022), 97, <https://architectus.pwr.edu.pl/files/numery/71_10.pdf>, accessed 30 August 2024.

AI is the possibility of developing a more direct and 'literary' approach to the adaptation of source texts into films, taking advantage of the textual nature of the T2I and T2V generative processes. However, transforming literary texts into suitable text prompts for AI systems requires careful intralinguistic translation to avoid the pitfalls caused by poetic and metaphorical language, which generative AI often misinterprets. This highlights the intricate interplay between human creativity and AI capabilities and underscores the importance of human oversight in guiding the generative processes to achieve a coherent adaptation of a literary source.

This approach also acknowledges translation as a multifaceted process that encompasses not only linguistic elements but also technological, cultural and creative dimensions. Consequently, it encourages translators to collaborate with other professionals to ensure the continued functionality of translations in the context of ongoing complexity and technological advancement. The increasing sophistication of technological tools, coupled with the growing number of professionals engaged in cultural projects that utilise AI, underscore the necessity for the development or adoption of a working method that can engage and optimise the performance of not only the machine but also the professionals and technicians involved.

The project under examination, AI*neid, Virgil's* Aeneid *in the Age of AI*, proposes a model in which a plurality of voices contribute to the creation of meaning across a range of semiotic systems. This model has the potential to inspire others, leading to innovative interpretations and translations that challenge traditional boundaries.

This contribution emphasises the importance of a multidisciplinary collaborative approach, involving professionals from various fields, when creating audiovisual content using generative AI tools. This collaborative aspect has not always been highlighted in previous research, which has tended to focus more on the technical aspects of the AI software and systems. This evolution reflects a broader cultural shift towards recognising the interconnectedness of different modes of communication in contemporary discourse and possibly vitalising and redefining the role of linguistics in the creative industry.

References

'Aeneas Route – Cultural Routes – Www.Coe.Int', Cultural Routes, <https://www.coe.int/en/web/cultural-routes/aeneas-route-4>, accessed 2 September 2024.

Ahmad, Imran Shafiq, Nazia Siddiqui and Boubakeur Boufama, 'A Comparative Study of Text-to-Image Generative Models', in 2024 IEEE 12th International Symposium on Signal, Image, Video and Communications (ISIVC) (Marrakech: Morocco, 2024), 1–6, <https://ieeexplore.ieee.org/document/10577779/>, accessed 3 September 2024.

Arkan, Gamze Nil, 'Cinema Literary Adaptations as a Narrative Form', *Contemporary Issues of Communication 2/2 (2023), 50–58* <https://dergipark.org.tr/tr/pub/conicom/issue/80112/1351082>, accessed 6 September 2024.

Barnden, John A., 'Metaphor and Artificial Intelligence: Why They Matter to Each Other', in Raymond W. Gibbs Jr., ed., *The Cambridge Handbook of Metaphor and Thought* (London: Cambridge University Press, 2008), 311–38.

Barnden, John A., 'Metaphor and Context: A Perspective from Artificial Intelligence', in Andreas Musolff and Jörg Zinken, eds, *Metaphor and Discourse* (London: Palgrave Macmillan, 2009), 79–94.

Bidgoli, Ardavan, Eunsu Kang, and Daniel Cardoso Llach, 'Machinic Surrogates: Human-Machine Relationships in Computational Creativity', arXiv (New York: Cornell University, 2019), <https://arxiv .org /abs /1908.01133>, accessed 26 August 2024.

Cahir, Linda Costanzo, *Literature into film: Theory and practical approaches* (Jefferson: McFarland, 2006).

Calcani, Giuliana, *Dal Mito alla Storia. La Rappresentazione della leggenda di Enea tra adattamenti e varianti* (Roma: Edizioni Efesto, 2017).

Camps, William Anthony, *An introduction to Virgil's «Aeneid»* (London: Oxford University Press, 1969).

Casini, Tommaso, 'Tra lessico pittorico e iconografia: Annibal Caro e la fortuna della traduzione dell'Eneide', *Gli dèi a corte - letteratura e immagini nella Ferrara estense* (Firenze: Istituto di Studi Rinascimentali, 2009), 115–134.

comfyanonymous, 'Github.Com-Comfyanonymous-ComfyUI_-_2023 -12-04_17-57-46', (2023), <http://archive.org/details/github.com

-comfyanonymous-ComfyUI_-_2023-12-04_17-57-46>, accessed 3 September 2024.

Curiosity Podcast, 'The Future of Generative AI Video with Cristóbal Valenzuela, CEO and Co-Founder of Runway', Founders in Arms Podcast (2023), <https://foundersinarms.substack.com/p/the-future-of-generative-ai-video>, accessed 29 August 2024.

D'Isa, Francesco, *La rivoluzione algoritmica. Arte e intelligenza artificiale* (Bologna: Luca Sossella Editore, 2024).

Danesi, Marcel, 'AI-Generated Cinema', in Marcel Danesi, *AI-Generated Popular Culture* (2024), 45–65, <https://link.springer.com /10 .1007 /978 -3-031 -54752 -2_3>, accessed 22 August 2024, (Springer Nature Switzerland, 2024).

Desmond, John M., and Peter Hawkes, *Adaptation: Studying Film and Literature* (Michigan: McGraw-Hill, 2005).

Ding, Ming, Zhuoyi Yang, Wenyi Hong, Wendi Zheng, Chang Zhou, Da Yin, and others, 'CogView: Mastering Text-to-Image Generation via Transformers', *arXiv* (New York: Cornell University, 2021), <https://arxiv.org/abs/2105.13290>, accessed 29 August 2024.

Dusi, Nicola, 'Intersemiotic Translation: Theories, Problems, Analysis', *Semiotica*, 2015/206 (2015), 181–205, <https://www .degruyter .com / document /doi /10 .1515 /sem -2015 -0018 /html>, accessed 19 August 2024.

Esser, Patrick, Johnathan Chiu, Parmida Atighehchian, Jonathan Granskog, and Anastasis Germanidis, 'Structure and Content-Guided Video Synthesis with Diffusion Models', in 2023 IEEE/CVF International Conference on Computer Vision (ICCV) (Paris, 2023), 7312–22, <https://ieeexplore .ieee.org /document /10377444/>, accessed 30 August 2024.

Fan, Kaifang, and Wang Chunlei, 'Translation Studies in the Era of AI: Characteristics, Fields and Significance', *International Journal of Translation and Interpretation Studies*, 3/4 (2023), 68–77, <https://al-kindipublisher.com/index.php/ijtis/article/view/6349>, accessed 28 August 2024.

Fortuna, Daniele, 'The iconography of Aeneas' escape from Troy in the European figurative culture', in Sandra Gatti, ed., *Aeneas in the Troas and Latium Regions. Mythology and Archaeology, Proceedings of the*

International Symposium Edremit 26 October 2021 (Roma: Edizioni Ponte Sisto, 2022), 223-245.

Gafni, Oran, Adam Polyak, Oron Ashual, Shelly Sheynin, Devi Parikh, and Yaniv Taigman, 'Make-A-Scene: Scene-Based Text-to-Image Generation with Human Priors', in Shai Avidan, Gabriel Brostow, Moustapha Cissé, Giovanni Maria Farinella, and Tal Hassner, eds, *Computer Vision – ECCV 2022*, (Springer Nature Switzerland, 2022), 89–106, <https://link .springer.com /10 .1007 /978 -3 -031 -19784 -0_6>, accessed 23 August 2024.

Gallina, Paolo, *La protoarte dei robot: Quando l'arte, la robotica e l'intelligenza artificiale si intrecciano* (Mimesis: Milano, 2023).

Gozalo-Brizuela, Roberto, and Eduardo C. Garrido-Merchán, 'A Survey of Generative AI Applications', arXiv (New York: Cornell University, 2023), <https://arxiv .org /abs /2306 .02781>, accessed 30 August 2024.

Hao, Yaru, Zewen Chi, Li Dong, and Furu Wei, 'Optimizing Prompts for Text-to-Image Generation', arXiv (New York: Cornell University, *2022),* <https://arxiv.org/abs/2212.09611>, accessed 21 August 2024.

Hutcheon, Linda, *A Theory of Adaptation* (New York: Routledge, 2006).

Jakobson, Roman, *On Linguistic Aspects of Translation* (Harvard University Press eBooks, 1959), <https://doi.org/10.4159/harvard.9780674731615 .c18>, accessed 27 August 2024.

Jaruga-Rozdolska, Anna, 'Artificial Intelligence as Part of Future Practices in the Architect's Work: Midjourney Generative Tool as Part of a Process of Creating an Architectural Form', *Architectus* 3/71 (2022), <https://architectus.pwr.edu.pl/files/numery/71_10.pdf>, accessed 30 August 2024.

Liu, Vivian, and Lydia B. Chilton, 'Design Guidelines for Prompt Engineering Text-to-Image Generative Models', *CHI Conference on Human Factors in Computing Systems* (2022), 1–23, <https://doi.org/10 .1145/3491102.3501825>, accessed 26 August 2024.

Llano, Maria Teresa, D'Inverno Mark, Yee-King Matthew, McCormack Alon, Ilsar, Jon, Pease Alison and others, 'Explainable Computational Creativity', arXiv (New York: Cornell University: 2022), <https://arxiv .org/abs/2205.05682>, accessed 5 September 2024.

Madonna, Sergio, Nisio, Stefania, Fenelli, Maria, Jaia, Alessandro and Ebanista Laura, 'Enea and Turno; the landscape of myth between geology and archaeology', *Memorie Descrittive della Carta Geologica d'Italia*, 109 (2022), 123–136.

Manovich, Lev, AI image and generative media: Notes on ongoing revolution', in Lev Manovich and Emanuele Arielli, eds, *Artificial aesthetic: A Critical Guide to AI, Media and Design (2023)*, <http://manovich.net/index.php/projects/artificial-aesthetics-book>, accessed 2 September 2024.

Manovich, Lev, 'What is Digital Cinema?', in Shane Denson, and Julya Leyda, eds, *Post-Cinema. Theorizing 21st-Century Film* (Falmer: REFRAME Books 2016), 20–50, <https://doi .org /10 .25969 /mediarep /13459>, accessed 10 September 2024.

Manovich, Lev, *The Language of New Media* (Cambridge, Massachusetts; London, England: The MIT Press, 2001).

McFarlane, Brian, 'Novel to film: an introduction to the theory of adaptation', *Choice Reviews Online* 34/06 (1997), 34-3224, <http://choicereviews.org/review/10.5860/CHOICE.34-3224>, accessed 2 September 2024.

Midjourney, <https://www.midjourney.com/home/>, accessed 5 September 2024.

MIRO | The Innovation Workspace, <https://miro.com/>, accessed 1 September 2024.

Oppenlaender, Jonas, 'A Taxonomy of Prompt Modifiers for Text-to-Image Generation', *Behaviour & Information Technology* (2023), 1–14, <https://www.tandfonline.com/doi/full/10.1080/0144929X.2023.2286532>, accessed 11 August 2024.

Personal Cloud Storage & File Sharing Platform – Google, <https://www.google.com/drive/>, accessed 25 August 2024.

Runway | Tools for Human Imagination, <https://runwayml.com/>, accessed 13 August 2024.

Runway AI Film Festival, <https://aiff.runwayml.com>, accessed 18 August 2024.

Singh, Aditi, 'A Survey of AI Text-to-Image and AI Text-to-Video Generators', *2023 4th International Conference on Artificial Intelligence, Robotics and Control (AIRC)*, (Egypt: Cairo, 2023), 32–36, <https://ieeexplore.ieee.org/document/10303174/>, accessed 13 August 2024.

Smith, Andrew L., Felix Greaves, and Trishan Panch, 'Hallucination or Confabulation? Neuroanatomy as Metaphor in Large Language Models', *PLOS Digital Health* 2/11 (2023), <https://dx.plos.org/10.1371/journal.pdig.0000388>, accessed 3 September 2024.

Soysal, Fırat, 'Enhancing Translation Studies with Artificial Intelligence (AI): Challenges, Opportunities, and Proposals', Karamanoğlu Mehmetbey Üniversitesi Uluslararası Filoloji ve Çeviribilim Dergisi 5/2 (2023), 177–91, <http://dergipark.org.tr/en/doi/10.55036/ufced.1402649>, accessed 8 September 2024.

Strauss, Barry, *The Trojan War: A new history* (New York: Simon & Schuster, 2007).

Sui, Peiqi, Eamon Duede, Sophie Wu, and Richard So, 'Confabulation: The Surprising Value of Large Language Model Hallucinations', in Lun-Wei Ku, Andre Martins, and Vivek Srikumar, eds, *Proceedings of the 62nd Annual Meeting of the Association for Computational Linguistics* 1 (Thailand: Bangkok, 2024), 14274–84, <https://aclanthology.org/2024.acl-long.770>, accessed 9 September 2024.

Veale, Tony, and Cardoso F. Amílcar, eds, *Computational creativity: The philosophy and engineering of autonomously creative systems* (Cham: Springer, 2019).

Veale, Tony, and Rafael Pérez Y Pérez, 'Leaps and Bounds: An Introduction to the Field of Computational Creativity', *New Generation Computing* 38/4 (2020), 551–63, <http://link.springer.com/10.1007/s00354-020-00116-w>, accessed 18 September 2024.

Virgil, *Aeneid*, trans. by Len Krisak (Philadelphia, PA: University of Pennsylvania Press, 2020).

Virgil, *Aeneid*, trans. by Shadi Bartsch (New York: Random House, 2021).

Virgil, *The Aeneid of Virgil*, trans. by Allen Mandelbaum (New York: Bantam Classics, 1981).

Virgil, *The Aeneid*, trans. and edited by Barry Powell (Oxford: Oxford University Press, 2015).

Virgil, *The Aeneid*, trans. and edited by David West (London: Penguin Classics, 1990).

Virgil, *The Aeneid*, trans. by A.S. Kline (Moscow, Idaho: Roman Roads Media, 2015).

Virgil, *The Aeneid*, trans. by David Ferry (Chicago: University of Chicago Press, 2017).

Virgil, *The Aeneid*, trans. by Patric Dickinson (New York: New American Library, 1961).

Williamson, Makyra, 'Virgil's Aeneid: The cornerstone of Roman identity', *Tenor of Our Times* 8 (2019), 159–171.

Zhu, Jichen, Antonios Liapis, Sebastian Risi, Rafael Bidarra, and G. Michael Youngblood, 'Explainable AI for Designers: A Human-Centered Perspective on Mixed-Initiative Co-Creation', 2018 IEEE Conference on Computational Intelligence and Games (CIG) (Maastricht, 2018), 1–8, <https://ieeexplore.ieee.org/document/8490433/>, accessed 9 September 2024.

6

AIneid, Narrating Mythology in the Age of AI: Exploring Human-Machine Collaboration from a Linguistic Perspective

Eleonora Gatto & Federica Villareale

Abstract

In the digital age that characterises the contemporary world, we are in daily contact with visual elements such as images or videos, and artificial intelligence (AI) is taking an increasingly crucial role in generating this type of content, showing the possibilities and limits of this process. In this article, analysing the AIneid, Narrating mythology in the Age of AI project, we investigate the world of generative AI in relation to the myth of the Virgilian Aeneid with the aim of studying the process of text-to-image conversion (intersemiotic translation), through a collaboration between researchers and the medium of artificial intelligence, to carry out a double investigation: on both visual and linguistic point of view.

1. Project and related issues

1.1 Introduction to the project

In the digital age that characterises the contemporary world, we are daily faced with visual elements such as images or videos. In this regard, Artificial Intelligence (AI) is playing an increasingly crucial role in generating this type of content. Moreover, traditional methods of storytelling and video creation are undergoing profound transformation, thereby proving the possibilities and limitations of this process, which consequently deserves further investigation[198]. Yet, could generative AI also be implemented to reinterpret classical

[198] Vincenzo De Masi, and Quinke Di, 'AI and the Future of Cinema: The Transformative Impact of *Our T2 Remake*', *LAB Research* (2024), 2.

texts and mythological stories? Arguably, AI-generated visual images could offer a new level of interaction with myth, thus creating a visual experience that intertwines with literary tradition. Indeed, the following project aims to investigate the world of generative AI in relation to Virgil's great myth of Aeneid, analysing the state of the art and assessing its current limitations, especially regarding archaeological accuracy and fidelity to historical context.

The project under analysis, *AIneid, Narrating mythology in the Age of AI*, seeks to investigate precisely such issues. Stemming from a collaboration between the *International Center for Research on Collaborative Translation* (IULM University, Milan) and Karma Lab (Koç University, Istanbul), this project is an experimental work which, through the creation of a video that reimagines the epic of the Aeneid, relates a myth – a Western classic – to the latest technologies. The objective is to observe the process of text-to-image transfer, more precisely referred to as 'intersemiotic translation', which involves a synergy between researchers and the artificial intelligence medium through a dual investigation: visual and linguistic[199].

The research team aims to reconsider the possibilities of storytelling in the digital age and the profound impact AI can have on the understanding of mythology. Furthermore, the video is an opportunity to reflect on the limits – perhaps only temporary – of artificial intelligence in the field of image creation when, as in this case, it is called to adapt to specific requirements of archaeological accuracy.

1.2 The experts involved

The project is the result of research conducted by PI Fabio Morotti to enhance the archaeological heritage of the places narrated in the *Aeneid* from drone images. In this journey, Morotti is joined by Sumru Deniz of Karma Lab (Koç University, Istanbul), and Francesco Laurenti, Director of the *International Center for Research on Collaborative Translation* (henceforth the 'Center') and Scientific Director of the Project.

---

199 The project-specific information presented in this article was obtained following several discussions the authors had with Fabio Morotti, Project Coordinator of *AIneid, Narrating mythology in the Age of AI.*

With this project, the Center aims to describe the intersemiotic translation of this creative process[200], to analyse the choice of the corpus used to create the video from a linguistic viewpoint – indeed, we speak of generative culture and generative media – and, finally, to generate subtitles specially for this new type of audiovisual product.

1.3 The reference work: the Aeneid and the cities explored

The reference text for this project is the *Aeneid*, a Latin epic poem consisting of twelve books, written by the Roman poet Virgil approximately between 29 and 19 b.C[201].

To make the video, the team selected some of the events narrated in the work, condensing the events lived by the protagonist, Aeneas, a demigod, son of Venus, the goddess of beauty, and Anchises, a shepherd. The plot of the video under analysis retraces some key episodes of Aeneas' journey, which can be conceptually divided into three macro-moments, based on the city in which they are set. In the opening scenes, Aeneas is at the gates of burning Troy (aerial view) fleeing with his family and many others. However, realising that he has lost Creusa, his wife, Aeneas returns to the city to look for her. He encounters only her ghost, who tells him his destiny, willed by the gods, is to reach Hesperia. This is the final moment of the Aeneid's chapter concerning Troy.

The second part focuses on Antandros, depicting the Trojan refugees who have escaped the fall of Troy. They journey toward Mount Ida and pause in this city, where they prepare their fleet before setting sail for Thrace. The third and final part depicts the arrival of the Trojan fleet on a new land, where Aeneas establishes his first city, Aeneid. Here, the viewer witnesses the revelation of Polydorus, who having been killed, warns Aeneas that the land

[200] The issue of the creative process in AI is highly debated; for more information see Section 1.5 of this chapter.

[201] Philip Gaskell, *Landmarks in Classical Literature* (Chicago: Fitzroy Dearborn Publishers, 1999).

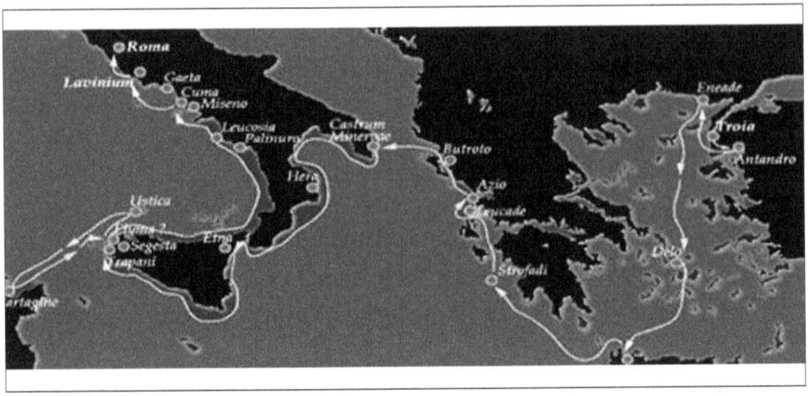

Figure 6.1 Aeneas' Route

is cursed. At this point, after paying funeral honours to Polydorus, Aeneas departs with his fleet, leaving those territories forever.[202]

1.4 Chasing a Route: how the project unfolds

The common thread of the project is a route established years ago, named the 'Aeneas' Route'[203]: an Aeneid-inspired physical path that has been recreated based on the places the Trojan hero passed through in the myth. This itinerary is officially recognised by the European Union and runs from the coasts of the northwestern Aegean Sea, in Turkey, to those of Latium, in Italy, embracing five countries in the Mediterranean area and important UNESCO sites, with a view to the enhancement and promotion of cultural heritage. Indeed, through this historical and fascinating itinerary, tourists have the opportunity to explore the locations visited by the Trojan hero and to learn about the mythology and history of the ancient world.

In the context of the project, the team focused on three of these places included in the Route and located in the Turkish region: Truva (Troy), Antandros

---

[202] 'Aeneas: myth and history', Aeneas Route Association, <https://www.aeneasroute.org/en/the-myth/#:~:text=The%20myth%20of%20the%20journey,crossed%20by%20countless%20routes%20of>, accessed 9 July 2024.

[203] <https://www.aeneasroute.org/en/>, accessed 14 June 2024.

(Antander), and Enez (Aeneid, in Thrace, which, on the border with Europe, is still today a borderland).

This was one of the four parameters for creating the video, as listed below:

- No cameras were allowed to make the video, only generative AI or post-production interventions;
- The voice-off – the narrative voice of the video – had to come from the English translation of the Aeneid (this involved a choice among the various available translations of the Virgilian text, along with an analysis of the most effective passages to use as prompts for generating the best images[204]);
- Settings and characters had to be created solely based on Virgil's words – which caused quite a few problems, due to the poor descriptions of the characters and the difficulty in reconstructing verisimilar settings from a historical and archaeological point of view[205]);
- The places to be described had to be limited to those that now fall within the borders of Turkey, where Fabio Morotti is located at the moment of writing to perfect the research.

As regards the latter, the representation of the cities is undoubtedly the true difficulty – if not hazard – of recounting the story. In the case of Troy, in particular, the extensive existing cinematic imagery strongly influences both the viewer and, consequently, the creator of the final product. Moreover, when it comes to working with videos and images, in scenes showing several characters or particular buildings, the consistency with the environments of the period is lost, due to missing images in the AI database. In fact, for this 'creative' process, the AI resorts to the collective imagery of the image, but visual references dating back to that period are scarce, creating an archaeologically verisimilitude narrative is not an easy task.

The narrow and specific geographic focus of the project enhances its value. Through aerial views, it was possible to reconstruct and represent this area, incorporating three modern Turkish cities into the video, which Morotti personally visited. The aim is to bring real geography within the final video

---

204 For more information on this subject, see Sections 3.1 and 3.2 of Chapter 3.

205 For more information on this subject, see Section 2.2 of Chapter 2.

through the use of drone cinematography, which allows for the representation of cities and spaces from a different perspective. Therefore, it serves a dual function: on the one hand, it facilitates the task of image and video creation, as it allows for objectivity, without risking delving into details that might not be faithfully reconstructed from an archaeological point of view; at the same time, the view from above is an expressive, imaginative and organisational potential of space, for centuries also referred to as the 'eye of God', essential in the field of arts and the formation of mythical and religious thought.[206] Further strengthening this external, omniscient viewpoint is the choice of an external narrator, which, on many occasions, helped avoid the use of lip-sync, a major challenge in creating videos with generative AI.

Overall, and given what has been presented so far, the style used by Fabio Morotti can be described as realistic. His approach to the work differed from what we are used to today; indeed, he did not resort to the classic fluid aesthetic seen daily but included an alienating element suggesting the birth of a new genre.

1.5 Generative culture and generative media: where does creativity lie?

Analysing what has been described so far, this seems to be the beginning of a revolution in media creation: the rise of 'generative media' or 'generative AI'. These terms refer to the process of creating new media objects, including images, animations, videos, texts, music, models and 3D scenes, with deep neural networks[207]. In the specific case of this research project, a true translation process took place, since a text was transposed into images, hence the definition of intersemiotic translation.

---

206 For more information on the subject, 'Drone Cinematography: How to create Cinematic Masterpieces', Drone U (2023), <https://www.thedroneu.com/blog/drone-cinematography-guide/#:~:text=In%20drone%20cinematography%2C%20only%20unmanned,visual%20impact%20to%20their%20projects and <https://editmentor.com/blog/aerial-shot-a-view-from-above/>, accessed 14 June 2024.

207 Lev Manovich, 'AI image and Generative Media: Notes on Ongoing Revolution', in Lev Manovich, and Emanuele Arielli, eds, *Artificial Aesthetics: Generative AI, Art and Visual Media* (2023), < chrome-extension://efaidnbmnnnibpcajpcglclefindmkaj/https://manovich.net/content/04-projects/175-artificial-aesthetics/manovich-ai-image-and-generative-media.pdf >, accessed 14 June 2024.

Figure 6.2 Image generated from the prompt '*the half-decomposed body of a person buried beneath the mound, black eyes open, grass and leaves, dark ambience, cinematic, very realistic --ar 16:9.*'

The question that arises, therefore, is: is it possible to speak of 'creation' and 'creativity' in the field of AI? According to the definition given by the Oxford dictionary, the term creativity is intended as 'the use of skill and imagination to produce something new or to produce art'[208]. Therefore, the question arises as to whether this term is the exclusive domain of human beings or can be reinterpreted through the lens of 'artificial intelligence'[209]. For decades AI was considered incapable of simulating artistic creativity, which was thought to be a uniquely human trait. However, in recent years, AI researchers have

208 'Creativity', Oxford Learner's Dictionaries, <https://www.oxfordlearnersdictionaries.com/definition/english/creativity#:~:text=%E2%80%8Bthe%20use%20of%20skill,new%20or%20to%20produce%20art>, accessed 14 June 2024.

209 Nell'era dell'AI che significa essere creativi?', LinkedIn (2023), <https://www.linkedin.com/pulse/nellera-dellai-che-significa-essere-creativi-francesco-elmi-sdjtf/>, accessed 14 June 2024.

managed to 'train' neural networks to generate text and images worthy of the best writers, artists, photographers or illustrators. Consequently, in wondering whether AI is 'creative' or if it just reproduces accumulated data based on the commands received from a human, the answer probably lies somewhere in between. After all, AI *simulates* creativity using the data it has been nurtured with[210]. What is certain is that artificial intelligence lacks decision-making power, a characteristic that precludes us from defining it as truly 'creative'. As a matter of fact, it is the result of the commands that are given to it, it is a tool, just like a mobile phone or a camera used to take pictures; working with AI, the artist, a specialist in the field, is in charge of giving commands to the machine, which it executes, again following the decision-making power of the person who guides and controls it. The use of AI, therefore, does not eliminate the role of the artist, who, on the contrary, remains the *primum movens* of the creative process (due to their creative abilities), thus expanding the possibilities of human artistic expression[211].

However, this is a complex matter that deserves further discussion; in the meantime, it can be said that AI is transforming the field of art, opening up new possibilities and challenges. The use of the term 'possibilities' lies in the idea that creators should not be intimidated by the advancement of these technologies. On the contrary, they should collaborate with them to bring to life what was previously unattainable or would have been too costly and time-consuming[212], all while enhancing their creativity. On the other hand, these challenges are mainly related to the limitations and constraints in the policies of the software chosen[213].

---

210 Vincenzo Franceschelli, *Creatività e Intelligenza Artificiale*, speech at the Stati Generali del Diritto di Internet e della Intelligenza Artificiale [General Assembly on Internet Law and Artificial Intelligence] (Roma: Luiss, 2023).

211 Angela Petrone, *To Use or Be Used: AI-Generated Content as a Human Technical Exercise*, speech at the conference *Artificial Creativity. Looking At the Future of Digital Culture* (Milan: SAE Institute, June 2024).

212 Paolo de Giglio, 'AI e arte: creatività e generazione di contenuti nell'età dell'intelligenza artificiale', Colibryx, <https://colibryx.com/blog/ai-e-arte-creativita-e-generazione-di-contenuti-nell-eta-dell-intelligenza-artificiale>, accessed 14 June 2024.

213 For more information on the subject, see Section 2.2 Chapter. 2

Within the project under analysis, an example of such creative input by the artist and the challenges they face when dealing with the machine is given by the creation of Polydorus. This character from the Aeneid presents himself to Aeneas only in the form of a voice or lament that comes from underground (while the hero is engaged in a sacrifice) and through the image of blood, which gushes from a shrub.[214] Due to the absence of references to its physical appearance, when generating images – a key aspect of the video – the team decided to give the character of Polydorus a face to make the scene more 'filmic' and more understandable. The outcome, shown below (Figure 6.2), is, therefore, a face emerging from the ground, depicted in dark colours (in shades of grey), creating the right setting for the character and allowing the viewer to better understand and visualise the narrated episode. This is a clear example that the artist's creativity comes into play in the creative process and that the choices made can influence the reception of the message: just as for 'classic' film production when two directors create different works although starting from the same 'script', the aforesaid happens with the use of generative AI. Indeed, after all, it is the prompts, and therefore the user's commands, that *create* a story to be told.

---

[214] For the sake of thoroughness, the reference to the passage from the Aeneid in question is provided below:
'I was making a sacrifice to the gods, and my mother Venus, Dione's daughter, with auspices for the work begun, and had killed a fine bull on the shore, for the supreme king of the sky-lords. By chance, there was a mound nearby, crowned with cornel bushes, and bristling with dense spikes of myrtle. I went near, and trying to tear up green wood from the soil to decorate the altar with leafy branches, I saw a wonder, dreadful and marvellous to tell of. From the first bush, its broken roots torn from the ground, drops of dark blood dripped, and stained the earth with fluid. An icy shiver gripped my limbs, and my blood chilled with terror. Again, I went on to pluck a stubborn shoot from another, probing the hidden cause within: and dark blood flowed from the bark of the second. Troubled greatly in spirit, I prayed to the Nymphs of the wild, and father Gradivus, who rules the Thracian fields, to look with due kindness on this vision, and lessen its significance. But when I attacked the third with greater effort, straining with my knees against the sand (to speak or be silent?), a mournful groan was audible from deep in the mound, and a voice came to my ears: "Why do you wound a poor wretch, Aeneas? Spare me now in my tomb, don't stain your virtuous hands, Troy bore me, who am no stranger to you, nor does this blood flow from some dull block. Oh, leave this cruel land: leave this shore of greed. For I am Polydorus. Here a crop of iron spears carpeted my transfixed corpse and has ripened into sharp spines.'

In conclusion, the creative process that characterised this project, i.e., the generation of images (and later of a video) from a written text, lies in the possibility of the creator's intervention, in the choices they make as a result of the inevitable (and innovative) human-machine collaboration, and the synergy between human and artificial intelligence – which raises questions of ethics and authenticity on the use of AI and creativity while leading constant and mutual dialogue and enrichment between humans and artificial intelligence.

2. The application process

2.1 Talking to the machine: a repository of Natural Language Prompts (NLP)

As Daniel Jurafsky and James H. Martin point out[215] since the pursuit of knowledge is a profoundly human aspiration, it is no surprise that as soon as computers were invented, people began to ask them questions. In particular, in recent times and with the advent of Artificial Intelligence, learning to talk to machines has become of paramount importance. For example, the development of text-driven diffusion models[216] in AI has enabled humans to create visually appealing computer-like images similar to those created by professional artists. The effectiveness of these models depends on the phrasing of the textual description and its relevant keywords – the prompt[217].

215 Daniel Jurafsky, and James H. Martin, *Speech and Language Processing. An Introduction to Natural Language Processing, Computational Linguistics, and Speech Recognition*, 3rd February 2024 draft, <https://web.stanford.edu/~jurafsky/slp3/ed3bookfeb3_2024.pdf>, accessed 6 June 2024.

216 A diffusion model is defined as a set of mathematical equations that attempt to estimate the propagation of an element or information within a population. Cf. Giulia Martinetto, *Stima dei modelli di diffusione nei servizi: applicazione al caso di una media company italiana*, Master's Thesis (Torino: Politecnico di Torino, 2019), <https://webthesis.biblio.polito.it/secure/10571/1/tesi.pdf>, accessed 6 June 2024.

217 Nikita Pavlichenko, and Dmitry Ustalov, 'Best Prompts for Text-to-Image Models and How to Find Them', arXiv (2022), <https://arxiv.org/abs/2209.11711>, accessed 6 June 2024.

Recent advances in natural language processing have made various applications of generative models possible[218], and one of the most promising is text-guided image generation (*text-to-image* models)[219]. However, human intervention is required to establish the ideal wording of the message and keyword combination. Generally, prompts consist of a short text sentence that is used to produce an image; a well-crafted prompt can help create unique and realistic images. There are basic prompts, consisting of single words, phrases or emoji, and more advanced prompts, which may include one or more image URLs, multiple text phrases and parameters if provided by the software used. In any case, when creating them, the following should be kept in mind:[220]

- Word choice is very important; often, more specific synonyms work better than general language.
- Plural words leave much to chance: better to specify precise figures or collective nouns.
- In general, it is more effective to describe what is desired rather than what is not, as the software does not interpret negative relationships (like 'without' or 'not') in the same way a human would. Every word in the prompt may be considered a possible element of the image.

Following is the analysis of the software chosen by the research team to develop the transition phase from the Virgilian text to 2D images.

---

218 Generative models try to understand everything about individual groups of elements and then generate an idea of what makes them unique. Supposing there are two sets of images, one containing only images of dogs and the other only images of cats, and you want to build a machine that, given a new image, can tell whether it is a dog or a cat, a generative model will try to learn what a dog looks like and what a cat looks like by studying the various images of cats and dogs. Then, when it has to analyse the image presented to it, it will try to 'generate' the idea of the animal based on what it has learnt and then decide which answer to give. 'Modelli generativi e discriminativi a confronto', Human And Artificial Intelligence (2023), <https://www.humai.it/modelli-generativi-e-discriminativi-a-confronto/>, accessed 6 June 2024.

219 Pavlichenko, and Ustalov, 'Best Prompts for Text-to-Image Models and How to Find Them', 1.

220 Rules for effective prompt writing apply to any software. For more information <https://docs.midjourney.com/docs/prompts-2>, accessed 6 June 2024.

2.2 Text-to-image (T2I) conversion: features and technical limitations of Midjourney software

Among the numerous image-generating tools on the market (i.e. Chatbot App[221], Microsoft Bing[222], Picsart[223], or Dall E[224]), the one that turned out to be most suitable and, therefore, was chosen and used for the text-to-image conversion of the project is Midjourney[225], an independent research lab 'exploring new mediums of thought and expanding the imaginative powers of the human species'[226], Midjourney is an artificial intelligence software that turns words into absolutely realistic images in less than 60 seconds through Discord, its official server[227]. Following prompt input, the software generates four versions of the same image to choose from.

One of the reasons for choosing Midjourney is its clarity in explaining how to phrase prompts, along with the large number of parameters that can be used within prompts, thus changing the way an image is generated (parameters can change the aspect ratio, templates, upscale, etc.)[228]. For instance, the -no[229] parameter instructs the machine on what not to include in the image, while with -cref[230] (a parameter added only recently and a breakthrough in image generation) images can be included in the prompts as a reference to a character, allowing for the generation of images featuring the same character in various situations or with different focal points.

---

221 <https://chatbotapp.ai/imagegeneration?utm_source=GoogleAds&utm_medium=cpc&utm_campaign={campaign}&utm_id=21156944805&utm_term=164296649201&utm_content=695813707413&gad_source=1&gclid=CjwKCAjwmYCzBhA6EiwAxFwfgFsc-1bJogAxHr9TsonH3db7TazDzaRcE_xaetvHE9fTJxA14D4ZHBoCXQsQAvD_BwE>, accessed 5 June 2024.

222 <https://www.microsoft.com/it-it/bing?form=MA13FV>, accessed 5 June 2025.

223 <https://picsart.com/ai-image-generator/>, accessed 5 June 2024.

224 <https://openai.com/index/dall-e/>, accessed 5 June 2024.

225 <https://www.midjourney.com/home>, accessed 3 June 2024.

226 <https://www.midjourney.com/home>, accessed 3 June 2024.

227 <https://discord.com/servers/midjourney-662267976984297473>, accessed 3 June 2024.

228 <https://docs.midjourney.com/docs/prompts-2>, accessed 3 June 2024.

229 For more information, see <https://docs.midjourney.com/docs/no>, accessed 3 June 2024.

230 For more information, see <https://docs.midjourney.com/docs/character-reference>, accessed 3 June 2024.

In contrast, the -iw[231] parameter describes the degree of freedom granted to the machine to reinterpret a character (perhaps by switching from full-figure representation to close-up). After entering the '/image' command, together with a set of prompts, the user is shown a set of four preliminary images, each derived from the inputs provided: if any of the images are of interest, they can be modified or used to create additional versions.

However, if on the one hand such software allows for the generation of images that are very close to those pictured by the user, thanks precisely to the multitude of parameters, on the other hand, it is also true that several attempts are often required to turn the text into the desired image, both for issues related to the textual elements available (in this case, the reference is to the Aeneid – see Chapter 3) and for tool policy.

In fact, among the community guidelines of Midjourney, point 2 reads:

> *No adult content or gore. Please avoid making visually shocking or disturbing content. We will block some text inputs automatically.*[232]

Since the Aeneid is an epic poem – over half of which is about war, sacrifice and bloodshed – creating images that realistically describe the text may be challenging. This was the case of the representation of a moment of a bull's sacrifice to Venus. Through considerable creative effort (Figures 3 and 4), the team managed to generate images depicting the animal, but not exactly as they had wished for (e.g., the bull is always depicted alive, never dead or suffering; the framing differed from the one required) because Midjourney was 'self-censoring'.

Representing characters also proved complicated, due to the nature of the mythological text. As Schlegel points out, myth is a narrative fixed outside of time and history, with a recursive and repetitive character:[233] the events

---

231 For more information, see <https://docs.midjourney.com/docs/image-prompts>, accessed 5 June 2024.

232 <https://docs.midjourney.com/docs/terms-of-service>, accessed 4 June 2024.

233 Friedrich Schlegel, *Discorso sulla mitologia* (1800); Raffaella Bertazzoli, 'Natura universale del mito', in Piero Gibellini, and Raffaella Bertazzoli, eds, *Il mito nella letteratura italiana: miti senza frontiere*, vol. 5 (Brescia: Morcelliana, 2009), 5-25.

Figure 6.3 Image generated using the prompt '*marshland, bull sacrifice on the shore, whorshipping altar, blood, Trojans whorship the Gods, ancient village of Aeneade, dark ambience, cinematic, very realistic --no red colour --ar 16:09.*'

Figure 6.4 Image generated using the prompt '*eyes close up, bull sacrifice to Trojan gods, blood drips, bull on the ground, dark ambience, cinematic, very realistic, eye closed --ar 16:9.*'

narrated within myth have to involve as many people as possible and place no limits on the imagination of the listener. Such is the reason why more space is given to the descriptions of the feelings felt by the characters rather than to the descriptions of their physical appearance or the places where the action takes place. This poses a challenge when it comes to realistically representing the era of the narrative and its protagonists. In fact, for prompt generation, the scarcity of adjectives in the descriptions of the original text forced the study team to consult other articles that addressed the same historical period[234]. Only then was it possible to train the machine and generate satisfactory images.

However, despite being innovative artificial intelligence software, the technology is admittedly still perfectible. Indeed, in addition to the issue of self-censorship – a structural limitation that inevitably influences and constrains the narrative – to date, including more than one character in a single image is not feasible, as it risks distorting the secondary images. This posed a significant limitation that the research team had to address during the process.

2.3 Image-to-video (I2V) conversion: the Runway Gen-2 software

While for the T2I conversion process the research team relied only on Midjourney, during the I2V conversion phase, several AI software programs were integrated[235], although the main tool used was Runway Gen-2.

Runway is an easy-to-use platform that allows an image to be entered as a prompt and expanded. Due to its style transfer, camera motion, film language simulation, motion tracking and integration of multiple plug-ins and other functions[236], this results in short videos (approx. four sec.). Furthermore, it

[234] For more details on the linguistic aspect, see Chapter 3.

[235] Fabio Morotti, 'Towards new forms of visual narrative: AIneid, Virgil's *Aeneid* in the Age of AI', *Nova Science Publishing* (forthcoming).

[236] Biying Guo et al., 'A Comparative Study on the Features and Applications of AI Tools -Focus on PIKA Labs and RUNWAY', *International Journal of Internet, Broadcasting and Communication* 16/1 (2024), 86-91.

includes lip-sync functionality, a key feature for producing videos with talking characters, although its results are still limited by some input parameters.

However, as Morotti points out[237], tests conducted on the tool showed several difficulties and some instability, particularly when flipping characters or when animating blurred areas or subjects in the input image. Hence, the T2I process had to be adjusted to mitigate the impact of these constraints. Additionally, when inserting an image, Runway software provides brush tools that allow adjustments to specific areas, enabling the simulation of movements in objects, animals and humans, as well as creating facial expressions. This feature, combined with the software's ability to initiate a realistic generation process, played a key role in the final decision.

2.4 Creating consistent adaptation: other limitations of generative AI software

In addition to the issue of censorship arising from the tool policy and the very nature of the text they wanted to adapt, the team had to face – and somehow overcame – other challenges related to the structure of AI software, such as historical inconsistencies, photographic consistency of characters or the repurposing of the same characters in different contexts. Outlined below are the strategies the researchers implemented to overcome these challenges.

a. Historical inconsistency: the representation of the triremes

AI models are trained on sets of contemporary images that include a vast number of illustrations, but which may not have sufficient breadth and accuracy to represent the full spectrum of historical periods. As a result, they are unable to accurately generate objects, fashions and historical contexts that are not well represented in the training data[238].

Indeed, this was precisely the difficulty that arose at the time of the representation of the triremes, warships typical of Greek fleets from the sixth to fourth centuries b.C. – the term trireme refers to 'a long flat ship with three

237 Morotti, 'Towards new forms of visual narrative: AIneid, Virgil's *Aeneid* in the Age of AI'.

238 Morotti, 'Towards new forms of visual narrative: AIneid, Virgil's *Aeneid* in the Age of AI'.

rows of oars on each side'[239]. During the initial attempts, the outputs showed structural features resembling typical Viking or Renaissance ships, although a different type of vessel was specified in the prompt: the *penteconter*[240].

Only when the reference was added to an existing image produced by another university[241], depicting a digitally reconstructed trireme, the team was able to represent a vessel with the characteristics required.

b. Photographic consistency of the characters

When generating a character[242], it is important to assess its photographic consistency; to avoid compromising the credibility of the image, all visual elements – including facial expressions, anatomical proportions, but also lighting, shadows and textures – have to be consistent and realistic.

As mentioned in Section 2.2, if on the one hand, the researchers aimed to remain faithful to the source text when creating the characters, on the other hand, they had to contend with very few descriptions present, none of them detailed. For this reason, the instructions derived from the literary text and intended for prompts were rephrased by adding some information, while remaining true to the prevailing style and tone of specific scenes[243]. Nonetheless, the resulting images presented physical stereotypes and – oddly enough – resembled Hollywood stars. Moreover, the armours were inconsistent with the archaeological indications, since they evoked Roman, Mediaeval, or sixteenth-century styles, which did not correspond

239 'Trireme', Oxford Learner's Dictionaries, <https://www.oxfordlearnersdictionaries.com/definition/english/trireme?q=trireme>, accessed 24 July 2024.

240 The penteconter was a type of vessel used in ancient times, particularly in Phoenicia and ancient Greece. The penteconter was a mixed propulsion vessel, propelled by both sail and rowing. It was the first vessel suitable for long navigation. Its name derives from the fifty oarsmen arranged in a row of twenty-five on each side of the ship. 'Pentecontera', Nautipedia, <https://www.nautipedia.it/index.php/Pentecontera>, accessed 24 July 2024.

241 Image created by Hephaestus Lab <https://sketchfab.com/HLab>, accessed 2 August 2024.

242 Chen Xi, and Jeanhun Chung, 'A Study on Character Design using [Midjourney] Application', *International Journal of Advanced Culture Technology* 11/2 (2023), 409-14.

243 Morotti, 'Towards new forms of visual narrative: AIneid, Virgil's Aeneid in the Age of AI'.

Figure 6.5 Image generated using the prompt '*aerial footage, Mount Ida, refugees getting on an ancient penteconter fleet, 5 penteconters, dawn, cinematic, very realistic, 1080 p --ar 16:9.*'

Figure 6.6 Image generated using the prompt '*daylight, bright sailing,* https://s.mj.run/OBuWxpOnC4A *ancient trireme, one square sail, one line made of 20 oars, daylight, cinematic, very realistic, very detailed, 1080 p --no boat-tail --v 6.0 --ar 16:9.*'

Figure 6.7 Reference image for the representation of Figure 6.6

Figure 6.8 One of the first representations of the protagonist Aeneas using the prompt '*Aeneas, an ancient trojan man in armour, beautiful hair, joyful charmed eyes, noble face.*'

to the stylistic norms of the time. As a result, the team opted for a more flexible interpretation of the adaptation to avoid creating overly stereotypical results and to overcome the obstacle of the armour through photomontage.

3. Linguistic considerations

3.1 The reference text: the choice among different translations

As previously mentioned[244], an English translation of the Aeneid was used for both the narrative voice of the video and for the prompts to be entered into the generative AI software. Therefore, the team had to choose the reference text from the various translations of the Virgilian (Latin) text and analyse the most effective sections to craft prompts that would produce the best images[245].

The use of the English language certainly serves two purposes; similarly to myth, which inherently seeks to reach the widest audience, the first scope of this choice is to make the work as universally accessible as possible. The second reason is instead linked to the use of AI: the '*lingua franca*' of the IT world has always been English, which, is also the language that works best when prompting generative AI.

The work phases, in order, were as follows: analysis of English translations of the *Aeneid* and selection of the descriptively best version, e.g., that in which more nouns or adjectives were found, to make the generated image richer; use of the texts as *corpora* for the selection of the right words to be turned into prompts. Proceeding following a 'work in progress' situation, it was not always easy to identify the exact words to be used for the prompts and it was often necessary to make several attempts before finding the best solution.

Once the *corpora* had been chosen and the episodes for the narration had been selected, they were put together into a single text. This text was then analysed to highlight the sections suitable for the video's voice-over, the prompts, those that serve both functions, and the character dialogue, resulting in a comprehensive worksheet for the linguistic analysis.

---

[244] See Section 1.4 of Chapter 1.

[245] The translation chosen was that of A.S. Kline (2002). The translations considered instead were those of Dickinson (1961), Mandelbaum (1981), West (1990), Powell (2015), Ferry (2017), Krisak (2020) and Bartsch (2021).

The greatest constraint of this type of narration, which condenses many episodes from the *Aeneid* into just a few minutes, lies in the presentation of the characters, who had to be recognisable with just a few brief lines. This was possible by carefully deconstructing and recomposing the text and choosing images generated so that the audience could understand the plot and identify the characters from the explanation of their mutual relationships. Certainly, the music plays a fundamental role in understanding this video: thanks to the skilful variations of rhythm and sound, the viewers foresee what awaits them in the next scene.

3.2 Intersemiotic translation of the *Aeneid*: is it possible to talk about collaborative human-machine translation?

Each phase of the project featured a translation from the choice of the source text (in Latin) to that of the English translations to be fed to the generative AI software for image and video generation, up to the creation of subtitles in the languages of the countries where it is supposedly going to be disseminated (English, Turkish and Italian). More precisely, three forms of translation were done during the process. These correspond to the three ways of interpreting a linguistic sign described by Roman Jakobson in his essay *On Linguistic Aspects of Translation*[246]:

1) Intralingual translation;
2) Interlingual translation;
3) Intersemiotic translation.

Among these, the first type of translation used in the project under analysis is the interlingual translation, i.e. the interpretation of linguistic signs using the signs of another language: this is the translation in the strict sense, i.e. the English version considered instead of the Latin source text. Subsequently, the authors resorted to intralingual translation, the interpretation of linguistic signs using other signs of the same language. In this case, we speak of rewording, which is the process of creating a single text for the AI prompts, since,

[246] Roman Jakobson, 'On Linguistic Aspects of Translation', in Reuben Arthur Brower, ed., *On Translation* (Cambridge, MA: Harvard University Press, 1959), 233.

at this stage, the translated-English-version English had to be reworded to obtain another version in English optimised for the software[247].

Finally, an intersemiotic translation, also known as transmutation, was used, i.e. the interpretation of linguistic signs using non-linguistic sign systems: the written version was first translated into images and then into a video (with subtitles); the text was translated into several different languages, thus constructing a polyphonic pathway that effectively translated its interdisciplinary nature, giving rise to a reinterpretation of the source text according to new, multiple points of view.

Therefore, the end product of this process is a multimedia work resulting from a human-machine collaboration, a process in which the individual has to provide the machine with the necessary commands and rephrase the outputs, according to their decision-making power and creative spirit. From this perspective, the human and machine are two intelligences in constant dialogue, mutually nourishing and enriching each other, leading us to what could be defined as a collaborative translation between a person and an artificial intelligence. Now, in this context and for the above-mentioned specific purposes, the team developed a new working model to proceed with the intersemiotic translation required by the *AIneid* project: a model outlined in five key stages, in which, after choosing the most appropriate prompt terms to generate images, these were used to create an AI video that was subsequently edited manually.

However, given the intercultural context in which the final video was shown – encompassing English, Italian and Turkish cultures – the project also featured another phase of interlingual translation. During the same, subtitles were written in Italian and Turkish to translate the off-voice so that the video could also be enjoyed in non-English-speaking contexts. The analysis of this last interesting step is presented in the following section.

[247] See Section 2.2 Chapter 2 of this article.

3.3 Subtitles: Aegisub. The process and brief linguistic remarks

To complete this captivating translation journey – involving the transformation from the Latin source text into English translations, into AI-generated images and, lastly, into a video recounting the main events of the hero Aeneas – only one last step remains to be described, namely the creation of the subtitles. The aim was to be as universally accessible as possible and to reach a wide audience, hence the choice of subtitles in several languages and, in particular, in addition to English, also in Italian and Turkish[248].

The process[249] carried out was the following: first, the English script, complete with the narrator's voice of the video and the characters' lines, was retrieved and inserted on Aegisub, a multi-platform programme for creating subtitles for video files. Then, the audio and video sequences were synchronised with the subtitles, thus creating an English version that matched as faithfully as possible the English translation of the *Aeneid* chosen for the narrator's voice, i.e. that of A.S. Kline.

At this point, the text excerpts were translated into Italian. As the words pronounced in the video precisely match the English translation, for the subtitles an attempt was made to remain as close as possible to the already published Italian translation.

Initially, four Italian translations of the *Aeneid* were considered: those by Catena,[250] Bacchielli,[251] Vivaldi[252] and Sermonti.[253] Following a thorough linguistic analysis, the translation chosen was that of Cesare Vivaldi, since:

- In Carlo Catena's translation, although dating back to 2008, the lexicon and sentence structure in Italian are excessively complex and pretentious, thus not immediately comprehensible. Therefore, it was not suitable for

---

248 The subtitles in English and Italian were created and translated by the article's authors.

249 The reference is to the Italian versions ed. by Eleonora Gatto and Federica Villareale.

250 Virgilio, *Opere*, Carlo Catena, ed. (Torino: UTET, 2008).

251 Virgilio, *Eneide. Versione poetica, introduzione e commento di Adriano Bacchielli* (Torino: Paravia, 1963).

252 Virgilio, *Eneide. Versione poetica di Cesare Vivaldi* (Torino: Edisco, 1995).

253 Vittorio Sermonti, *L'Eneide di Virgilio* (Milano: BUR, 2007).

subtitling a video which shows only a small part of the myth and can, therefore, be difficult to follow;

- In Adriano Bacchielli's *Aeneid* which dates back to 1963 the lexicon is overall more appropriate, almost more contemporary, but the sentence structure is still not straightforward. Indeed, its rephrasing would have inevitably led to excessive divergence from the original text, which was to be avoided as much as possible;
- Sermonti's translation (2007) is perhaps the closest version to the English text, but the length of the sentences in Italian would have required cuts and rewording to meet the subtitling rules, thus leading to a text potentially too different from the original;
- In Cesare Vivaldi's 1995 translation the sentence structure and vocabulary were overall the best: adaptation to video required minimal changes, ensuring higher fidelity to the text.

Table 6.1 Comparison of the Italian versions

English version (A.S. Kline)	Catena's translation	Bacchielli's translation	Vivaldi's translation	Sermonti's translation[254]
I went there, and founded my first city named Aeneadae from my name.	Mi portò colà e le mura incomincio a porre di una città, e il nome di Eneade, dal mio nome, le creo. (En, III, 16-18) [It took me there and the walls I began to lay of a city, and the name Aenead, after my name, I created them.]	Là mi volsi, e presto sorsero le prime mura che dal mio nome Eneade chiamai. (En, III, 24-27) [There I turned, and soon the first walls arose, which I called Enead after my name.]	Qui dunque vado a sbarcare, edifico le prime mura di una città che chiamo Eneade, dal mio nome. (En, III, 23-25) [Here, therefore, I go to disembark and build the first walls of a city that I call Aenead, after my name.]	Lì mi ritrovo e sulla spiaggia curva pongo le prime pietre di una città; dal mio nome le assegno il nome di Eneade. (En, III,15-17) [There I find myself and on the curved beach I lay the first stones of a city; after my name I name it Aenead.]

However, some adjustments were necessary, both for reasons of consistency and to adapt lexical choices that would have created an estrangement effect, and for the restrictions of subtitling; thus, reading all four versions proved to be essential to create effective subtitles. Below is a brief analysis of some of the strategies implemented.

- **Condensation or rephrasing:** the most frequently used technique in this work is that of condensation (or rephrasing), which aims to synthesise the text, avoiding loss of information. For instance, as shown in the table below, in the second segment several sentences have been modified to reduce the number of characters, due to the length limits imposed by the subtitling.
- **Deletion:** through cuts and omissions, a total reduction of certain parts of the text, considered 'expendable', was made. For example, the adjective

254 All translations into English have been made by the authors.

'fitta' [thick] was omitted, in favour of a shorter sentence that complied with CPS,[255] in the sentence 'C'era lì vicino una macchia fitta' [There was nearby a thick bush].

- **Additions:** rarely – where it was necessary and feasible for reasons of fidelity to the text, it was chosen to add elements that resembled the English version, to avoid the loss of information when switching from one language to another. For instance, in the first segment, specifying that the action took place 'tra le rovine' [among the ruins] of the city was necessary for the setting of the scene.
- **Inversion:** on one occasion, the element order of the sentence (which did not coincide between Italian and English) had to be inverted so that the viewer could benefit from the information while being presented by the voice-over. This was the case of the second segment in which the sentence 'Oh Enea, caro marito' [oh Enea, dear husband] was brought forward (here, the vocative 'Oh Enea' was added for the reasons described in the previous point).
- **Change of verb tenses:** for text standardisation (and fidelity to the English off-voice), some verb tenses were changed, mostly from the present to the 'passato remoto' [remote past]. Consequently, some deictics were also adapted, such as 'there' instead of 'here'.
- **Lexical modifications:** in some cases, for greater fidelity to the English (and Latin) text or for a better and immediate understanding of certain terms (considering that the translation of the *Aeneid* used as reference dates back to 1995, some lexical modifications were necessary. For example, 'primavera' [spring] which became 'estate' (as in Latin, *aestas*, summer) or 'polloni' [shoots] which became 'germogli' [sprouts].

The above-mentioned examples can be found in Table 6.2.

[255] Characters per second.

Table 6.2 Examples of modifications

Strategy	Aeneid, A.S. Kline (2002)	Eneide, Cesare Vivaldi (1995)	Adaptation for subtitles AIneid (2024)
Condensation or rephrasing	This has not happened without the divine will Yours is long exile, and you will come to Hesperia's land.	Ciò che accade **l'ha deciso la ferma volontà dei celesti**. **Dovrai affrontare** un lunghissimo esilio, **e infine** arriverai al paese di Esperia. [What happens **has been decided by the firm will of the celestials.** **You will have to face** a very long exile, **and finally** you will arrive in the country of Esperia.]	Ciò che accade **segue il volere degli dèi**. **Affronterai** un **lungo** esilio e arriverai a Esperia. [What happens **follows the will of the gods.** **You will face** a **long** exile and arrive in the country of Esperia.]
Deletion	There was a mound nearby.	C'era lì vicino una macchia fitta, [There was nearby a thick bush,]	C'era lì vicino una macchia ~~fitta~~, [There was nearby a bush,]
Addition	Among the city roofs, the unhappy ghost and true shadow of Creusa appeared before my eyes.	**[...] per tutte le case** della città, mi apparì l'immagine infelice di Creusa, l'immenso suo fantasma. [**[...] throughout all the houses** of the city, appeared to me the unhappy image of Creusa, the immense ghost of her.]	**Tra le rovine** della città, mi apparì l'immagine infelice di Creusa, l'immenso suo fantasma. **[Among the ruins** of the city, the unhappy image of Creusa, her immense ghost, appeared to me.]

Strategy	**Aeneid, A.S. Kline (2002)**	**Eneide, Cesare Vivaldi (1995)**	**Adaptation for subtitles AIneid (2024)**
Inversion (+ addition)	Oh Eneas, sweet husband, what use is it to indulge in such mad grief?	Perché ti lasci andare ciecamente al dolore, **caro marito**? [Why do you blindly give in to pain, **dear husband**?]	**Oh Enea, caro marito**, perché ti lasci andare ciecamente al dolore? **[Oh Aeneas, dear husband**, why do you blindly give in to pain?]
Change of verb tenses	I went there and founded my first city named Aeneadae from my name.	Qui dunque **vado** a sbarcare, **edifico** le prime mura di una città che **chiamo** Eneade, dal mio nome. [Here, therefore, I **go** to **disembark**, and **build** the first walls of a city that I call Aenead, after my name.]	**Lì** ~~dunque~~ **sbarcai, edificai** le ~~prime~~ mura di una città che **chiamai** Eneade, dal mio nome. [**There** I **disembarked**, and **built** the first walls of a city that I **called** Aenead, after my name.]
Lexical modifications	Here a crop of iron spears carpeted my transfixed corpse, and has ripened into sharp spines.	Una ferrea messe di dardi qui mi ha trafitto, ed è cresciuta con tenaci radici e sottili **polloni**. [A fierce mass of darts here pierced me, and it grew with tenacious roots and thin **shoots**.]	Una ferrea messe di dardi qui mi ha trafitto, ed è cresciuta con tenaci radici e sottili **germogli**. [A fierce mass of darts here pierced me, and it grew with tenacious roots and thin **sprouts**.]

4. Conclusions

The creative potential of AI is increasingly enabling a more 'literary' approach to adapting original texts into video content, also due to the textual nature of text-to-image (T2I) and image-to-video (I2V) conversion processes[256].

However, given the temporal distance between the present moment and the period of the text under analysis (over 3,000 years ago) and aiming to create audiovisual content based on the precise indications provided by literary sources, it is clear that AI software still has crippling technical limitations that affect aesthetic and narrative choices. This is particularly true in phases where certain parameters have to be met to achieve a specific outcome. As a matter of fact, the further back in the past, the scarcer the available data are, and the generative process seems to be much less accurate than it is possible in archaeological investigation. This aspect imposes a fundamental role on the human side, which acts as a form of '*figurative checker*'[257] that collaborates with the machine.

Another issue with this software is the limitations arising from biases, content policies and regulations, which, in turn, make the task of converting text into images and video more difficult, thus requiring greater creativity from the human. Despite all these challenges, the potential of generative AI software along with its attractiveness in the various fields of investigation drives scholars to experiment with it, giving rise to innovative and fascinating products, as in the case of the video generated for this project.

In conclusion, to rephrase Morotti's own words, we are witnessing the advent of a new phase, that of a pre-cinema age of AI. Much like in the early days of cinema, today's pioneering enthusiasm for AI figuration, coupled with the desire to achieve natural and realistic results[258], has made the primary focus of software development verisimilitude, photographic credibility

256 Morotti, 'Towards new forms of visual narrative: AIneid, Virgil's *Aeneid* in the Age of AI'.

257 Morotti, 'Towards new forms of visual narrative: AIneid, Virgil's *Aeneid* in the Age of AI'.

258 Stephen Neale, *Cinema and Technology: Image, Sound, Colour* (Bloomington: Indiana University Press, 1985).

and the two-dimensional illusion of space and movement[259], which could exponentially enhance the already remarkable potential of generative AI.

References

Bertazzoli, Raffaella, 'Natura universale del mito', in Piero Gibellini, and Raffaella Bertazzoli, eds, *Il mito nella letteratura italiana: miti senza frontiere*, vol. 5 (Brescia: Morcelliana, 2009), 5-25.

De Masi, Vincenzo, and Quinke Di, 'AI and the Future of Cinema: The Transformative Impact of *Our T2 Remake*', *LAB Research* (2024), 2.

Franceschelli, Vincenzo, *Creatività e Intelligenza Artificiale*, intervento presso gli Stati Generali del Diritto di Internet e della Intelligenza Artificiale (Roma: Luiss, 2023).

Gaskell, Philip, *Landmarks in Classical Literature* (Chicago: Fitzroy Dearborn Publishers, 1999).

Guo, Biying et al., 'A Comparative Study on the Features and Applications of AI Tools -Focus on PIKA Labs and RUNWAY', *International Journal of Internet, Broadcasting and Communication* 16/1 (2024), 86-91.

Jakobson, Roman, 'On Linguistic Aspects of Translation', in Reuben Arthur Brower, ed., *On Translation* (Cambridge, MA: Harvard University Press, 1959), 232-39.

Jurafsky, Daniel, and James H. Martin, *Speech and Language Processing. An Introduction to Natural Language Processing, Computational Linguistics, and Speech Recognition*, 3rd February 2024 draft, <https://web.stanford.edu/~jurafsky/slp3/ed3bookfeb3_2024.pdf>, accessed 6 June 2024.

Manovich, Lev, 'AI image and Generative Media: Notes on Ongoing Revolution', in Lev Manovich, and Emanuele Arielli, eds, *Artificial Aesthetics: Generative AI, Art and Visual Media* (2023), <https://manovich.net/content/04-projects/175-artificial-aesthetics/manovich-ai-image-and-generative-media.pdf>, accessed 25 September 2024.

[259] Curiosity Podcast (7 December 2023), *The future of generative ai video with Cristóbal Valenzuela, ceo and co-founder of Runway* [Substack newsletter], Curiosity's Substack,<https://curiositypodcast.substack.com/p/the-future-of-generative-ai-video>, accessed 20 August 2024.

Martinetto, Giulia, *Stima dei modelli di diffusione nei servizi: applicazione al caso di una media company italiana*, Tesi di Laurea Magistrale (Torino: Politecnico di Torino, 2019), <https://webthesis.biblio.polito.it/secure/10571/1/tesi.pdf>, accessed 6 June 2024.

Morotti, Fabio, 'Towards new forms of visual narrative: AIneid, Virgil's *Aeneid* in the Age of AI', *Nova Science Publishing* (forthcoming).

Neale, Stephen, *Cinema and Technology: Image, Sound, Colour* (Bloomington: Indiana University Press, 1985).

Pavlichenko, Nikita, and Dmitry Ustalov, 'Best Prompts for Text-to-Image Models and How to Find Them', arXiv (2022), <https://arxiv.org/abs/2209.11711>, accessed 6 June 2024.

Petrone, Angela, *To Use or Be Used: AI-Generated Content as a Human Technical Exercise,* speech at the conference *Artificial Creativity. Looking At the Future of Digital Culture* (Milan: SAE Institute, June 2024).

Schlegel, Friedrich, *Discorso sulla mitologia* (1800).

Sermonti, Vittorio, *L'Eneide di Virgilio* (Milano: BUR, 2007).

Virgil, *Aeneid,* trans. by Shadi Bartsch (New York: Random House, 2021).

Virgil, *The Aeneid,* trans. by Patric Dickinson (New York: New American Library, 1961).

Virgil, *The Aeneid,* trans. by David Ferry (Chicago: University of Chicago Press, 2017).

Virgil, *The Aeneid,* trans. by A.S. Kline (Moscow, Idaho: Roman Roads Media, 2015).

Virgil, *The Aeneid of Virgil*, trans. by Allen Mandelbaum (New York: Bantam Classics, 1981).

Virgil, *Aeneid*, trans. by Len Krisak (Philadelphia, PA: University of Pennsylvania Press, 2020).

Virgil, *The Aeneid*, trans. and edited by Barry Powell (Oxford: Oxford University Press, 2015).

Virgil, *The Aeneid,* trans. and edited by David West (London: Penguin Classics, 1990).

Virgilio, *Eneide. Versione poetica di Cesare Vivaldi* (Torino: Edisco, 1995).

Virgilio, *Eneide. Versione poetica, introduzione e commento di Adriano Bacchielli* (Torino: Paravia, 1963).

Virgilio, *Opere*, Carlo Catena, ed. (Torino: UTET, 2008).

Xi, Chen, and Jeanhun Chung, 'A Study on Character Design using [Midjourney] Application', *International Journal of Advanced Culture Technology* 11/2 (2023), 409-14.

Websites

'Aeneas: myth and history', Aeneas Route Association, <https://www.aeneasroute.org/en/the-myth/#:~:text=The%20myth%20of%20the%20journey,crossed%20by%20countless%20routes%20of>, accessed 9 July 2024.

'Creativity', Oxford Learner's Dictionaries, <https://www.oxfordlearnersdictionaries.com/definition/english/creativity#:~:text=%E2%80%8Bthe%20use%20of%20skill,new%20or%20to%20produce%20art.>, accessed 14 June 2024.

De Giglio, Paolo, 'AI e arte: creatività e generazione di contenuti nell'età dell'intelligenza artificiale', Colibryx, <https://colibryx.com/blog/ai-e-arte-creativita-e-generazione-di-contenuti-nell-eta-dell-intelligenza-artificiale>, accessed 14 June 2024.

'Drone Cinematography: How to create Cinematic Masterpieces', Drone U (2023), <https://www.thedroneu.com/blog/drone-cinematography-guide/#:~:text=In%20drone%20cinematography%2C%20only%20unmanned,visual%20impact%20to%20their%20projects>, accessed 14 June 2024.

'Modelli generativi e discriminativi a confronto', Human And Artificial Intelligence (2023), <https://www.humai.it/modelli-generativi-e-discriminativi-a-confronto/>, accessed 6 June 2024.

'Nell'era dell'AI che significa essere creativi?', LinkedIn (2023), <https://www.linkedin.com/pulse/nellera-dellai-che-significa-essere-creativi-francesco-elmi-sdjtf/>, accessed 14 June 2024.

'Pentecontera', Nautipedia, <https://www.nautipedia.it/index.php/Pentecontera>, accessed 24 July 2024.

Podcast episode: Curiosity Podcast (7 December 2023), *The future of generative AI video with Cristóbal Valenzuela, CEO and co-founder of Runway* [Substack newsletter], Curiosity's Substack, <https://curiositypodcast.substack.com/p/the-future-of-generative-ai-video>, accessed 20 August 2024.

'Trireme', Oxford Learner's Dictionaries, <https://www.oxfordlearnersdictionaries.com/definition/english/trireme?q=trireme>, accessed 24 July 2024.

Aeneasroute, <https://www.aeneasroute.org/en/>, accessed 14 June 2024.

Chatbotapp.ai,<https://chatbotapp.ai/imagegeneration?utm_source=GoogleAds&utm_medium=cpc&utm_campaign=%7bcampaign%7d&utm_id=21156944805&utm_term=164296649201&utm_content=695813707413&gad_source=1&gclid=CjwKCAjwmYCzBhA6EiwAxFwfgFsc-1bJogAxHr9TsonH3db7TazDzaRcE_xaetvHE9fTJxA14D4ZHBoCXQsQAvD_BwE>, accessed 5 June 2024.

Discord, <https://discord.com/servers/midjourney-662267976984297473>, accessed 3 June 2024.

Openai, <https://openai.com/index/dall-e/>, accessed 5 June 2024.

Picsart <https://picsart.com/ai-image-generator/>, accessed 5 June 2024.

Sketchfab, <https://sketchfab.com/HLab>, accessed 2 August 2024.

7

A New Frontier of Human-Machine Interaction: Simultaneous Interpreting in Virtual Reality

Valentina Baselli, Manuela Comoglio, Claudio Russello

Abstract

In recent years, the interest in the Metaverse and the use of Virtual Reality (VR) for training purposes has notably increased. These immersive environments represent a new frontier of human-interpreter interaction, where interpreters immerse themselves in new worlds and interact using their avatars and VR headsets. This contribution aims to shed light on the dynamics of the interpreter-VR interaction and to present the results of a case study conducted at IULM University during interpreters' training in VR. In these sessions, MA students in Conference Interpreting had the opportunity to take part in experimental classes focused on practising activities such as sight translation, shadowing and simultaneous interpreting within simulated realistic working environments, including a conference hall equipped with interpreting booths, all within the immersive setting of the metaverse.

Introduction

Throughout history and across various cultures, interpreting has enabled communication between different peoples and regions, overcoming language barriers, and solving the problem of incommunicability among human beings. However, the development of interpreting as a profession is quite recent and has always gone hand in hand with technological innovation. In the 1920s, discoveries in the field of electronics paved the way for the invention of voice transmission systems that were later adapted to simultaneous interpreting (SI). 'In simultaneous mode, the interpreter sits in a booth with a clear view of the meeting room and the speaker and listens to and simultaneously interprets the speech into a target language'[260].

In traditional SI, interpreters listen to the speaker's speech through headphones and translate it into a microphone for the audience, who listens to the target text through earphones. However, over time, new forms of SI (such as oversound, bidule and remote interpreting, have developed thanks to technological advances. The digitalisation of activities has also affected interpreting, which has recently gone through a technological turn[261].

In recent years, particularly in the wake of the COVID-19 pandemic, there has also been a significant interest in a new technology that had previously received little attention in interpreting and interpreters' training: virtual reality (VR) and virtual learning environments (VLEs). These immersive technologies 'can be exploited to support individual and collaborative learning, especially by providing a social "space" where learning can take place. VLEs aspire to create a sense of presence or immersion'[262] and have emerged as a promising avenue for interpreters' education.

From this perspective, virtual reality and virtual learning environments for interpreters' training can be understood as innovative tools for human-machine interaction, i.e. the interaction between technologies and interpreters.

In human-machine interaction, people and technology interact in the pursuit of a shared overarching goal, with technology being considered part of this system[263]. In this context, 'technology facilitates this collaboration across time and space, with multiple parties able to work independently and

260 Kilian Seeber, 'Simultaneous Interpreting', in Holly Mikkelson, and Renée Jourdenais, eds, *Routledge handbook of interpreting* (London / New York: Taylor and Francis, 2015), 80.

261 Claudio Fantinuoli, 'Interpreting and technology: the upcoming technological turn', in Claudio Fantinuoli, ed., *Interpreting and Technology* (Berlin: Language Science Press, 2018), 1-12.

262 Sabine Braun, Elena Davitti, and Catherine Slater, 'It's like being in bubbles: Affordances and challenges of virtual learning environments for collaborative learning in interpreter education', *The Interpreter and Translator Trainer* 14/3 (2020), 1.

263 Christopher D. Mellinger, 'Embedding, extending and distributing interpreter cognition with technology', in Gloria Corpas Pastor, and Bart Defrancq, eds, *Interpreting Technologies – current and future trends* (Amsterdam / New York: John Benjamins Publishing Company, 2023); John M. Carroll, *HCI Models, Theories, and Frameworks:*

extend their capabilities beyond what is possible individually'[264]. Against this backdrop, interpreter-technology interaction is essential for the execution of simultaneous interpreting, which would be unfeasible without a microphone, headsets, earphones, console, soft console and all the equipment necessary for SI.

As previously mentioned, the new technological breakthrough of virtual reality is getting increasingly closer to interpreting. This new technology involves the use of VR headsets to join virtual environments and the metaverse through the creation of avatars. However, while the potential of VR in education has already been widely investigated[265], further exploration is needed

Toward a Multidisciplinary Science (New York: Elsevier, 2003); Phil Turner, *HCI Redux: the Promise of Post-Cognitive Interaction* (Berlin: Springer, 2016).

264 Mellinger, 'Embedding, extending and distributing interpreter cognition with technology', in Corpas Pastor, and Defrancq, eds, *Interpreting Technologies – current and future trends*, 206; for further details, see Itiel E. Dror, and Stevan Harnad, *Cognition distributed: How Cognitive Technology Extends Our Minds* (Amsterdam / Philadelphia: John Benjamins Publishing Company, 2008).

265 Marco Romano, Alessandro Frolli, Alessandro Aloisio, Claudio Russello, Angelo Rega, Francesco Cerciello, and Fabio Bisogni, 'Exploring the Potential of Immersive Virtual Reality in Italian Schools: A Practical Workshop with High School Teachers', *Multimodal Technologies and Interaction* 7/12 (2023), 111; Venus Chan, 'Using a virtual reality mobile application for interpreting learning: Listening to the students' voice', *Interactive Learning Environments* 32/6 (2022), 2438–51; Venus Chan, 'Investigating the impact of a virtual reality mobile application on learners' interpreting competence', *Journal of Computer Assisted Learning* (2023), 1–17; Sabine Braun, Catherine Slater, Robert Gittins, Panagiotis Ritsos, and Jonathan C. Roberts, 'Interpreting in Virtual Reality: designing and developing a 3D virtual world to prepare interpreters and their clients for professional practice', in Don Kiraly, Silvia Hansen-Schirra, and Karin Maksymski, eds, *New Prospects and Perspectives for Educating Language Mediators* (Berlin: Gunter Narr Verlag Editors, 2013), 93–120; Sabine Braun, Catherine Slater, and Nicholas Botfield, 'Evaluating the pedagogical affordances of a bespoke 3D virtual learning environment for training interpreters and their clients', in Suzanne Ehrlich, and Jemina Napier, eds, *Interpreter Education in the Digital Age: Innovation, Access, and Change* (Washington: Gallaudet University Press, 2014), 39–67; Sabine Braun, and Catherine Slater, 'Populating a 3D virtual learning environment for interpreting students with bilingual dialogues to support situated learning in an institutional context', *The Interpreter and Translator Trainer* 8/3 (2014), 469–85; Braun, Davitti, and Slater, 'It's like being in bubbles: Affordances and challenges of virtual learning environments for collaborative learning in interpreter education', 1-18.

in simultaneous interpreting training using VR technology along with the 'avatar-interpreter' in virtual reality events. Therefore, this contribution intends to foreground the human interpreter-VR interaction, by outlining this new type of interpreters' training. In particular, the first section provides an overview of VR, its main features and its possible applications in education, followed by a description of different forms of interpreter-VR interaction, namely interpreting in virtual events, augmented interpreting and interpreters' training (Section 2). Section 3 presents a case study on interpreters' training in VR where simultaneous interpreting with VR headsets was also experimented, while the closing addresses the main difficulties experienced and the potential for future research on this topic.

1.What is Virtual Reality

1.1 Definition, characteristics and applications

VR has emerged as a transformative technology with far-reaching implications across various fields, including simultaneous interpreting. However, to fully understand the potential impact of these technologies, it is crucial to define VR and distinguish between related concepts and subclasses. As Milgram and Kishino state, 'the VR label is frequently used in association with a variety of other environments, to which total immersion and complete synthesis do not necessarily pertain'[266]. These include Augmented Reality (AR), Mixed Reality (MR) and the metaverse. This section provides an overview of such technologies, exploring their definitions, key characteristics and existing applications in education across various fields.

In this context, as the authors suggest, virtual reality can be defined as a computer-generated simulation of a three-dimensional environment that can be interacted with in a way that makes it appear real by the person using special electronic equipment, such as a headset with a stereoscopic screen. Therefore in VR, the user is completely immersed in a simulated environment, typically through a head-mounted display (HMD) that excludes the physical world from sight.

[266] Paul Milgram, and Fumio Kishino, 'A taxonomy of mixed reality visual displays', *IEICE Transactions on Information Systems* 77/12 (1994), 1321–9.

Augmented reality, in contrast to VR, enhances the physical world with virtual content. In an AR system, the user can still perceive the real world, but with additional digital information overlaid onto it. Augmented reality does not necessarily need HMDs, which users may still find heavy and uncomfortable, as reported in the questionnaires of our study (see §3.3). Instead, it can be achieved through smartphones, tablets or even smart glasses, which are becoming increasingly popular and affordable in the marketplace.

Mixed reality can be seen as a more advanced form of AR, where virtual objects can, not only be overlaid on the real world, but can also interact with it. In MR, real and virtual worlds are more seamlessly blended, allowing for more complex interactions between physical and digital elements[267].

The metaverse is a concept that goes beyond individual VR, AR or MR experiences. While there is no single, universally accepted definition of a metaverse[268], the 'metaverse' concept refers to a shared three-dimensional virtual environment where people can interact with each other and with digital objects in an immersive manner. Key features of the metaverse include the presence of multiple scenarios and worlds, social interaction through avatars, the existence of a virtual economy and the possibility of customising personal avatars and spaces. Another key feature of the metaverse is that it is a persistent and continuous environment remaining active even when users disconnect.

1.2 Key characteristics: immersion, interactivity and sensory engagement

The efficacy of virtual reality experiences is commonly referred to in the literature based on the following key characteristics: immersion, interactivity and sensory engagement. The following section presents an analysis of these key characteristics, with a focus on their relevance for interpreters.

The term 'immersion' is used to describe the sensation of being physically present within a non-physical environment. In the context of VR, this sense

[267] Milgram, and Kishino, 'A taxonomy of mixed reality visual displays'.

[268] Romano, Frolli, Aloisio, Russello, Rega, Cerciello, and Bisogni, 'Exploring the Potential of Immersive Virtual Reality in Italian Schools: A Practical Workshop with High School Teachers'.

of immersion, or the 'illusion of being there'[269], is primarily achieved through multisensory stimulation, mainly based on visual and auditory inputs. In the case of interpreters, a high level of immersion can favour the highest level of concentration, together with a more nuanced comprehension of the context and subtleties of the source material, thereby enhancing their ability to convey meaning accurately. Often, the degree of immersion can be assessed by how well this virtual environment manages to 'switch off' or reduce sensations and distractions from the real world.

Another defining feature of VR is its interactivity, which enables users to engage with and influence their surroundings. Currently, such interaction is commonly achieved by tools such as hand controllers and/or gesture recognition systems. The degree of interactivity is of paramount importance in influencing the user's sense of presence and overall engagement within the virtual environment as it enables a more personalised and dynamic experience. The ability to interact with their surroundings is also critical for interpreters who frequently find themselves relying on objects and equipment, interacting with people around them, moving around their workplace, and so forth. Indeed, AR/MR solutions that enable interactivity – as shown in the following sections (see §2.2) – are the most promising for the interaction between interpreters and virtual reality technologies.

Lastly, sensory engagement aims to involve multiple senses in order to create a persuasive illusion of reality. While contemporary consumer VR systems are still focused on visual and auditory stimulation, ongoing research is exploring additional modalities such as haptic feedback, simulated temperature changes and olfactory stimulation[270]. For interpreters, engaging multiple senses can enhance comprehension, memory activation and retention, but also recall, which are critical for effective interpretation. These advancements are designed to further enhance the sensory experience, making VR not just a visual or auditory medium but rather a holistic environment that engages users, as well as future interpreters, on multiple levels.

---

269 Mel Slater, 'Immersion and the illusion of presence in virtual reality', *British Journal of Psychology* 109/3 (2018), 431–3.

270 Jordan Tewell, and Nimesha Ranasinghe, 'A Review of Olfactory Display Designs for Virtual Reality Environments', *ACM Computing Survey* 56/11 (2024), article 276.

1.3 VR applications in education

The potential of VR in education has been recognised across various disciplines and 'an ongoing stream of literature champions the success of VR-enhanced instruction, showcasing improved outcomes compared to traditional lecture-based formats'[271]. A recent study carried out at the UNINT University of Rome[272] explored the potential of immersive VR in Italian schools through a practical workshop with high school teachers. The study underscored considerable interest in VR technology within various educational domains, suggesting its potential as a powerful tool for student skills development. However, the authors emphasised that targeted training and purposeful curriculum design would be necessary for a more seamless integration of VR into educational practices. This section aims to present three VR applications that the authors find beneficial for the design of training curricula.

Distance learning: VR platforms like Horizon Workrooms by Meta[273] offer immersive virtual classrooms where students and teachers can interact as if they were physically present in the same space. These environments allow for the use of body language, virtual whiteboards and the share of resources from personal computers, potentially addressing issues of disengagement often associated with traditional online learning.

Immersive videos: 360-degree videos and interactive VR experiences can transport students to different locations and historical periods, providing contextual learning experiences that would be impossible or impractical in the real world. For example, students can take virtual tours of museums, explore ancient civilisations or even visit other planets, enhancing their understanding and retention of complex subjects.

---

271 Romano, Frolli, Aloisio, Russello, Rega, Cerciello, and Bisogni, 'Exploring the Potential of Immersive Virtual Reality in Italian Schools: A Practical Workshop with High School Teachers', 2.

272 Romano, Frolli, Aloisio, Russello, Rega, Cerciello, and Bisogni, 'Exploring the Potential of Immersive Virtual Reality in Italian Schools: A Practical Workshop with High School Teachers'.

273 Horizon Workrooms, <https://www.meta.com/it-it/experiences/meta-horizon-workrooms-beta/2514011888645651/>, accessed 4 September 2024.

Situated learning: VR allows learners to engage with content in authentic settings that reflect real-world scenarios. This is crucial for situated learning, which posits that knowledge is best understood when applied in relevant contexts, allowing for a learning-by-doing approach[274]. For instance, VR can simulate environments in fields such as engineering, medicine and language learning, enabling learners to practise skills in a safe, controlled manner that mirrors real-life situations and promotes monitoring and feedback by trainers[275].

The applications of VR in education extend beyond these examples, with potential uses in many fields including interpreter training, as explored in the next sections (see § 2.3).

2. Interpreter-VR interaction

The emerging VR technologies described in the previous sections are opening up new frontiers in how language interpretation is implemented and taught. This emerging intersection of cutting-edge technology and the age-old practice of facilitating cross-language communication presents both exciting opportunities and unique challenges for the interpreting profession.

This section will present an analysis of the three main reasons why the interpreting field and VR/AR technologies are increasingly interacting, transforming the work of interpreters. First, it will consider how these innovations are changing the contexts in which interpreting can take place (the setting). Second, it will examine the impact of new VR technologies on the performance and effectiveness of interpreting itself (the process). Third, it will analyse how new technologies are influencing the training of future interpreting professionals (the training), with an overview of previous studies revealing generally favourable attitudes among users towards the functionality, usability and immersive learning experiences within VR environments.

274 Hayne W. Reese, 'The learning-by-doing principle', *Behavioral Development Bulletin* 17/1 (2011), 1–19.

275 Pingping Hu, Bin Gao, and Ke Li, 'Learning interpreting in virtual reality: a scoping review', *Interactive Learning Environments* (2024), 1–20.

2.1 Interpreting in VR

As virtual reality technologies become widespread for holding remote events across industries, a new frontier is emerging in the field of interpretation: interpreting within VR environments. This novel approach, on which the case study in the following sections is based (see §3), presents both opportunities and challenges for the profession.

The primary advantage of interpreting in VR is the potential for enhanced spatial presence. In traditional remote interpreting setups, interpreters often feel disconnected from the event they are interpreting. VR can bridge this gap by placing the interpreter in a virtual representation of the actual venue, complete with 360-degree views of speakers, audience and visual aids. This immersive experience can improve the interpreter's understanding of the context and situational details, leading to more accurate and nuanced renditions. Additionally, the sense of immersion of VR environments can also improve the ability to stay focused only on the speakers to be interpreted, preventing potential distractions from the physical environment such as movements in the conference hall, activity inside the interpreting booths, annoying lights and so forth[276].

However, interpreting in VR also presents unique challenges. The technology requires interpreters to adapt to new interfaces and potentially manage additional cognitive load. For instance, interpreters may need to navigate virtual spaces, interact with digital objects, or manage their virtual presence while simultaneously performing their primary task of interpretation. Additionally, the need to manage any technical difficulties arising from using VR headsets and controllers could potentially affect the interpreters' performance and lead to the so-called 'cybersickness'. Many of these drawbacks have been confirmed in the questionnaires of our case study (see §3.3).

Another consideration is the potential for VR to alter the dynamics of interpreter-client relationships. In traditional settings, interpreters often rely on subtle physical cues and face-to-face interactions to build rapport and trust

[276] Erik Camayd-Freixas, 'Cognitive theory of simultaneous interpreting and training', *Proceedings of the 52nd Conference of the American Translators Association* (New York: ATA, 2011).

with clients. VR interpreting necessitates new strategies for establishing this critical professional relationship in a virtual space.

2.2 Augmented Interpreting

Augmented interpreting refers to the enhancement of the interpreter's capabilities through the use of technology, particularly augmented reality. This innovative approach combines the human interpreter's skills with immersive and interactive features to create a more efficient and effective interpretation process.

A recent pilot study conducted by researchers at the ZHAW (the Zurich University of Applied Sciences) explores the potential of AR technology to support interpreters[277]. The study focuses on using AR glasses to display suggestions in the target language for the most common problem triggers in interpreting, namely technical terms, numbers or proper names, whenever they are uttered by the speaker in the source language. This approach aims to solve a critical problem in simultaneous interpreting: the need for interpreters to redirect their visual attention away from the speaker to consult glossaries or computer screens. As project leader Anne Catherine Gieshoff explains,

> Regardless of whether the interpreter uses a glossary or a CAI-tool, they still need to redirect their visual attention because the glossary or the CAI output is displayed on a computer screen which is usually much lower in the interpreter's field of vision than the speaker is.[278]

This shift in attention can momentarily destabilise the interpreter, disrupting the delicate balance between comprehending the source text and producing the target text. The ZHAW study involved professional conference

277 Anne Catherine Gieshoff, and Martin Schuler, 'The augmented interpreter: a pilot study on the use of augmented reality in interpreting', *3rd HKBU International Conference on Interpreting: Interpreting and Technology, Hong-Kong (Online), 7-9 December 2022* (2022).

278 Anne Catherine Gieshoff, 'The augmented interpreter: The future of simultaneous interpreting?', Zürcher Hochschule für Angewandte Wissenschaften (2022), <https://blog.zhaw.ch/languagematters/2022/12/22/augmented-reality/>, accessed 4 September 2024.

interpreters interpreting a technical talk while wearing AR glasses. During the interpretation, they received suggestions for technical terms, numbers or proper names, which appear in the target language whenever the speaker uses them in the source language. The words appear in a semi-transparent blue box that can be positioned anywhere in the interpreter's field of view, allowing for customisation based on individual preferences.

It appears plausible to hypothesise that the rapid advancements in smart glasses technology, coupled with the growing adoption of Computer-Assisted Interpreting tools (CAI tools) among interpreters, will give rise to a novel form of interpreting assistance. In this envisioned scenario, future interpreters may utilise smart glasses rather than traditional laptops or tablets to access CAI software. The suggestions and support provided by these tools would be seamlessly integrated into the interpreter's field of view, without the need for a separate display. This integration would allow interpreters to receive real-time assistance, such as terminology suggestions or speech transcriptions, without drawing attention from the speaker and the audience. Consequently, interpreters may be able to enhance their performance in a natural and unnoticeable manner, leveraging the capabilities of CAI tools through smart glasses technology.

2.3 Interpreters' Training

VR and AR technologies offer unprecedented opportunities for enhancing the training of interpreters. VR addresses the gap in traditional interpreter training methods by providing immersive, realistic simulations that can be customised to meet specific learning objectives. Key advantages include the ability to create and practice in diverse and challenging scenarios, develop the essential skill of maintaining focus amidst distractions and stressful circumstances, incorporate advanced feedback mechanisms and facilitate peer learning and remote mentoring.

One illustrative example is the project of situated learning implemented by a group of researchers at Monash University, concerned with the development of a VR training program for community interpreters engaged in the field of family violence (FV)[279]. This initiative aims to address the pressing need for effective interpreter training, particularly in the many contexts of community interpreting, where interpreters often face complex emotional and situational challenges. The authors assert that the VR project offers 'evidence-based, pedagogically sound, authentic, situated learning scenarios in a safe, virtual environment', which is crucial for adequately preparing students to navigate the complexities of their role effectively. The training enables interpreters to engage in simulated tasks involving victims of FV, social workers, police and other pertinent stakeholders. This immersive experience was designed to enhance the interpreters' skills in real-world scenarios, thereby improving their readiness to assist culturally and linguistically diverse (CALD) communities, who are particularly vulnerable in FV situations.

The significant attention gained over the last two decades by integrating VR, VLEs and immersive technologies in interpreting training is reflected in the academic contributions published in recent years. In addition to the aforementioned studies conducted within the Universities of Zurich and Monash, the present literature review summarises key findings from studies that explore the opportunities and challenges of these innovative approaches.

One of the pioneering projects in virtual reality learning environments for interpreters' training was led by Sabine Braun as early as 2012 and presented in a number of papers in the following years[280]. This project resulted in the development of the IVY/EVIVA resource, a virtual learning environment designed to support students in business and community interpreting training.

---

[279] Leah Gerber, Jim Hlavac, Irwyn Shepherd, Paul McIntosh, Alexander Avella Archila, and Hyein Ellen Cho, 'Stepping into the future: virtual reality training for community interpreters working in the area of family violence', *Journal of Specialised Translation* 36b (2021), 252–75.

[280] Braun, Slater, Gittins, Ritsos, and Roberts 'Interpreting in Virtual Reality: designing and developing a 3D virtual world to prepare interpreters and their clients for professional practice', in Kiraly, Hansen-Schirra, and Maksymski, eds, *New Prospects and Perspectives for Educating Language Mediators*; Braun, Slater, and Botfield. 'Evaluating the pedagogical affordances of a bespoke 3D virtual learning environment for training interpreters and their clients', in Ehrlich, and Napier, eds, *Interpreter Education in the Digital Age: Innovation, Access, and Change*; Braun, and Slater, 'Populating a 3D virtual learning environment for interpreting students with bilingual dialogues to support situated learning in an institutional context'.

IVY/EVIVA was created using the 3D environment 'Second Life', which was accessed through a standard computer screen rather than a headset. While this approach had its advantages, such as wider accessibility, it might lack the immersive experience that modern virtual reality headsets can provide.

More recently, Hu, Gao and Li[281] performed a scoping review on learning to interpret in virtual reality. Their analysis identified key themes in VR use for interpreters' training, highlighting its potential to foster engagement and improve outcomes, while calling for further research to establish best practices.

In two papers published in 2022 and 2023, Chan[282] investigates the effectiveness of a mobile-based virtual reality application designed to enhance interpreting competence among learners. It reports significant improvements in students' self-rated language and interpreting proficiency following the use of the application.

Braun, Davitti and Slater[283] examined the affordances and challenges of VLEs for collaborative learning in interpreters' education. Their study revealed that VLEs support situated and autonomous learning, emphasising user experience. The research highlighted VLEs' potential to enhance practical skills through role-play simulations.

Kohn[284] also highlighted the effectiveness of role plays in videoconferencing and virtual reality for interpreter training. The study emphasised practical experiences in developing interpreting skills, suggesting that immersive environments significantly enhance learning.

Finally, as early as 2012 and 2013, two contributions by a group of researchers led by Ritsos[285] explored virtual worlds for training interpreters,

---

281 Hu, Gao, and Li, 'Learning interpreting in virtual reality: a scoping review'.

282 Chan, 'Using a virtual reality mobile application for interpreting learning: Listening to the students' voice'; Chan, 'Investigating the impact of a virtual reality mobile application on learners' interpreting competence'.

283 Braun, Davitti, and Slater, 'It's like being in bubbles: Affordances and challenges of virtual learning environments for collaborative learning in interpreter education'.

284 Kurt Kohn 'Role Plays in Videoconferencing and Virtual Reality', *European project - Interviews, CHECK.point eLearning, Special for ONLINE EDUCA BERLIN 2014* (2014).

285 Panagiotis D. Ritsos, Robert Gittins, Sabine Braun, Catherine Slater, and Jonathan C. Roberts, 'Training Interpreters Using Virtual Worlds', *Lecture Notes in Computer Science*

demonstrating how these environments could simulate real-life scenarios. Their findings indicated that virtual worlds facilitate collaborative learning and provide valuable skill development opportunities.

As these technologies continue to evolve, the literature on the topic is likely to be enriched soon with more contributions and insights on the integration of VR and AR technologies in interpreters' training and practice. While challenges remain, particularly in terms of technology adoption and the need for curriculum redesign, the potential benefits in terms of enhanced learning experiences, improved performance and expanded professional opportunities are substantial.

3. Case study and preliminary results

3.1 Training description

In the 2023/2024 academic year, the authors organised an interpreter training in virtual reality for the first-year students of the IULM master's degree programme in Specialised Translation and Conference Interpreting. The training was conducted as part of the activities of the International Center for Research on Collaborative Translation, directed by Francesco Laurenti. Ten students (nine female and one male) with Italian as their A-language and English and German as their B-languages took part in the training. The ten-hour training lasted from March 2024 to May 2024 and ended with a mock conference.

The training comprised an overall understanding of the VR headsets' functionality and use. During the training, ten 128 GB Meta Oculus Quest 3 were used. These VR headsets weigh 515 grams, and their battery life is up to two hours on average. Once switched on, students learned how to use the VR headsets, starting with the two default programmes First Steps[286] and

(2013), 21–40; Panagiotis D. Ritsos, Robert Gittins, Sabine Braun, Catherine Slater, and Jonathan C. Roberts, 'Using Virtual Reality for Interpreter-mediated Communication and Training', *2012 International Conference on Cyberworlds*, Darmstadt, Germany (2012), 191–8.

286 First steps, <https://www.meta.com/en-gb/experiences/first-steps/1863547050392688/>, accessed 30 August 2024.

First Contact[287]. After becoming familiar with them, students were asked to log in to Spatial[288] in order to create their own spaces and avatars. These tasks helped them understand the rudiments of 'existing' and moving in a virtual space. They had to perform various tasks, i.e. add a mirror to improve their body language, a screen to broadcast a video and create a portal to teleport to another space.

In addition to Spatial, students logged into Learnbrite[289] and MootUp[290] by Hyperspace[291], a 3D virtual event platform. The advantage of Hyperspace is that it allows users to host both virtual and hybrid events. This also gives the possibility of adding objects, such as an interpreting booth, which provides students with a deeper insight into conference interpreting in virtual reality.

Furthermore, the students also used the YouTubeVR app, watching immersive videos and practising activities such as shadowing President Obama in the video 'People's House. Inside the White House with Barack and Michelle Obama'[292].

Another application used during the training was Virtual Speech[293], an immersive platform for soft skill training with the integration of Artificial Intelligence. Virtual Speech offers the possibility to practise public speaking and sight translation at different speech speeds and to record one's own delivery. Another feature tested within the training was role playing, which involves user interaction with AI-generated avatars. This functionality encompasses different scenarios, from spontaneous conversation situations to simulations of job interviews and buying and selling. In addition to being able to choose the avatar's language proficiency level and speaking speed, this

---

287 First contact, <https://www.meta.com/en-gb/experiences/oculus-first-contact/2188021891257542/>, accessed 30 August 2024.

288 Spatial, <https://www.spatial.io/>, accessed 30 August 2024.

289 LearnBrite, <https://www2.learnbrite.com/>, accessed 4 September 2024.

290 MootUp, <https://mootup.com/>, accessed 4 September 2024.

291 Hyperspace, <https://hyperspace.mv/virtual-event-spaces-in-hyperspace/>, accessed 4 September 2024.

292 'The people's house. Inside the White House with Barack and Michelle Obama', <https://www.youtube.com/watch?v=bqW2qm02jwI>, accessed 4 September 2024.

293 Virtual Speech, <https://virtualspeech.com/>, accessed 4 September 2024.

function also allows users to start recording role plays and receive real-time feedback on their performance.

3.2 Mock conference in Virtual Reality

The last hour of the training was dedicated to a mock conference in the metaverse using the platform Learnbrite by Hyperspace. In this mock conference, the ten students were physically divided into five booths and virtually into five platform channels to simultaneously interpret two speeches from English and German using VR headsets. The students were physically present in a classroom equipped with booths while their avatars took part in the virtual event.

Prior to the mock conference, an online meeting was organised by the authors and Hyperspace to set up the virtual environments. With the support of Hyperspace, three rooms were configured: a briefing room, a conference room where the speakers' videos to be interpreted were uploaded and a debriefing room.

On the day of the mock conference, the students wore their VR headsets equipped with proper earphones and joined the virtual briefing room where the setup of the mock conference was explained. Afterwards, their avatars

Figure 7.1 Virtual interpreting booths – Hyperspace

were teleported to the virtual conference room, where each interpreter pair entered the predefined channel. The interpreters' avatars sat down in the virtual booths while the interpreters' voices were being heard from the different channels. The interpreters listened to and translated in shifts a ten-minute video from English into Italian and another ten-minute video from German into Italian. The video used to interpret from English into Italian was the first part of Mark Zuckerberg's speech held at the event 'Facebook Connect 2021' titled 'The Metaverse and How We'll Build It Together'[294] while the German speech was titled 'Forschung im Dialog: Metaverse – Wie wir uns im digitalen Raum der Zukunft begegnen werden'[295]. To the best of the authors' knowledge, it was the first time simultaneous interpreting through VR headsets was experienced in a virtual reality conference, where avatar-interpreters actively joined the event and performed simultaneous interpreting.

3.3 Questionnaires and students' feedback

After the training, the students were asked to complete a Google Form questionnaire on their experience and simultaneous interpreting in VR, which included five open-ended questions. The following section shows a summary of the responses given by the students.

Almost all students were curious and eager to see how this new technology works and how it could be successfully used during interpreter training and in the interpreting world of the future. Moreover, they expected a new immersive type of interpreting.

In relation to the activities conducted, students indicated that practising shadowing in VR, interacting with an AI-generated avatar in Virtual Speech and performing SI in a virtual conference room were the tasks they appreciated the most.

With reference to the activities conducted, students highlighted some signs of cybersickness among the drawbacks of training in VR. For instance, the process of sight translation was identified as a challenging task due to

---

294 Mark Zuckerberg, 'The Metaverse and How We'll Build It Together' (2021), <https://www.youtube.com/watch?v=Uvufun6xer8&t=221s>, accessed 30 August 2024.

295 Aljosa Smolic, 'Forschung im Dialog: Metaverse – Wie wir uns im digitalen Raum der Zukunft begegnen werden' (2023), <https://www.youtube.com/watch?v=EnglnQ3OXko&t=191s>, accessed 30 August 2024.

Table 7.1 Question 1

What were your expectations from the training?	• Experiencing a new immersive type of interpreting, so that in the future, even if the interpreter is not physically present at a meeting, it actually feels as if he/she was. • Getting to know a little about interpreting in a virtual world. • Being curious to see concretely how virtual reality could provide valuable help to the interpreter or interpreting student by trying out this technology first-hand. • Discovering a new world to engage with, which could represent a future innovation not only in technology, but also in the interpreting world. • Learning more about VR and how to use it as a tool for interpreter training. • Didn't know what to expect, as it was never experienced before.

Table 7.2 Question 2

What tasks and activities did you appreciate the most during the training?	• The shadowing activity, looking at the videos of Obama and the solar system on YouTube VR. • Interpreting as if I were sitting in front of the person I was working with. • The Virtual Speech application, not only because it gives you the possibility to practise sight translation and receive instant feedback generated with Artificial Intelligence, but also because it offers an endless variety of exercises that help with certain skills (e.g. eye contact, breathing or gestures). • The final session where we had the opportunity to perform simultaneous interpreting using VR headsets in a virtual conference room. • Creating the avatar.

the participants' reports of headaches and difficulty in maintaining focus. Furthermore, VR headsets were perceived as being heavy to wear.

It is worth noting that the possibility of integrating VR and Artificial Intelligence, especially AI-based CAI tools, was highly appreciated by the students, as it allowed them to explore the cutting-edge paradigm of the

Table 7.3 Question 3

What tasks and activities did you appreciate the least during the training?	• The sight translation activity. It was hard to focus because I got a headache almost right away. • Initial activities around the device itself. • The creation of the room in Spatial. • The shadowing session. The physical classroom was not large enough, and the background noise was quite distracting. • VR headsets are a little bit uncomfortable to wear.

Table 7.4 Question 4

What programmes and apps were the most helpful for interpreting as a profession?	• Besides Virtual Speech, which is very useful for the interpreter's preparation or even more so for interpreting students, the most useful application for an interpreter is Spatial. It is intuitive and easy to use, useful as it also provides the possibility to integrate CAI tools. • I think Spatial was essential for the success of our sessions. • YouTube VR and Virtual Speech, because it was possible to practise a foreign language with an AI-based avatar.

Table 7.5 Question 5

What's your overall feedback on the training?	• Very positive! It's a great alternative way of interpreting and it could be useful to make sure that the interpreter feels like he/she is actually physically present in the meeting. However, over long periods of time, it can cause problems such as headaches. • Positive start in an industry that in 25/30 years could play a significant role. • I was really excited to participate in this training, not only because it gave me the opportunity to learn about and explore virtual reality technology, but also because it allowed me to realise how valuable technology can be for an interpreter if used consciously. • Overall, it was a truly educational experience that I had the privilege and pleasure to participate in. I think it was useful for broadening perspectives and understanding how the interpreting profession is constantly evolving, yet still keeping pace with new technologies. • Excellent • Although sometimes I had nausea due to the heavy headset, it was interesting and definitely an enriching opportunity to deal with something that will be part of our future.

augmented interpreter. The same applies to the integration of Virtual Reality and Artificial Intelligence tested in Virtual Speech with an AI-based avatar.

Although some participants were not accustomed to using VR headsets and showed little discomfort in the VR training, the overall response to this question was very positive. They highlighted the pleasure of participating in the training and the usefulness of the experience. Students' expectations have been fulfilled, demonstrating how important it is to continue researching in training and simultaneous interpreting with VR headsets.

3.4 Trainers' Considerations

Notably, the students displayed considerable enthusiasm for the opportunity to utilise this new technology and great interest in the topic of VR in general and, more specifically, towards the integration of VR solutions in the field of interpreting.

The authors also perceived particular attention towards a more specific aspect related to virtual reality technologies, i.e. the possibilities of integrating VR/AR and CAI tools, hence towards augmented interpreting.

However, it must be acknowledged that technical difficulties were encountered during the training, including the technical setup of simultaneous interpreting for the mock conference. In fact, at the time of writing, no platform with channels for simultaneous interpreting is available on the market. On the other hand, in addition to the expected cybersickness due to the prolonged use of VR headsets, the students also experienced technical problems when joining the platform and listening through VR headsets.

Nevertheless, due to the highly immersive environment, some students' performance was perceived by the trainers as notably better in VR than in traditional SI training. As observed both by the authors and the participants, some outputs showed a higher level of accuracy and fluency, although they were not recorded and assessed.

4. Conclusion

This study evaluated the potential of interpreter training in VR and simultaneous interpreting using VR headsets as a new form of human-machine interaction in the context of collaborative learning and interpreters' training.

Our findings suggest that the training was greatly appreciated by the students, who found the new activities helpful for learning and practising interpretation techniques. However, some of the challenges encountered during the training led to several limitations and adjustments to the training schedule. Factors such as the time spent recharging the VR headsets and the limited number of accesses to the VR apps need to be considered in future training and studies.

Furthermore, interpreters' training and simultaneous interpreting with VR headsets is still in its infancy. Although the authors have not found any event platforms for VR/metaverse events already equipped with integrated simultaneous interpreting channels, the field is rapidly evolving. New comprehensive studies and the training sessions planned for the next academic year at IULM University could bridge this gap and further investigate the potential for integrating VR and AI, especially AI-based CAI tools.

Finally, future research and *ad hoc* training courses may provide more significant insights into this field by shedding more light on the interpreter-VR collaboration as a new form of human-machine interaction.

Acknowledgments

The authors would like to thank the International Center for Research on Collaborative Translation (IULM) for the ongoing financial, logistic and organisational support prior to and during the training and Hyperspace for providing free and unlimited access during the mock conference.

References

Braun, Sabine, Catherine Slater, Robert Gittins, Panagiotis Ritsos, and Jonathan C. Roberts, 'Interpreting in Virtual Reality: designing and developing a 3D virtual world to prepare interpreters and their clients for professional practice', in Don Kiraly, Silvia Hansen-Schirra, and Karin Maksymski, eds, *New Prospects and Perspectives for Educating Language Mediators* (Berlin: Gunter Narr Verlag Editors, 2013), 93–120.

Braun, Sabine, Catherine Slater, and Nicholas Botfield, 'Evaluating the pedagogical affordances of a bespoke 3D virtual learning environment for training interpreters and their clients', in Suzanne Ehrlich, and Jemina Napier, eds, *Interpreter Education in the Digital Age: Innovation,*

Access, and Change (Washington: Gallaudet University Press, 2014), 39–67.

Braun, Sabine, and Catherine Slater, 'Populating a 3D virtual learning environment for interpreting students with bilingual dialogues to support situated learning in an institutional context.', *The Interpreter and Translator Trainer* 8/3 (2014), 469–85.

Braun, Sabine, Elena Davitti, and Catherine Slater, 'It's like being in bubbles: Affordances and challenges of virtual learning environments for collaborative learning in interpreter education', *The Interpreter and Translator Trainer* 14/3 (2020), 259-78

Dror, Itiel E., and Stevan Harnad, eds, *Cognition distributed: How Cognitive Technology Extends Our Minds* (Amsterdam / Philadelphia: John Benjamins Publishing Company, 2008).

Camayd-Freixas, Erik, 'Cognitive theory of simultaneous interpreting and training', *Proceedings of the 52nd Conference of the American Translators Association* (New York: ATA, 2011).

Carroll, John M., *HCI Models, Theories, and Frameworks: Toward a Multidisciplinary Science* (New York: Elsevier, 2003).

Chan, Venus, 'Using a virtual reality mobile application for interpreting learning: Listening to the students' voice', *Interactive Learning Environments* 32/6 (2022), 2438–51.

Chan, Venus, 'Investigating the impact of a virtual reality mobile application on learners' interpreting competence', *Journal of Computer Assisted Learning* (2023), 1–17.

Fantinuoli, Claudio, 'Interpreting and technology: the upcoming technological turn', in Claudio Fantinuoli, ed., *Interpreting and Technology* (Berlin: Language Science Press, 2018), 1–12.

Gerber, Leah, Jim Hlavac, Irwyn Shepherd, Paul McIntosh, Alexander Avella Archila, and Hyein Ellen Cho, 'Stepping into the future: virtual reality training for community interpreters working in the area of family violence', *Journal of Specialised Translation* 36b (2021), 252–75.

Gieshoff, Anne Catherine, and Martin Schuler, 'The augmented interpreter: a pilot study on the use of augmented reality in interpreting', *3rd HKBU International Conference on Interpreting:*

Interpreting and Technology, Hong-Kong (Online) 7-9 December 2022 (2022).

Gieshoff, Anne Catherine, 'The augmented interpreter: The future of simultaneous interpreting?', Zürcher Hochschule für Angewandte Wissenschaften (2022), <https://blog.zhaw.ch/languagematters/2022/12/22/augmented-reality/>, accessed 4 September 2024.

Hu, Pingping, Bin Gao, and Ke Li, 'Learning interpreting in virtual reality: a scoping review', *Interactive Learning Environments* (2024), 1–20.

Kohn, Kurt 'Role Plays in Videoconferencing and Virtual Reality', *European project - Interviews, CHECK.point eLearning, Special for ONLINE EDUCA BERLIN 2014* (2014).

Mellinger, Christopher D., 'Embedding, extending and distributing interpreter cognition with technology', in Gloria Corpas Pastor, and Bart Defrancq, eds, *Interpreting Technologies – current and future trends* (Amsterdam / Philadelphia: John Benjamins Publishing Company, 2023), 195–216.

Milgram, Paul, and Fumio Kishino, 'A taxonomy of mixed reality visual displays', *IEICE Transactions on Information Systems* 77/12 (1994), 1321–9.

Reese, Hayne W., 'The learning-by-doing principle', *Behavioral Development Bulletin* 17/1, (2011), 1–19.

Ritsos, Panagiotis D., Robert Gittins, Sabine Braun, Catherine Slater, and Jonathan C. Roberts, 'Training Interpreters Using Virtual Worlds', *Lecture Notes in Computer Science* (2013), 21–40.

Ritsos, Panagiotis D., Robert Gittins, Sabine Braun, Catherine Slater, and Jonathan C. Roberts, 'Using Virtual Reality for Interpreter-mediated Communication and Training', *2012 International Conference on Cyberworlds*, Darmstadt, Germany (2012), 191–8.

Romano, Marco, Alessandro Frolli, Alessandro Aloisio, Claudio Russello, Angelo Rega, Francesco Cerciello, and Fabio Bisogni, 'Exploring the Potential of Immersive Virtual Reality in Italian Schools: A Practical Workshop with High School Teachers', *Multimodal Technologies and Interaction* 7/12 (2023), 111.

Seeber, Kilian, 'Simultaneous Interpreting', in Holly Mikkelson, and Renée Jourdenais, eds, *Routledge handbook of interpreting* (London / New York: Taylor and Francis, 2015), 79–95.

Slater, Mel, 'Immersion and the illusion of presence in virtual reality', *British Journal of Psychology* 109/3 (2018), 431–3.

Tewell, Jordan, and Nimesha Ranasinghe, 'A Review of Olfactory Display Designs for Virtual Reality Environments', *ACM Computing Survey* 56/11 (2024), article 276.

Turner, Phil, *HCI Redux: the Promise of Post-Cognitive Interaction* (Berlin: Springer, 2016).

Notes on Contributors

Valentina Baselli

Valentina Baselli is a conference interpreter trainer and Doctoral Researcher at IULM University. After obtaining an MA Degree in Specialised Translation and Conference Interpreting from IULM University, she has worked as a conference interpreter (English – Italian – German). She is a member of the Italian Association for Translators and Interpreters (AITI) and has been teaching English-Italian simultaneous and consecutive interpreting as well as translation at IULM and Istituto di Alti Studi SSML Carlo Bo since 2010. She also teaches Computer-Assisted Interpreting and Remote Simultaneous Interpreting (RSI) within the MA Programme in Specialised Translation and Conference Interpreting, collaborating with the RSI platform provider Converso. She has participated in different research projects organized by the Department of Humanities and the International Center for Research on Collaborative Translation (IULM). Her research is focused on new AI-based technologies for interpreters, Computer-Assisted Interpreting (CAI) tools, Remote Simultaneous Interpreting, Interpreting in Virtual Reality/Metaverse, and Collaborative Translation.

Manuela Comoglio

Manuela Comoglio is the Head of Teaching at Istituto di Alti Studi SSML Carlo Bo in Milan. She holds an MA Degree in Conference Interpreting from IULM University and an MA Degree in Modern European and American Languages and Literature from the University of Eastern Piedmont "Amedeo Avogadro" (UPO) in Vercelli. Since 2009, she has been working as a professional conference interpreter in English and German. She teaches consecutive and simultaneous translation at Istituto di Alti Studi SSML Carlo Bo and IULM University in Milan. She cooperates with the International Center for Research on Collaborative Translation (IULM), where she convenes regular seminars on the use of new technologies in interpreting. In addition to her academic role, she developed an online course to teach English as a second language at the university level for students and professors for SSML Carlo Bo. Her research interests focus on new AI-based technologies for interpreters and language students, and Interpreting in Virtual Reality/Metaverse.

Lara Delle Foglie
Lara Delle Foglie is a Research Collaborator at the International Center for Research on Collaborative Translation (IULM University, Milan). Her research focuses on extreme translations, transcreation, literary translation, creativity in translation and ethics in MT and AI. In 2023, she won the IULM Talent & Creativity Challenge (II edition) for the Best Audiovisual Translation. In April 2024, she was a speaker at the "How Can AI Translate?" International Conference (University of Naples Federico II), with a contribution titled *Are machines fit for extreme translations? Comparing English-Italian human translation to MT and AI output*. This contribution is available in *Testo a Fronte. Teoria e pratica della traduzione n. 69 – II semestre 2023. Leo S. Olschki Editore, Firenze.* In May 2024, Delle Foglie was a speaker at the "Collaborative Translation Award" International Conference (IULM University, Milan), giving a presentation titled *Extreme Translations and transcreation: a collaborative approach.*

Eleonora Gatto
Eleonora Gatto is a researcher at the International Center for Research on Collaborative Translation (IULM). She is also an academic assistant for the Editorial Translation courses (Spanish I and Spanish II) of the master's degree in Specialised Translation at IULM University in Milan, where she graduated in July 2023.

In addition to her work at the university, she works as an editorial translator. She collaborated with Professor Elena Liverani to translate *Perla, la cagnolina magica* (Feltrinelli), the Italian translation of Isabel Allende's new children's picture book. She has also translated for Salani Editore the Spanish novel *Tierra* by Eloy Moreno.

Her studies focus on children's literature (with a thesis on the translation and commentary of the Spanish work *Historias de la otra tierra* by Paloma Orozco Amorós, a collection of short stories that is in the process of being published). She is also interested in collaborative translation, audiovisual translation and ecolinguistics. She is currently investigating the relationship between translation and AI, supporting the research of Fabio Morotti with the project "AIneid".

Laura Giordani
Laura Giordani is a novelist, dialogue adapter and audio describer. She is a member of the College of Experts at the AIDAC (Italian Association of Film

and Television Dialogue Adapters). Her tenure in RAI state television started in 2009. She has also been an audio description and dialogue adaptation professor at several universities since 2016. She participated in drafting the Italian Guidelines for Audio Description in collaboration with organisations representing visual impaired and low-vision individuals. In 2021, the jury of the International Dubbing Festival recognised and celebrated her career as an audio describer by awarding her a prize for her professional achievements.

Francesco Laurenti

Francesco Laurenti is an associate professor in Comparative Literature. He is the Director of the "International Center for Research on Collaborative Translation" (IULM University, Milan). Since 2021 he has been the Head of the "Collaborative Revision of Texts in Translation" Lab at IULM.

The outcomes of his research have been presented at international conferences and published in monographs, collected volumes and articles in international peer-reviewed academic journals. He is a member of the editorial and advisory boards of several academic peer-reviewed journals, and he has edited special journal issues and collected volumes on translation.

Fabio Morotti

Fabio Morotti is a Doctoral Researcher at the IULM University Doctoral Programme of Visual and Media Studies. His academic and professional background is based on a multidisciplinary approach, employing anthropological categories for the analysis and understanding of contemporary visual culture. His fields of study encompass cinema, AI, intangible heritage, Cambodian culture, aerial cinematography and travel literature. He has taught English language at La Sapienza University and is a freelance translator. He is also the author of several novels and a monograph about Cambodian performing arts.

Claudio Russello

Claudio Russello is a professional interpreter and translator and a lecturer at the UNINT University of Rome, where he currently teaches computer-assisted interpreting, real-time subtitling, virtual reality and metaverse for interpreters, video game localisation and interpreting theory. He also collaborates with the Universities of Roma Tre, IULM, Bergamo and Macerata as a trainer for specialised courses and seminars. He is the Director of the

Master Course in 'Artificial Intelligence and Technologies for Interpreters and Translators' at UNINT.

In addition to his academic role, he regularly conducts workshops and training sessions on CAI and generative AI tools for national and international associations of interpreters and translators and is an official trainer for the CAI software InterpretBank. His research interests focus on the interaction between new technologies and interpreting and translation, and he has published several articles on his research in professional journals.

Federica Villareale

Federica Villareale is a Doctoral Researcher in Visual and Media Studies at IULM University. After earning her degree in Specialized Translation at IULM University, Federica Villareale has been working with the International Center for Research on Collaborative Translation (IULM) to explore the connection between translation and AI, as well as the effectiveness of collaborative translation tools in academia.

After graduating, she convened a series of seminars for the course in Editorial Translation (English I and English II) and participated in several conferences, such as the II International Congress on Translation and Cultural Sustainability (University of Salamanca), with a poster titled "Evaluation of Collaborative Translation in Academic/Training Context", and the conference “Teaching translation for Multimedia Scenarios” (IULM University), with a paper titled "Strumenti per la traduzione collaborativa: tra ambienti virtuali e nuove tecnologie" (Tools for collaborative translation: between virtual environments and new technologies).

www.ingramcontent.com/pod-product-compliance
Ingram Content Group UK Ltd.
Pitfield, Milton Keynes, MK11 3LW, UK
UKHW020641041026
15590UKWH00001B/24